Cyber Empires

Cyber Empires

How Nations Are Fighting for Digital Supremacy

By

Arjun Deshmukh

Vij Books

New Delhi (India)

Published by

Vij Books
(Publishers, Distributors & Importers)
4836/24, 3rd Floor, Ansari Road
Delhi - 110 002
Phone: 91-11-43596460
Mobile: 98110 94883
e-mail: contact@vijpublishing.com
www.vijbooks.in

ISBN: 978-93-90349-67-8 (PB)

This book was developed using advanced writing tools to support the drafting and ideation process. All content has been thoughtfully curated, refined, and reviewed to ensure quality and relevance.

Contents

Introduction

A blackout is rarely silent. The hum of appliances dies, the glow of screens extinguishes, and a city becomes aware of its own dependence. In Kiev, in 2015, entire districts went dark not because of a storm or a strike but because malicious code was threaded into the arteries of the grid. Operators stared at consoles that no longer obeyed them. Elsewhere, in Baltimore, a ransomware infection paralysed municipal offices, halting property sales and crippling emergency systems. No bombs fell, no buildings crumbled, yet lives were disrupted, trust eroded, and the cost of repair soared into tens of millions. These were not isolated acts of mischief: they were episodes in a quiet war, fought without sirens, waged through fibre and silicon.

The paradox is stark. We inhabit an age of unprecedented technological capability, yet our most sophisticated infrastructures can be crippled by tools improvised on laptops. In the hands of state actors, cyber operations promise deniability with devastating impact. In the hands of criminals, they blur into geopolitical leverage. And for ordinary citizens—teachers, nurses, small business owners—the consequences arrive suddenly, personally, and often irreversibly. We are all targets, though most of us never signed up to be soldiers in this conflict.

To grasp what is unfolding, it helps to think historically. Great powers once sought dominion over land and sea lanes; today, they fight over cables and clouds. Empires were once carved with steel and gunpowder; now they are assembled with data, standards, and lines of code. Territory has not disappeared—it has shifted. And the contests over it, though bloodless on the surface, determine wealth, power, and dignity for generations.

The New Frontiers of Conflict

Every generation must name its wars. For the twentieth century, we spoke of the Cold War and the nuclear balance. For the twenty-first, the labels are less settled: cyber war, information war, hybrid war. Yet each term struggles with the same dilemma: when espionage, crime, and sabotage can be carried out by the same actors, using the same tools, how do we know when war has begun?

This book confronts that problem directly. It examines the thresholds where an intrusion becomes an attack, where inconvenience becomes coercion, and where deniable interference morphs into overt aggression. Such boundaries matter because mislabelling creates danger in both directions: a hospital outage mistaken for war risks escalation; a strategic breach dismissed as crime leaves states paralysed. To navigate this fog, leaders and citizens alike must learn new literacies—how intent is inferred from packet traces, how proportionality can be judged when no craters mark the ground.

The architecture of the digital world also demands a new kind of map. Chips, cables, clouds, code, and clicks: these are the five layers on which modern power rests. Each layer hosts its own chokepoints. A scarce lithography machine in the Netherlands matters as much to geopolitics as a strait in the Middle East. A submarine cable snaking across the Atlantic carries more daily value than most shipping lanes. An app store gatekeeping billions of devices functions as a kind of customs office, shaping what knowledge circulates and what does not. Seeing the stack in this way explains why familiar spending priorities often miss the decisive bottlenecks.

Ambiguity itself becomes a weapon. Cyber operations thrive in the grey space between plausible accident and deliberate sabotage. False flags—code deliberately salted with another nation's language or time-zone fingerprints—complicate attribution. Proxy groups, tolerated or directed by states, muddy accountability further. Decision-makers are asked to act under radical uncertainty. The classic Clausewitzian fog of war is reborn at the packet level, with misperception and miscommunication amplified by speed and scale.

From Data to Empire

If war defines one axis of cyber power, empire defines another. States and firms now engage in what might be called data colonialism. Instead of minerals extracted from the ground, it is behavioural and industrial data extracted from populations. The analogy is exacting: first comes surveying—tracking what people do, what machines report, what patterns emerge. Then enclosure—defining terms of access, building platforms, requiring consent that is rarely informed. Finally, taxation—monetising flows, deciding who pays and who profits.

This process is not abstract. In many parts of the world, "free" digital services arrive as infrastructure, only to create dependencies that cannot easily be escaped. Consent becomes a fig leaf covering structural imbalances. Just as empires once drew borders, so too do standards and protocols draw invisible lines across the internet. Decisions about encryption defaults or identity schemes determine which actors can enter, which must pay tariffs, and who is locked out altogether. Few citizens notice such details; fewer still have any influence over them. Yet these hidden choices shape sovereignty in the digital century.

The law, always slower than code, is strained to breaking point. Where data is stored, which jurisdiction claims it, and how subpoenas or sanctions cross borders—all these questions are manipulated by firms adept at jurisdiction shopping. The result is a geopolitical economy where territory is not land but cloud region, where compliance is a bargaining chip, and where the sovereignty of nations is tested daily by the sovereignty of platforms.

The State Hacker and the Supply Chain

The anatomy of the modern state hacker reveals a peculiar fusion of bureaucracy and improvisation. Units within ministries sit alongside contractors and tolerated criminals. Some specialise in deep infiltration, others in mass collection, others still in disruptive effect. Budgets are significant, but the tools are often purchased on open grey markets where zero-day exploits are priced like rare commodities. Talent is recruited from universities, or, failing that, borrowed from underground forums. Proxies provide deniability but also risk: a gang might follow its own profit motive, misaligning with state strategy.

The supply chain itself has become the attack surface of choice. Software today is a lattice of dependencies, maintained by volunteers or underfunded teams. A single compromised package can cascade across industries. Trusted update channels, once regarded as the very guarantee of safety, have been turned into weapons. Even hardware—the chips soldered into everyday devices—carries suspicions of backdoors, though the reality is often less cinematic than the fear. Resilience, not inspection, becomes the rational goal: minimal trust, verifiable builds, staged rollouts, continuous audit.

Algorithms with Teeth

No survey of contemporary conflict is complete without attention to artificial intelligence. Algorithms are no longer passive tools; they are active participants. They scale persuasion campaigns, generate synthetic media, and target messages with precision that older propagandists could only dream of. Cognitive operations now compete with kinetic ones in their ability to unsettle societies.

At the same time, autonomous systems threaten to compress decision-making timelines to intolerable speeds. If machines decide before humans can deliberate, accountability is lost, and escalation becomes more likely. The temptation to remove humans from loops of judgement, in the name of efficiency, risks ceding not just control but ethics. Defensive uses of AI—anomaly detection, honeypots, deception systems—offer promise but also risk overconfidence. When data itself is corrupted, poisoned at the source, the most elegant models falter.

What rules, then, should govern the use of such tools? Who verifies, who audits, who decides when proportionality is breached? These questions echo those that once surrounded nuclear arms, yet their answers will be shaped in boardrooms and standards committees as much as in treaties.

Surveillance, Ransomware, and Infrastructure

The bargain between security and liberty, once thought to be a matter of public policy, is now embedded in everyday design choices. Surveillance capitalism rivals state intelligence in scope, assembling dossiers on individuals that outstrip what most agencies could ever manage. Smart cities and predictive policing promise efficiency but often deliver power without accountability. Citizen scoring—whether for loans, jobs, or political loyalty—risks turning social trust into a mechanism of control.

Ransomware gangs, meanwhile, have become instruments of foreign policy. Tolerated within certain jurisdictions, they serve as levers against rivals. Payment rails, from cryptocurrencies to mixers, determine whose sanctions bite and whose do not. Municipalities and hospitals, the very symbols of civic life, are held hostage, revealing how deeply national security is now domestic. Negotiation routines have emerged: grim playbooks followed by harried administrators under impossible pressure. Disruption operations, when they succeed, demonstrate that even in cyberspace, alliances matter, timing matters, law enforcement matters.

And beneath it all lie the physical substrates: grids, pipelines, ports, aviation systems, satellites. Each is a network of networks, fragile in ways often invisible until failure occurs. Recovery is not only about restoring power but about restoring trust. A blackout ends when lights return; a cyber blackout ends only when confidence does.

Quantum Gambits and New Alignments

The horizon bristles with further challenges. Quantum computing threatens to break cryptosystems that undergird not just military secrecy but banking, healthcare, and governance. Post-quantum migration is not a technical footnote; it is a generational project demanding inventories, pilots, and organisational will. States fund labs as if they were arsenals, while smaller nations seek consortia or niches that grant them leverage in the next order.

As these contests unfold, a new non-alignment emerges. Not every country wishes to choose between rival superpowers. Some seek neutral corridors, shared clouds, or standards diplomacy as hedges against dependency. Norms—verifiable prohibitions on attacking hospitals, tampering with elections, or corrupting update channels—offer at least a scaffold of restraint. Whether such norms can be enforced is a question of both forensics and diplomacy.

The Citizen at the Centre

Amid the machinery of states and corporations, the citizen remains the pressure point. Elections are disrupted not by tanks but by troll farms. Clinics are paralysed not by bombs but by ransomware. Schools are compromised not by spies but by phishing emails. The front line runs through homes, small businesses, and civic institutions. Shielding citizens—through threat modelling, sensible device hygiene, and insurance that incentivises safety rather than complacency—is not charity but strategy.

Yet protection cannot be left to individuals alone. The final arc of this book insists on dignity as the measure of digital order. Dignity means systems designed with agency and consent as constraints, not afterthoughts. It means institutions with real power to enforce rights. It means funding models that reward resilience over exploitation. And it means treating citizens not merely as consumers but as participants—organising, voting, contributing to standards, shaping norms.

What This Book Offers

This book is not a catalogue of threats for their own sake. It is a guide to reading power in a digital century, a lens for discerning strategy in what otherwise appears as chaos. Its chapters combine historical parallels with technical detail, ethical argument with practical playbooks. They are meant to equip not only policymakers and practitioners but also citizens who suspect, rightly, that their daily lives are entangled in contests once thought distant.

Urgency is clear. Blackouts and breaches, disinformation and ransomware, are no longer speculative scenarios. They are lived experience. Yet timelessness is also present: the same questions of sovereignty, legitimacy, and human dignity recur, merely transposed into new media. Empires have always been built on the control of flows—of goods, of people, of information. Today, those flows run through cables and code. The contest for them will shape the century.

As you read, I invite you to hold a set of questions close. How do we distinguish crime from war when both arrive as code? How do we balance liberty and security when the same sensors promise both protection and control? Can small states find agency in a world dominated by digital duopolies? And what does dignity mean when every click, every dataset, every standard embeds values as surely as any law?

The chapters ahead do not offer easy answers. But they offer, I hope, the tools to see more clearly, to decide more wisely, and to act with more confidence in a world where silence can be the sound of war, and where empires are rebuilt not with steel, but with silicon.

Chapter 1

The War Without Sirens

The first signs are rarely cinematic. No explosion splits the skyline, no siren pierces the air. Instead, a hospital's booking system begins to stutter, forcing staff back to pen and paper. A port authority finds its cargo management software frozen, leaving containers stranded on quays. A city's email servers fail, paralyzing council meetings and delaying emergency permits. To the outside observer, life continues with deceptive normality; yet beneath the surface, the machinery of daily existence has been thrown into disarray. The aggressor is faceless, the weapon invisible, and the theatre of conflict—our most ordinary institutions—feels unsettlingly intimate.

This is warfare without warning sirens, where thresholds blur and definitions collapse. Is the hospital outage a criminal shakedown, an intelligence-gathering probe, or the opening shot of state-directed coercion? Was the frozen port system a blunder of chance, or a rehearsal for blockade? What counts as an *attack* in a world where the same lines of code can serve espionage, sabotage, or extortion? Such questions are not pedantic: they determine whether governments respond with police warrants, diplomatic protests, or military force. Yet our legal categories, forged in an age of craters and casualties, lag far behind a technical reality that leaves no visible scars.

The difficulty of naming is only the beginning. Behind every incident lies a deeper puzzle of attribution and intent. Code travels easily; fingerprints can be forged. A keystroke in one time zone may be staged to mimic another. An intrusion may be exploratory or preparatory, its meaning legible only in hindsight. Leaders are thus forced to decide under uncertainty: when to attribute, when to retaliate, when to hold back. Too little confidence risks paralysis, too much risks escalation. In this new theatre of conflict, mislabelling is not just a semantic error; it is a strategic hazard.

If naming the act is one problem, mapping the terrain is another. The digital world is not a formless cloud but a layered architecture—chips, cables, clouds, code, and clicks. Each layer hosts its own chokepoints and incentives. The chip foundries that etch nanometres of silicon are geopolitical treasures as decisive as oil fields once were. Submarine cables, thin as garden hoses, carry the economic lifeblood of nations. Cloud platforms, operated by a handful of firms, decide where data rests and which laws govern it. The code itself—open-source fragments maintained by unpaid volunteers—constitutes both the fuel of innovation and the seeds of exposure. And at the surface, the clicks of billions of citizens, shaped by app stores and algorithms, create pressure points more powerful than tanks in the street.

Yet security spending, political rhetoric, and public imagination often fixate on the wrong layers. Firewalls are installed while dependencies in chips go unexamined. Budgets flow to visible protections while the decisive bottlenecks remain neglected. To see the stack clearly is to understand where control truly resides, and why defending it requires more than patching the symptoms of each breach. The five layers introduced here will act as the through-line of this book, a map by which to navigate the conflicts ahead.

Ambiguity, of course, is not merely a by-product but a weapon in its own right. Where Clausewitz once spoke of the fog of war, today's commanders and policymakers confront packet-level uncertainty. False flags can be seeded into code repositories; deniable proxies can masquerade as independent gangs. Signalling, always fraught in international politics, becomes treacherous when the signals themselves can be forged. The very conditions that make cyberspace fertile ground for espionage—speed, concealment, adaptability—make it a treacherous medium for diplomacy. Decisions must be taken without clarity, and misperceptions, once made, can cascade with frightening speed.

Then there is the question of cost. A few lines of code, cheaply developed and endlessly reused, can impose outsized recovery expenses. A ransomware intrusion may cost attackers a fraction of a salary but force hospitals into months of recovery and millions in losses. For logistics networks, downtime is measured not in hours but in supply chains disrupted, shelves emptied, and livelihoods stalled. Offence benefits from surprise and re-use; defence must guard every doorway, every weak credential, every overlooked vendor. The asymmetry of costs is not an academic curiosity; it is the structural condition that shapes the strategy of states, insurers, and businesses alike. It explains why attackers persist and why defenders often feel perennially behind.

And at the centre of it all stand ordinary citizens. Their clinics, schools, and town halls have become pressure points in conflicts far larger than themselves. A ransomware infection that halts chemotherapy appointments or cancels GCSE exams may be tactically trivial but politically devastating. Panic is not collateral damage; it is the goal. By targeting the infrastructures of everyday life, adversaries exploit the thin line between civic disruption and strategic coercion. National security, once imagined as the preserve of armies and intelligence agencies, has become a domestic matter. The front line now runs through the very institutions that anchor communal trust.

This chapter begins with these dilemmas because they are the conditions of all that follows. If we cannot agree on what counts as an attack, we cannot build doctrines of response. If we do not see the stack clearly, we cannot identify the bottlenecks that matter. If we ignore ambiguity, we are destined to misread signals. If we underestimate asymmetry, we will design strategies that fail. And if we neglect citizens, we will mistake the battlefield entirely.

The war without sirens is not science fiction; it is the soundtrack of our present. Yet to hear it clearly requires learning to listen differently—not for the roar of bombs, but for the silence of systems gone dark. What you will find in the pages ahead is not a catalogue of disasters but a framework for judgment. For once, we can distinguish between noise and signal, between nuisance and attack, between crime and coercion; we gain the clarity to act wisely in uncertainty. The questions opened here—about naming, mapping, signalling, costs, and citizens—will resonate throughout the book. They are the grammar of cyber conflict, and learning to speak it may be the only way to prevent silence from becoming a catastrophe.

What Counts as an Attack?

In June 2017, a piece of malicious code later dubbed *NotPetya* raced through networks worldwide. Within hours, it had frozen shipping terminals, grounded flights, and forced hospitals back to pen-and-paper triage. The cost was immense—over ten billion dollars in damages by conservative estimates. Yet here is the paradox: though the scale rivalled that of a natural disaster, few governments declared it an act of war. Insurance firms refused to pay out under "war clauses", arguing it was a crime. Intelligence agencies hinted at state responsibility, but public attribution was delayed and contested. Victims, meanwhile, cared little for the labels; their concern was survival.

This incident captures the heart of the problem: in cyberspace, the line between espionage, crime, and warfare is porous. A tool written to steal passwords may be reused to disable hospital systems. An operation intended for sabotage may be passed off as extortion. Legal frameworks forged in an age of visible violence—where bombs left craters and armies wore uniforms—struggle to accommodate attacks that leave no physical trace yet disable care, disrupt governance, and destabilise economies. We are left asking, with increasing urgency: what truly counts as an attack?

The law offers some guidance but little clarity. The United Nations Charter speaks of "armed attacks" and "use of force", concepts that presuppose kinetic violence. International humanitarian law draws distinctions between combatants and civilians, distinctions blurred when a teenager in a basement can disable a hospital from across the world. Even national statutes often collapse categories—treating some cyber incidents as crime, others as espionage, others as warfare—without recognising that the same intrusion can embody all three. Technical reality outruns legal imagination.

Attribution complicates matters further. To act responsibly in international affairs, one must know *who* is behind an incident and with what intent. Yet tracing digital fingerprints is fraught. Malware can be recycled, command-and-control servers hijacked, code comments inserted deliberately in foreign languages to mislead. Forensic evidence, while improving, is rarely definitive. Intelligence may provide context, but rarely in a form that can be shared publicly. Leaders are forced into a delicate balance: disclose too little and appear weak, disclose too much and compromise sources. The uncertainty is not incidental; it is engineered. Adversaries exploit it to buy time, sow division, and avoid accountability.

Proportionality—another cornerstone of just conduct in war—becomes equally tangled. If a cyber operation disables a hospital system but causes no direct casualties, is it equivalent to a missile strike? If a ransomware attack cripples municipal services, what is the measured response? Retaliation in kind is rarely possible: a state cannot credibly threaten "hacking back" against criminals dispersed across borders. Military retaliation risks escalation. Diplomatic protest often feels inadequate. The spectrum of possible responses is wide, but the criteria for choosing among them remain murky.

Intent complicates the picture still further. Consider a breach of a power grid. Was it reconnaissance—an intelligence probe mapping vulnerabilities? Was it coercion—a show of capability meant to intimidate?

Or was it preparation for war, a sleeper access awaiting activation in crisis? Each interpretation suggests a different response. Yet at the moment of discovery, the intent is unknowable. Analysts infer meaning from patterns of behaviour, historical precedent, and the balance of risks. But inference is not certainty. Leaders act under ambiguity, knowing their choices will be judged not only by adversaries but by allies, publics, and markets.

The stakes of mislabelling are high. To call a criminal intrusion an "act of war" risks overreaction, escalation, and the erosion of credibility. To dismiss a state-sponsored operation as mere nuisance risks paralysis and vulnerability. Insurance markets face similar dilemmas: payouts hinge on whether an incident is categorised as war, terrorism, or crime. Victims find themselves caught in definitional limbo, denied restitution by semantics. Even language itself becomes a battlefield, with adversaries exploiting categories to delay or divide.

Real-world cases highlight the fragility of thresholds. The Stuxnet operation that sabotaged Iranian centrifuges in 2010 was arguably the first state use of cyber tools to achieve physical destruction. It raised a profound question: if disabling a weapons system with code counts as legitimate military action, what about disabling a hospital or a water supply? Conversely, the SolarWinds intrusion of 2020, which compromised US federal agencies and corporations, was described by some as espionage, by others as an act of aggression. The difference lay not in the technical facts but in the interpretation of scale, intent, and harm.

Historical parallels are instructive but limited. Espionage has always been tolerated as a "grey zone" activity, condemned when exposed but rarely treated as war. Sabotage, by contrast, has often been considered an act of aggression. Yet in cyberspace the same technique—say, exploiting a software vulnerability—can serve both purposes, depending only on what the intruder chooses to do once inside. The very fungibility of tools collapses categories.

Philosophically, the problem touches on deeper questions of sovereignty and legitimacy. What does it mean for a state to promise protection when the instruments of harm are invisible, borderless, and deniable? Citizens expect care to be safeguarded, elections to be defended, schools to be resilient. Yet governments hesitate, fearing that strong declarations will tie their hands, while silence leaves citizens uncertain. The absence of clear thresholds corrodes trust—not only between states but between governments and their people.

The difficulty is not only conceptual but practical. Escalation management depends on shared understandings of thresholds. During the Cold War, doctrines of deterrence relied on clarity: an attack of one kind would trigger a predictable response of another. In the digital age, that clarity is absent. States improvise, hoping their improvisation will not be misunderstood. The risk is that each side, fearing weakness, responds too strongly—or, fearing escalation, fails to respond at all. Both pathways undermine stability.

So, what counts as an attack? Perhaps the answer is not a fixed threshold but a set of questions: Who is responsible, and can that responsibility be credibly established? What was the scale of harm—not only in material terms but in civic trust? What was the intent—exploitation, coercion, preparation, or destruction? And what response safeguards security without triggering uncontrollable escalation? These are the judgements this book will revisit in later chapters, as we examine how nations signal, retaliate, and restrain themselves in a domain without sirens.

For now, it is enough to recognise that the absence of craters does not mean the absence of violence. Code can disable care as surely as bombs can. Yet the categories we use to describe these acts remain contested, and the decisions made in the grey zones between them will shape the future of conflict. The challenge is to learn how to act wisely when the labels fail—to distinguish between nuisance and threat, espionage and war, inconvenience and coercion.

And perhaps the deeper question lingers still: if the very grammar of conflict is changing, what new language will we need to speak of war, peace, and everything that lies in between?

The Five Layers of Control

A single company in the Netherlands manufactures the machines that etch the smallest circuits on the world's most advanced chips. Without these lithography systems, no nation can build the processors that power artificial intelligence or advanced weapons. One firm, one supply chain, one chokepoint—yet its significance rivals that of oil wells in the twentieth century. At the other end of the spectrum, a different bottleneck: a handful of app stores control which software billions of citizens may download, shaping not only convenience but the boundaries of political speech. The paradox is that the most strategic assets of the digital age are often invisible, scattered across domains so technical that even policymakers struggle to grasp their implications. To see the true terrain of cyber power, we must learn to read it as a stack.

The digital world is not flat. It is layered, structured, and hierarchical, like a nervous system with distinct pathways. At the foundation are *chips*: the silicon logic units that translate design into physical capacity. Above them run the *cables* that connect continents and cities, the arteries through which data flows. Over cables sit the *clouds*, monopolised by a few providers whose data centres decide jurisdiction, resilience, and reach. Next comes *code*—open-source, proprietary, patched, and repurposed—that animates every application. Finally, at the surface, there are the *clicks* of billions of human users, mediated by platforms that decide what rises to attention and what vanishes unseen.

Each layer hosts its own incentives, vulnerabilities, and leverage points. Together, they form the architecture of digital control. Yet security debates often ignore this architecture, focusing on visible symptoms rather than the structural chokepoints. The result is a misallocation of resources: billions spent hardening endpoints while critical dependencies remain fragile. By disaggregating the layers, we can see where power is concentrated and why conflicts play out as they do.

Take chips. For decades, the assumption was that semiconductors would flow freely, produced by global supply chains too complex for any single actor to dominate. That assumption has collapsed. Taiwan, home to the most advanced fabrication plants, is now a strategic fulcrum in global politics. Export controls on advanced lithography machines reveal how knowledge itself becomes a geopolitical weapon. Unlike oil, chips cannot simply be drilled elsewhere: decades of investment, talent, and infrastructure create barriers to entry. Control of chip production is not merely economic but strategic, determining who can develop supercomputers, train large-scale AI, or modernise military arsenals. The bottleneck is not distributed; it is singular, precise, and fiercely contested.

Move up a layer and the cables appear. Few citizens realise that more than 95 per cent of international data traffic travels not through satellites but through submarine cables, strands of fibre lying on ocean floors. These cables are laid, owned, and maintained by a small consortium of companies, many of them now backed by nation-states or tech giants. A single fault—whether accidental or deliberate—can disrupt an entire region. The act of tapping or cutting a cable is not dramatic in imagery, yet its effect is as decisive as blockading a port. Here again, chokepoints abound: narrow straits where cables converge, coastal stations where they land, repair vessels limited in number and easily monitored. Whoever controls the cables controls the arteries of the digital economy.

Above the cables, the clouds dominate. To describe them as "distributed" is misleading; in reality, cloud computing is one of the most concentrated industries in the world. A handful of firms run hyperscale data centres, with contractual terms that decide where data resides, which jurisdiction applies, and how swiftly information can be retrieved or seized. The choice of cloud region becomes a political act, determining which laws protect or expose sensitive information. For governments, this raises existential questions: how much sovereignty can be outsourced before it is forfeited? For corporations, it defines the limits of compliance and liability. Cloud dominance is not merely technical efficiency—it is a form of jurisdictional power.

Then comes code. It is easy to imagine software as infinitely malleable, but the reality is that modern applications are built atop libraries and dependencies maintained by scattered communities. A trivial open-source module, written years ago by a volunteer, can become embedded in critical infrastructure. When vulnerabilities are discovered, they cascade through supply chains. Here the chokepoints are not physical but human: a few overworked maintainers whose unpaid labour secures vast empires of commerce and governance. At the other end of the spectrum, proprietary codebases act as fortresses, closed to scrutiny but open to coercion by their owners. The paradox is that code is both the most open and the most closed of the layers—transparent in theory, opaque in practice, fragile in ways few appreciate.

Finally, at the surface, lie the clicks—the choices of billions of users mediated by platforms that decide visibility. App stores dictate which programmes may be installed, often enforcing political bans under the guise of "content moderation". Social platforms rank posts in ways that amplify outrage, suppress dissent, or serve state requests for censorship. Advertising models monetise attention, turning clicks into commodities that can be steered, harvested, and weaponised. The layer of clicks is where abstract power meets human experience: elections swayed by targeted disinformation, protests mobilised or suppressed by platform algorithms, public opinion shaped invisibly by unseen curation. At this layer, the sovereignty of citizens collides with the incentives of corporations.

What unites the five layers is the principle of chokepoints. Each contains nodes whose control confers disproportionate influence. Yet these nodes are distributed across technical, legal, and cultural domains, making them hard to defend with uniform strategy. Spending billions on endpoint protection does little to secure lithography monopolies or submarine cables. Training users in password hygiene does not solve the dependence on a few open-source libraries. Policymakers and boards often fail to see the layers as interlocking, preferring to address each problem in isolation. This blindness is costly: it leaves societies vulnerable to the most decisive bottlenecks, while lavishing attention on the most visible but least critical.

To think in layers is to recover perspective. Just as geologists read strata to understand deep time, or doctors trace systems to diagnose disease, so too must we map the digital stack to see where control lies. The five layers are not a metaphor; they are the operational reality of twenty-first century power. Each has its custodians, its vulnerabilities, and its politics. Together, they explain why cyber conflict rarely plays out as imagined in Hollywood—no sudden apocalyptic strikes, but instead struggles over factories, contracts, standards, and platforms.

Yet the mapping is unfinished. Who will govern the lithography chokepoints—one company, one country, or a consortium? Will cables remain private consortia or become nationalised infrastructure? Can clouds be made sovereign without fragmenting the internet? Will open-source code be supported as a public good or continue as a precarious volunteer effort? And at the surface, can the clicks of billions be insulated from manipulation, or will attention itself remain the currency of power?

The stack is a map, but it is also a set of questions. By following its layers, we glimpse both the hidden vulnerabilities of our world and the possibilities of resilience. To ignore it is to mistake symptoms for causes, noise for signal. To see it clearly is to recognise that the war without sirens will be fought not in one domain but across five—and that understanding their interdependence is the first step towards control.

The Fog of Cyber War

In the summer of 2007, Estonia—a small, digitally advanced state—found its government websites, banks, and news outlets paralysed. The flood of traffic was relentless, overwhelming servers and silencing services. Suspicion fell immediately on Russia, given the political tensions of the time, yet proof was elusive. The attacks bore hallmarks of nationalist hacktivists, perhaps acting with encouragement, perhaps independently. No missile had crossed the border, no soldier had advanced, but the state found itself under siege nonetheless. Was this war? Was it crime? Was it a protest that spiralled out of control? Estonia was forced to respond in the fog, improvising alliances and doctrines in real time.

The ambiguity that haunts cyber conflict is not accidental; it is engineered. In conventional war, the smoke of battle obscures troop positions, intentions, and outcomes. Clausewitz named this the "fog of war": the uncertainty that clouds commanders' judgements. In cyberspace, the fog is thicker still—not the residue of smoke, but the deliberate layering of deception at the level of packets, protocols, and proxies. Ambiguity becomes a weapon, wielded to sow hesitation in adversaries, to buy time, and to erode trust.

False flags are the most obvious manifestation. Malware may include Cyrillic characters or Chinese time stamps, planted to misdirect forensic investigators. Command-and-control servers can be routed through a dozen jurisdictions, each requiring laborious legal processes to access logs, by which time the trail has gone cold. Code snippets borrowed from prior operations create misleading genealogies, suggesting attribution that is at best tenuous. In this environment, appearances are not evidence; they are bait. Analysts must decide whether what they see is genuine trace or calculated misdirection.

Proxies further deepen the haze. States rarely act alone in cyberspace; they lean on contractors, intelligence fronts, or tolerated criminal groups. Such actors provide deniability, but at a cost: their actions may diverge from state intent, creating ambiguity not only for adversaries but for their own sponsors. A ransomware gang shielded by a state may pursue profit on one day and political disruption on another. Governments confronted with such groups face a dilemma: treat them as criminals, as combatants, or as something in between? Each choice carries risks of escalation or impotence.

Even signalling—the basic grammar of deterrence—falters in this domain. During the nuclear age, states developed rituals of communication: missile tests, military exercises, declarations of red lines. The signals were visible, deliberate, and designed to be understood. In cyber operations, signals are easily missed or misread. An intrusion into a power grid might be intended as reconnaissance, a show of capability, or a threat of future escalation. To the target, all three interpretations appear plausible. Lacking clarity, leaders may underreact, emboldening the aggressor, or overreact, triggering escalation. Deterrence relies on shared meanings; cyberspace undermines them.

The psychological effects are equally corrosive. A denial-of-service attack, though technically unsophisticated, can feel to citizens like a siege. The absence of information—government portals down, news sites inaccessible—creates a void easily filled by rumour and fear. This cognitive fog amplifies the technical one: uncertainty about attribution breeds suspicion, suspicion erodes trust, and trust is the foundation of both governance and alliance. Adversaries exploit this dynamic precisely because it is cheap, effective, and difficult to counter without appearing heavy-handed.

Case studies illustrate the stakes. The 2014 attack on Sony Pictures, later attributed by Washington to North Korea, was initially dismissed by many analysts as the work of hacktivists. The delay in attribution weakened the credibility of the response and fuelled conspiracy theories. In 2015, the blackout in western Ukraine, widely considered the first confirmed case of cyber-induced power outage, raised questions about whether it was a demonstration or a rehearsal for larger acts. Analysts still debate whether it was primarily a warning shot, a tactical disruption, or the visible tip of a broader strategy. Each interpretation carries different policy implications. The fog does not lift even years after the fact.

For leaders, the challenge is radical uncertainty. Decisions must be taken before evidence is complete, before attribution is conclusive, before intent is clear. Waiting for certainty is often not an option: hospitals cannot suspend care, militaries cannot postpone defence, markets cannot tolerate prolonged ambiguity. Yet acting prematurely risks miscalculation. This is the cruel geometry of cyber strategy: every choice is made in partial light.

Philosophically, this uncertainty forces us to revisit the very idea of knowledge in conflict. Clausewitz assumed that the fog could be penetrated with experience, intuition, and reconnaissance. In cyberspace, the fog may be permanent, not because information is absent, but because information is manipulated. Evidence is no longer merely incomplete; it is adversarial. Leaders must cultivate a different skill set: not the pursuit of certainty, but the ability to act responsibly without it. Judgement, resilience, and proportionality become more important than definitive proof.

The temptation, of course, is to seek technological solutions. Better forensics, faster sensors, automated attribution—all promise to cut through the fog. Yet none can eliminate the core problem: that adversaries adapt, that evidence can be forged, and that interpretation always remains contested. Technology may sharpen vision, but it cannot guarantee clarity. The fog is not an accident of poor lighting; it is the battlefield itself.

And so the enduring question remains: how does a state maintain stability, credibility, and deterrence when the very ground of knowledge is unstable? How do leaders communicate resolve when they cannot prove what they suspect, or when adversaries exploit hesitation to their advantage? These questions echo through every crisis, from Estonia to Ukraine, from Sony to SolarWinds. They will shape the doctrines of the century ahead.

Perhaps the most unsettling thought is this: in cyber conflict, uncertainty is not a temporary hindrance but a permanent condition. Leaders must act not when they *know*, but when they *cannot know*. The fog is not waiting to be lifted; it is waiting to be navigated. And the way we learn to navigate it—cautiously, creatively, or recklessly—will determine not only the outcomes of single skirmishes but the stability of the international order itself.

Asymmetry of Costs

In 2019, a ransomware attack on the city of Baltimore locked municipal workers out of critical systems. The ransom demand was modest—about $76,000 in Bitcoin. Baltimore refused to pay. The recovery bill, however, spiralled towards $18 million. Payroll was delayed, property sales suspended, emergency services hampered. A trivial sum, demanded by anonymous intruders with off-the-shelf malware, metastasised into a crisis that strained the city's finances for months. The paradox was stark: it cost almost nothing to break, but a fortune to fix.

This imbalance is the defining feature of cyber conflict. Offence thrives on surprise, re-use, and scale. A single intrusion kit can be redeployed against countless targets; a single vulnerability, once discovered, can be exploited indefinitely until patched. Defence, by contrast, demands relentless vigilance. To succeed, defenders must be right across an entire estate—every server, every endpoint, every neglected supplier. To fail, attackers need only find one overlooked doorway. The asymmetry is structural, not accidental, and it reshapes the incentives of criminals, states, insurers, and victims alike.

Hospitals offer some of the most harrowing examples. In 2017, the WannaCry worm raced through the UK's National Health Service, cancelling thousands of operations and appointments. The malware itself was crude, unsophisticated, and in fact contained a kill-switch that abruptly halted its spread. Yet the disruption was severe: ambulances diverted, records inaccessible, doctors reverting to pen and paper. The attackers earned little; the NHS shouldered recovery costs measured in hundreds of millions. In health care, time is not only money but life. An attacker needs only a few lines of code to halt chemotherapy schedules or to freeze blood transfusion databases. Defenders must spend endlessly to ensure such interruptions never occur.

The logistics sector is equally vulnerable. In June 2017, the NotPetya attack, initially targeted at Ukrainian firms, spilled into global shipping. Maersk, the world's largest container company, saw its terminals paralysed. The malware destroyed servers so thoroughly that engineers had to locate a single surviving domain controller in a remote office to restore operations. Losses ran to hundreds of millions. The attack cost the intruders almost nothing beyond the effort of weaponising stolen code. For Maersk, recovery meant reinstalling 45,000 PCs and 4,000 servers—an operation of Herculean scale. The economic logic is brutal: destruction is cheap, resilience costly.

Cities, too, reveal the imbalance. When Atlanta was hit by ransomware in 2018, the ransom demand was about $50,000. The eventual recovery bill exceeded $17 million. Systems underpinning courts, utilities, and payroll were crippled. Citizens queued for services that had reverted to manual paperwork. The city's reputation for competence eroded in real time. A small gang of hackers had extracted outsized disruption from trivial resources.

Why does this asymmetry persist? The first reason is reuse. An exploit or toolkit, once written, can be applied endlessly with marginal cost near zero. A phishing campaign, for example, costs pennies per message; if one employee clicks, the return is enormous. Defence, by contrast, cannot reuse so efficiently. Every system must be patched individually, every employee trained, every supply chain monitored. The unit cost of prevention is stubbornly high.

The second reason is surprise. Attackers choose the time, place, and method; defenders must spread resources across every possibility. A zero-day exploit—an unknown vulnerability—renders even the most advanced defences porous. Once revealed, defenders scramble to patch, test, and deploy fixes across vast estates. The attacker moves on; the defender lags.

The third reason lies in incentives. Attackers operate without regard for law or liability; defenders must comply with both. A hospital cannot simply shut down its IT systems pre-emptively; lives depend on their continuous operation. A logistics firm cannot halt operations indefinitely; global trade depends on continuity. Attackers exploit this asymmetry of urgency: they can wait, experiment, retreat. Defenders cannot.

Insurance markets have become laboratories of this imbalance. Cyber insurance was once seen as a way to absorb risk. But insurers now recoil at the magnitude of claims. Premiums rise, exclusions multiply, and the line between crime and state activity becomes decisive. If an incident is categorised as "war", policies may refuse payout. Victims find themselves entangled not only in recovery but in definitional battles. The asymmetry of costs extends into semantics: the words used to describe an incident can shift millions in liability.

Philosophically, the imbalance forces a reconsideration of deterrence. In traditional warfare, deterrence rested on reciprocity: an attack would be met with equal or greater force. In cyberspace, reciprocity is elusive. How does one reciprocate for a ransomware attack that demanded $50,000 but cost $20 million in recovery? To respond in kind would be disproportionate; to remain silent invites repetition. States experiment with sanctions, indictments, and disruption operations, but the cost curve remains lopsided. Offence still enjoys the cheap advantage.

Yet asymmetry is not absolute. Some strategies can mitigate it. Resilience—building systems to fail gracefully, to restore quickly, to compartmentalise damage—shifts the equation. An organisation that can recover in days rather than months changes the calculus of attackers. Likewise, intelligence sharing among allies multiplies defensive effectiveness. If one victim's experience can inoculate others, the attacker's cost of reuse rises. The asymmetry narrows, if never fully closes.

Still, the imbalance exerts a gravitational pull on strategy. For criminals, the lure of profit is irresistible. For states, the appeal of tools that disrupt rivals cheaply is obvious. For insurers, the difficulty of pricing risk becomes existential. And for citizens, the reality is sobering: institutions they rely on can be crippled not by great armies but by small groups with minimal resources.

The deeper question is whether societies can afford to live with such imbalance. Can we design infrastructures where defence does not require perfection, only sufficiency? Can insurance evolve from indemnity to governance, aligning incentives for resilience rather than payouts? Or must we accept that in digital conflict, unlike physical war, the cost of defence will always outweigh the cost of attack?

The paradox remains: the cheapest code can create the most expensive crises. And as long as that asymmetry endures, attackers will probe, defenders will strain, and societies will pay the price. The question that hangs in the air is not whether we can prevent every intrusion—clearly we cannot—but whether we can rewrite the economics of cyber conflict so that the balance of costs begins, finally, to tilt away from the attacker's favour.

Why Citizens Are Targets

In 2016, a wave of fabricated news stories spread across social media platforms in the United States, some originating from obscure servers in Eastern Europe. They claimed that a presidential candidate ran a secret paedophile ring from a Washington pizzeria, that ballots were being stuffed in favour of one party, that shadowy elites controlled both sides. Absurd as these rumours seemed, they reached millions. One man, armed with a rifle, entered the restaurant to "investigate" for himself. The episode, ludicrous and tragic, revealed something more profound: ordinary citizens had become the decisive terrain of twenty-first century conflict.

Cyber operations need not topple satellites or paralyse grids to achieve strategic effect. A hospital locked by ransomware, a school system paralysed by phishing emails, a town hall shut down by malware—these may appear small compared with traditional military targets. Yet their disruption generates leverage, panic, and headlines. Unlike hardened military facilities, civilian institutions are often ill-defended, deeply trusted, and intimately tied to everyday life. Attackers have realised what generals once knew: the surest way to pressure a government is to frighten or inconvenience its people.

The ethics of targeting civilians in war have long been codified. The Geneva Conventions prohibit direct attacks on non-combatants. Yet in cyberspace, the boundaries blur. Is shutting down a hospital IT system an "attack on civilians" if no bomb falls and no blood is spilled? If an electoral database is altered—not to change votes, but to undermine confidence in results—is that sabotage or propaganda? The law struggles to categorise these acts, but their effects are plain. Trust is eroded, fear spreads, and leaders feel compelled to respond.

Elections illustrate this starkly. Democracies depend not only on secure ballots but on shared belief in the legitimacy of outcomes. In 2016 and again in subsequent cycles, hostile actors sought not primarily to change votes but to amplify polarisation, sow doubt, and delegitimise institutions. The target was not the ballot box but the minds of citizens. If enough people believe their system is rigged, the democratic compact frays. No army needs to cross a border; the damage is done from within.

Healthcare systems have also become pressure points. The 2021 ransomware attack on Ireland's Health Service Executive forced doctors to cancel appointments, delay diagnostics, and revert to manual records. Patients felt the impact immediately: postponed surgeries, delayed cancer treatments, uncertain access to care. The ransom demand was measured in millions, but the true cost was measured in lives disrupted and trust shaken. For attackers, hospitals offer leverage disproportionate to their size: governments cannot ignore suffering patients, and the moral outrage multiplies pressure.

Schools and universities, too, are frequent targets. A ransomware infection that delays student records or locks down online classrooms reverberates through families and communities. Education is both symbolic and practical: when disrupted, it suggests that even the most basic institutions of civic life are vulnerable. Moreover, schools often operate on tight budgets, with limited IT capacity, making them attractive soft targets. The consequence is that children and parents are conscripted into conflicts they neither started nor understood.

Small businesses occupy another vulnerable tier. A hacked payroll system or compromised invoicing software can devastate firms with little margin for recovery. For states, these businesses may seem peripheral; for attackers, they represent entry points into larger supply chains or political narratives. A single breached vendor can cascade into national infrastructure. Here again, citizens—the owners, employees, customers—bear the immediate brunt.

Why, then, are citizens such effective targets? The answer lies in political returns. A blackout at a military base can be classified, contained, and managed. A blackout at a hospital or city hall becomes a national story within hours. Citizens complain, journalists amplify, opposition parties seize upon failures. Leaders are forced onto the defensive, compelled to explain why basic services failed under their watch. In this way, attackers harness democratic accountability against democracies themselves.

There is also a cognitive dimension. Panic spreads faster than information, and in the absence of clarity, rumours thrive. A cyber incident in one school district becomes fuel for anxiety in others. A minor disruption in election reporting snowballs into conspiracy theories about the entire system. The human mind, primed to seek patterns, fills gaps with suspicion. Adversaries exploit this psychological vulnerability as carefully as they exploit technical ones.

The ethical stakes are immense. Targeting civilians in cyberspace may not kill directly, but it corrodes the social fabric. When patients fear that medical systems can be frozen at will, when voters doubt that ballots are secure, when parents wonder if schools can protect their children's data, trust in government withers. National security is no longer a matter of defending distant borders; it is about safeguarding the daily rhythms of ordinary life. Defence ministries may still talk of tanks and planes, but the true front line runs through clinics, classrooms, and town halls.

This shift reframes citizenship itself. Once, to be a citizen under threat meant the possibility of conscription or rationing during wartime. Today, it means carrying the risks of cyber conflict in one's everyday interactions—opening emails, visiting hospitals, paying bills, casting votes. Citizens are not merely collateral damage; they are intentional pressure points. Understanding this is essential if societies are to respond intelligently.

And so the paradox endures: the more digital convenience and connectivity citizens enjoy, the more they become the preferred targets of those who wish to coerce states. National security is now domestic security. The question is whether societies can protect their most ordinary institutions without curtailing the liberties that make them worth defending. The answer, still unwritten, will decide whether citizens remain pawns in conflicts beyond their control—or whether they can become participants in shaping the resilience of their democracies.

Chapter 2

Data Is Territory

In 1884, European powers gathered in Berlin to carve Africa into spheres of influence. Maps were redrawn with straight lines that ignored rivers, languages, and lives. The logic was simple: survey the land, mark it as property, and extract what lay beneath—minerals, crops, labour. Fast forward to today, and another partition is underway. This time there are no rivers to cross or borders to fence. The new resource is data—our movements, preferences, purchases, and communications—and it too is being surveyed, enclosed, and taxed. The lines on the map are not drawn in ink but encoded in standards, contracts, and cloud jurisdictions.

The parallel with empire is not rhetorical flourish. When a platform enters a new market offering "free" connectivity or low-cost devices, it echoes the arrival of colonial companies trading beads for land. Access is exchanged for dependence. The value does not lie in a single person's clicks but in the aggregation, the concentration of information into datasets that can predict behaviour, shape markets, and influence politics. The logic of extraction has shifted from the ground to the cloud, but the asymmetry of power—between those who harvest and those who are harvested—remains remarkably consistent.

Why does this matter? Because privacy, so often framed as an individual preference, is increasingly a matter of sovereignty. A government that cannot control how its citizens' data is collected, processed, and exported has ceded a dimension of self-determination. Just as weak states once found their mines and forests commandeered by foreign firms, today their digital commons are mined by corporations whose terms of service effectively function as law. Consent, when it exists at all, is thin cover for structural dependence. Citizens click "agree" not because they understand, but because opting out is impossible without exclusion from modern life.

This chapter traces how data became territory and why its governance is now a geopolitical struggle. We begin with the analogy to empire: how extraction shifted from minerals to metadata, from surveying landscapes to mapping attention. The transition is not merely metaphorical but practical: the techniques of control—classification, enclosure, taxation—are replicated in digital form. Companies map user behaviour with the precision once reserved for cartographers; they enclose ecosystems through proprietary formats and platforms; they tax activity by taking a cut of every transaction.

We then turn to case studies of what might be called *data colonialism*. In low-regulation markets, firms have deployed services that appear benevolent—cheap internet access, health apps, educational platforms—while ensuring dependence on their infrastructure. The trade is uneven: connectivity in exchange for continuous extraction. Consent, when demanded, is performative. Users "agree" to terms they cannot negotiate or even read, much as colonial subjects once signed treaties in languages they did not speak. The lesson is clear: governance vacuums invite rule by contract, and in cyberspace, contracts often serve as constitutions written by corporations.

Standards, too, operate as borders. The choice of encryption defaults, the protocols governing identity schemes, the decisions of obscure technical committees—these determine who may enter a network, what tolls they must pay, and what protections they can expect. Like borders, standards are political instruments disguised as neutral technicalities. They create winners and losers quietly, deciding which firms dominate, which governments gain visibility, and which citizens enjoy protection. To read standards as politics rather than plumbing is to understand a hidden architecture of power.

Cloud sovereignty is another front. Where data rests determines whose laws apply. Firms exploit this fluidity, shopping for jurisdictions that favour secrecy or weak enforcement. Governments respond with localisation laws, demanding that data about their citizens remain within their borders. Yet clouds, by definition, transcend geography, and multi-region architectures enable companies to arbitrage between competing regimes. Subpoenas, treaties, and mutual legal assistance processes struggle to keep pace. For policymakers and chief technology officers alike, procurement decisions now carry strategic weight: the choice of a cloud provider can determine the reach of a nation's laws.

Finally, we confront the *consent trap*. Liberal democracies often treat consent as the ultimate safeguard: if a user agrees, then exploitation is legitimate. Yet bounded rationality, dark patterns, and asymmetries of information render such consent hollow. The decision to click "accept" is rarely informed, almost never free of coercion. Structural protections—robust regulation, default safeguards, collective bargaining rights for data subjects—matter far more than the ritual of the click. Recognising this trap shifts the debate from individual responsibility to systemic accountability.

Taken together, these threads form the fabric of a new territorial order. Data is not simply a by-product of digital life; it is the terrain upon which political power, economic advantage, and social control are being contested. To misunderstand this is to misread the stakes. To grasp it is to see why battles over privacy, standards, and cloud governance are not arcane disputes but central struggles over sovereignty in the twenty-first century.

The question, then, is not whether data will be governed—it always is—but who will govern it, by what rules, and to whose benefit. As we move deeper into this chapter, we will see how today's choices about extraction, consent, and sovereignty echo the territorial grabs of the past, and how the lines being drawn now will shape not only markets but the contours of freedom itself.

From Land Grabs to Data Grabs

In the late nineteenth century, when European powers carved Africa into colonial possessions, explorers travelled inland with survey maps and steel compasses. Their mission was not only to chart rivers and mountains but to claim what lay beneath: seams of gold, veins of copper, fertile ground for plantations. The act of surveying was not a neutral science; it was the prelude to extraction. To map was to enclose, and to enclose was to control. Today, the resource is no longer mineral or agricultural. It is data: intimate patterns of human life, industrial flows of logistics, environmental readings from sensors embedded in cities. The same logic persists. To map is still to enclose, and to enclose is still to control.

The transition from land to data reveals a striking continuity of imperial techniques. Just as colonial officers once counted heads and hectares to impose taxes, digital firms now count clicks, locations, and transactions. Entire populations are surveyed continuously through devices they willingly carry. To the individual, the act seems trivial—another app downloaded, another form completed. But at scale, this aggregation creates datasets whose value far exceeds any single record. A miner does not profit from a single rock, but from tonnes hauled out of the earth; in the same way, platforms do not profit from a lone search query, but from billions accumulated, correlated, and modelled.

This shift reframes privacy. In liberal discourse, privacy is often imagined as an individual's right to withhold or share. But if value and harm are concentrated in datasets, not in fragments, then privacy is no longer merely personal. It becomes collective, political, even territorial. A nation that loses control over how its citizens' data is gathered and exported has ceded sovereignty, just as surely as a state that cannot guard its oilfields or forests. The personal merges into the geopolitical.

Consider how global platforms extract and organise. Social media firms map networks of friendship, influence, and persuasion with a precision once reserved for intelligence services. E-commerce giants log purchasing flows that reveal not just tastes but vulnerabilities—what people crave, what they fear, when they are willing to pay more. Cloud providers capture industrial telemetry, learning how supply chains pulse, when factories idle, and where bottlenecks lurk. Each act of collection deepens informational asymmetry: firms know more about populations than governments do, and sometimes more than populations know about themselves.

The analogy to empire extends to enclosure. Colonial regimes fenced off land, excluding traditional users in order to commodify its yield. Today, digital ecosystems are enclosed through proprietary standards, app stores, and ecosystems that bind users into dependence. Once inside, exit is costly. Data does not flow freely back to those who generated it; it remains locked, enriched, and monetised by its custodians. The logic is strikingly familiar: resources flow one way, profits flow another, and the governed find themselves bound by rules they did not write.

Taxation completes the imperial triad. Colonial administrations imposed head taxes and hut taxes, payable in coin, to compel participation in their economies. Modern platforms extract rents by taking percentages of transactions, by selling access to datasets, or by charging for visibility in crowded marketplaces. The tax is not denominated in shillings but in data points and fees, yet the principle is the same: those who control the infrastructure set the levy.

The paradox of the digital empire is that citizens participate willingly. They carry the sensors that record them, install the applications that track them, and click "agree" to contracts that legitimise extraction. Yet the voluntariness is thin. To abstain from participation often means exclusion from communication, commerce, or social belonging. The choice is not free but structured: sign away data or accept isolation. Here lies the subtlety of modern extraction. Where land once required force to seize, data is surrendered through routine, through convenience, through the illusion of choice.

The ethical stakes are profound. If datasets confer power, then the aggregation of billions of lives into a handful of corporate hands represents not simply market concentration but political imbalance. These datasets shape advertising markets, yes, but also elections, credit scoring, and health policy. When predictive models are trained on the intimate traces of citizens, those citizens become subjects of governance without representation. The line between commerce and sovereignty dissolves.

Case studies underscore the pattern. In several African and Asian countries, technology firms have offered free internet access through curated platforms. Citizens receive connectivity, but only to a subset of sites chosen by the provider. On the surface, it is a gift; underneath, it is enclosure. The platform becomes the gateway to knowledge, commerce, and social life, setting rules as a private government. Data from millions of first-time users is harvested at the point of entry, shaping future markets and political landscapes. The empire-building is quiet but unmistakable.

This logic does not stop at consumer data. Industrial systems—ports, factories, energy grids—now run on platforms that collect telemetry at scale. A manufacturer's production schedule, a port's shipping flows, an energy grid's fluctuations: these are datasets of immense strategic value. Whoever controls them can anticipate shortages, influence prices, or apply coercion. The competition to host industrial data is thus geopolitical, echoing the contests once fought over rubber, coal, and oil.

To recognise the analogy is not to suggest a perfect continuity. Data, unlike land, is infinitely replicable. Its extraction does not deplete a field or a mine. Yet the value lies not in possession of raw data but in the capacity to aggregate, analyse, and act upon it. That capacity is scarce, and those who wield it can dominate others. Just as colonial empires leveraged railways, telegraphs, and gunboats to magnify control, digital empires leverage machine learning, cloud infrastructure, and global reach. The mechanics differ; the asymmetry of power does not.

What follows from this recognition is unsettling. If privacy is sovereignty, then its erosion is not simply a personal inconvenience but a collective dispossession. If datasets are territory, then governance cannot be left to the click of an individual consent box. The stakes demand political debate, institutional reform, and international contestation.

The open question is whether societies can design structures that prevent data extraction from becoming data empire. Can states assert sovereignty without sliding into authoritarian control? Can citizens regain agency without sacrificing participation in digital life? Can firms profit from data without reproducing the dynamics of colonial exploitation? These questions linger, unresolved, at the heart of the data age.

One truth is already clear: the map of the twenty-first century will not be drawn primarily in land, but in datasets. Whoever surveys, encloses, and taxes them will wield power far beyond their formal boundaries. And as with empires of old, the legacy will not be measured solely in profit or innovation, but in the balance—or imbalance—of freedom, trust, and sovereignty for generations to come.

Case Studies in Data Colonialism

In 2015, a programme known as Free Basics promised to connect millions of people in the Global South to the internet at no cost. Launched by Facebook, it was presented as a philanthropic effort: the gift of digital opportunity to those without access. The catch was subtle but decisive. Users could only visit websites selected by the company and its partners. For many first-time users, Facebook itself became the internet, shaping how they discovered news, commerce, and even public services. On the surface, it looked like inclusion. In practice, it was enclosure. What was "free" came at the price of dependence, as data from these populations flowed to a single corporate centre with minimal oversight.

This paradox—that the infrastructure of digital generosity often conceals a deeper pattern of extraction—defines what can aptly be called *data colonialism*. Just as earlier empires offered railways or schools while securing access to resources, digital platforms provide connectivity or services while ensuring that the data generated accrues to them. The asymmetry is profound. Those in low-regulation markets gain short-term functionality, while the long-term benefits—predictive models, targeted advertising, competitive insights—are centralised elsewhere.

Consider India's initial confrontation with Free Basics. Civil society groups argued that the programme violated the principle of net neutrality, creating a tiered internet in which corporate-curated content was privileged. In 2016, regulators banned the service. Yet by then, the strategic intent was clear: capture users early, shape their habits, and position the platform as indispensable infrastructure. Even without Free Basics, Facebook and similar platforms already commanded such scale that regulators faced an impossible dilemma: limit them and risk depriving citizens of services, or tolerate them and cede control over national data flows.

In Africa, parallel stories unfolded. Telecom operators, in partnership with global platforms, offered "zero-rating" services that exempted certain apps from data charges. For users with limited income, the choice was obvious: why pay for full access when Facebook, WhatsApp, or Twitter could be used without cost? Yet this arrangement entrenched a form of dependency. Local content providers, unable to strike the same deals, found themselves sidelined. The digital public sphere narrowed to a handful of global actors, while user data travelled outward, fuelling models and markets abroad. Once again, access was traded for autonomy.

China's Belt and Road Initiative has carried the logic further, exporting not only fibre-optic cables and surveillance systems but the platforms to run them. In several African and Asian capitals, Chinese firms have built "safe city" systems equipped with cameras, biometric databases, and centralised control rooms. Officially justified as tools for crime reduction or traffic management, they generate streams of data that are not always confined within national borders. Contracts are often opaque, and the governance structures weak. In effect, states purchase infrastructure while simultaneously embedding external dependence. The lesson is familiar: infrastructure is never neutral, and whoever designs it shapes the flows of power.

The education sector offers another telling case. In the aftermath of the COVID-19 pandemic, online learning platforms surged into markets across Latin America, South Asia, and Africa. Promoted as tools to bridge gaps in schooling, they also harvested vast quantities of data on students: attendance patterns, performance metrics, even keystroke dynamics. For governments with limited capacity to regulate, the promise of cheap or free digital education outweighed concerns about privacy. Yet the long-term implications are sobering. Entire cohorts of children are growing up as subjects of data regimes controlled by firms headquartered thousands of miles away. Their learning profiles, aggregated and analysed, become commodities traded in markets they will never see.

What unites these examples is the fig leaf of consent. Citizens are presented with lengthy terms of service, drafted in technical language, which they "accept" with a single click. The act is performative: no one reads, fewer understand, and fewer still have genuine alternatives. Consent in these contexts does not signify informed choice; it legitimises asymmetry. Platforms point to it as evidence of fairness, while regulators struggle to counter its hollowness. Much as colonial treaties were once signed under duress or incomprehension, digital contracts now function as instruments of rule, creating binding obligations without meaningful negotiation.

Governance vacuums exacerbate the pattern. In markets where data protection laws are absent, underfunded, or unenforced, corporate contracts effectively stand in for constitutions. They determine how data is stored, who may access it, and under what circumstances it may be shared. This is sovereignty outsourced. Where once rule was asserted through conquest, now it is asserted through clickwrap agreements and end-user licence terms. Rule by contract has replaced rule by decree.

There is, however, a counterpoint worth noting. For many users in low-income settings, these services are not luxuries but lifelines. A zero-rated app may provide the only affordable means of contacting family abroad, accessing emergency information, or conducting business. To dismiss such services as mere instruments of exploitation risks overlooking the agency of those who use them. The tension lies not in whether these services should exist, but in who sets the terms and whether those terms can be made accountable.

Still, the strategic infrastructure metaphor cannot be ignored. Just as railways were once built to transport minerals to ports rather than to connect local economies, today's digital networks are often optimised to capture and export value. The extractive logic is not concealed; it is embedded in the business model. What distinguishes data colonialism from earlier forms of exploitation is its subtlety: there is no visible frontier, no boundary fence, no explicit act of appropriation. Instead, dependence deepens through the routines of everyday life: the free app, the zero-rated service, the standardised platform.

The challenge is whether governance can catch up. Can regulators in fragmented markets impose conditions on firms whose scale dwarfs that of many states? Can international frameworks be built to ensure that data collected in the Global South is not merely funnelled outward, but reinvested in local capacities? Or will the current trajectory persist, with "free" services operating as Trojan horses, embedding dependence under the guise of inclusion?

The future hinges on these questions. If data is indeed the new territory, then the case studies of Free Basics, zero-rating, safe cities, and edtech platforms are not isolated experiments—they are the early phases of a new imperial cartography. The risk is not only that users surrender their data, but that entire nations find themselves governed by contracts written in corporate boardrooms far from their capitals. Whether these arrangements can be rebalanced will determine not just who profits from data, but who controls the infrastructures that increasingly define citizenship, sovereignty, and freedom itself.

Standards as Borders

In 1983, a quiet but decisive moment in the history of the internet unfolded: the global switch from NCP (Network Control Protocol) to TCP/IP. No armies marched, no treaties were signed, no monuments were erected. Yet in that moment, borders were drawn across the digital landscape. Those who adopted TCP/IP gained access to what would become the global internet. Those who clung to older protocols were gradually stranded in isolated enclaves. A technical standard, invisible to most of the world, performed the work of sovereignty. It decided who could enter, who was left out, and on what terms interaction was possible.

Such moments remind us that borders in the digital age do not always take the form of walls, checkpoints, or customs offices. They are encoded in protocols, encryption defaults, and identity schemes—rules that appear neutral but shape the distribution of power as surely as the cartographers of empires once did. To cross a border is to submit to its conditions. To design the border is to exercise power.

The everyday act of sending an email illustrates the point. Beneath the apparent simplicity lies a thicket of standards—SMTP for transmission, DNS for routing, TLS for encryption. Each standard embodies choices about interoperability, security, and trust. Those choices are not made in a vacuum. They are debated, negotiated, and sometimes fought over in committees whose membership and processes decide the direction of the internet. Participation in these arenas—whether at the Internet Engineering Task Force (IETF), the International Telecommunication Union (ITU), or the World Wide Web Consortium (W3C)—is therefore not simply technical housekeeping. It is politics by other means.

Consider encryption. When defaults are set to weak standards, as they often were in the 1990s under pressure from intelligence agencies, the effect is to create porous borders: states gain easier access, but so too do criminals. When defaults are strong—as in the case of end-to-end encrypted messaging apps—entire classes of surveillance are excluded. Here, the "border" is invisible yet decisive: a message either crosses securely, or it does not. Users rarely notice the negotiations behind these defaults, but governments do. Debates about "going dark," lawful intercept, and backdoors are not just about crime or terrorism; they are about who writes the rules of entry and exit in the global information space.

Identity schemes reveal another layer of politics. Take India's Aadhaar programme, which assigns biometric-linked numbers to over a billion citizens. For some, Aadhaar is a triumph of efficiency: streamlined welfare distribution, reduced fraud, universal identification. For others, it is a creeping border that mediates access to everyday rights—bank accounts, mobile phones, even food subsidies. Here, the standard is not a protocol buried in software but a database and biometric system that reconfigures citizenship itself. Whoever controls the system sets the terms of belonging, exclusion, and surveillance.

Borders, whether physical or digital, also create tariffs—sometimes literal, sometimes hidden. Standards around data localisation, for instance, can function as customs barriers. A country that mandates local storage of health or financial data effectively asserts control over that dataset, preventing firms from routing it to global centres where it might be mined for value. Conversely, cloud providers that design architectures optimised for jurisdiction shopping allow corporations to avoid such tariffs, moving data to wherever tax and regulation are most favourable. The architecture of standards thus doubles as an architecture of economic advantage.

The politics inside standards bodies is less visible but no less consequential. Representation is uneven: large technology firms can afford to send engineers to every meeting, to draft proposals, to shape the consensus process. Small states, by contrast, often lack the expertise or budget to participate meaningfully. The result is a quiet bias. Standards that favour scalability, proprietary ecosystems, or particular languages and technical assumptions tend to prevail. Winners and losers are picked not through open competition but through the subtle choreography of committees, working groups, and drafts.

There are rare moments when the hidden stakes become visible. In the early 2000s, the battle over mobile telephony standards pitted GSM, rooted in European governance, against CDMA, championed by American firms. Billions of dollars in licensing revenues and market dominance hinged on the outcome. In the end, GSM spread across much of the world, ensuring European companies a revenue stream for decades. What looked like a technical decision was, in fact, a geopolitical one: a border drawn across the future of wireless communication.

What makes standards powerful is their capacity to fade into the background. Once adopted, they appear as natural as the lines on a map, their origins forgotten, their alternatives erased. Few users today recall that the keyboard layout they type on—QWERTY—was a compromise shaped by the mechanical limitations of typewriters, yet it continues to govern digital interaction globally. Similarly, the choice of one identity scheme, one encryption default, one routing protocol, locks in advantages and disadvantages that persist long after the debate has ended.

For citizens, the opacity of these processes presents a profound challenge. We do not vote on encryption defaults. We do not deliberate on identity standards. Yet these rules determine the balance between privacy and surveillance, competition and monopoly, openness and exclusion. The politics of standards is rarely visible on campaign trails, but it quietly defines the conditions of our civic and economic life.

If standards are borders, the critical question is: who patrols them? At present, the answer tilts heavily towards a handful of corporations and states with the resources to dominate committees and deploy infrastructure. The rest of the world, whether individuals, small firms, or smaller states, must live with the consequences. Whether that imbalance can be redressed—whether standards can be made more inclusive, accountable, and transparent—remains an open question.

The stakes could not be higher. Borders, once drawn, are difficult to erase. Each technical choice today hardens into tomorrow's political geography. The struggle over standards is therefore not a peripheral skirmish but a central contest in the making of the digital order. And as with all borders, the most important truths are those not seen at first glance: the quiet rules of passage that determine who may cross, and at what price.

Cloud Sovereignty and Jurisdiction Shopping

When Microsoft announced in 2013 that it would challenge a United States warrant demanding access to emails stored on a server in Dublin, the case exposed a paradox that has haunted the digital age ever since: data may exist as electrical pulses on a server rack in one country, but legal authority over it may stretch across oceans. For years, businesses and governments alike had treated cloud storage as if it were weightless, borderless, beyond the reach of territorial logic. In that case, and the decade of disputes it triggered, revealed the opposite. The cloud is not immaterial. It is grounded in jurisdictions, entangled in treaties, and constrained by the politics of place.

This paradox—between the apparent placelessness of digital information and the stubbornly territorial reach of law—has become one of the defining struggles of the 21st century. A firm's decision about where to host its servers is no longer simply about latency, cost, or efficiency. It is about sovereignty, surveillance, and leverage. To store data in Frankfurt rather than California, or in Singapore rather than Sydney, is to bind it to one legal regime rather than another. The choice is strategic, and it is often irreversible.

The stakes can be life-and-death. Consider a hospital chain procuring cloud services for sensitive patient data. A server located in the United States may fall within the scope of the CLOUD Act, granting American authorities the right to demand access, even when that data belongs to non-Americans. A server in Germany, by contrast, is protected by stringent EU privacy law, but also subject to German government access rules. For the hospital, the difference could determine whether patients trust their information will remain confidential—or whether it might one day be pulled into a foreign court proceeding without their knowledge.

This tension gives rise to what might be called *jurisdiction shopping*. Global firms increasingly architect their systems not only for performance but also for regulatory arbitrage. Data is routed, partitioned, and mirrored across regions in order to exploit the gaps between laws. A financial institution might keep transaction records in Luxembourg to benefit from favourable tax secrecy provisions while hosting customer-facing services in the United States to take advantage of robust infrastructure. A social media platform may promise local data storage in India to comply with localisation mandates, while quietly backing up user profiles elsewhere to retain operational flexibility. The game is played across borders, and the rules are rarely transparent.

For policymakers, this creates a dilemma. Traditional instruments of legal cooperation—Mutual Legal Assistance Treaties (MLATs)—were designed for an earlier era, when physical documents or phone records could be requested through diplomatic channels. Today, the scale and speed of digital data overwhelm such processes. Requests for evidence in cybercrime investigations can languish for months or years, undermining prosecutions. In response, some states bypass international mechanisms altogether, compelling cloud providers directly. The providers, caught between conflicting jurisdictions, are left to decide whose laws they will honour and whose they will resist. These decisions, made in corporate boardrooms, effectively determine how justice is carried out across borders.

For technology leaders, the procurement question is equally fraught. To choose a cloud provider is to inherit its geopolitical entanglements. Opting for an American giant like Amazon Web Services or Google Cloud may bring scale and reliability, but it also means inheriting exposure to American law enforcement and intelligence requests. Choosing a regional provider may offer stronger alignment with domestic sovereignty, but potentially at the cost of resilience, global reach, or cutting-edge features. There is no neutral choice. Every procurement decision carries an implicit geopolitical bet.

Data localisation mandates complicate the picture further. Governments from Russia to Vietnam, from Brazil to India, have insisted that certain categories of data must remain within national borders. Their stated reasons vary: protecting citizens' privacy, ensuring national security, fostering local industry. Yet localisation often functions as leverage. It gives governments direct access to data they might otherwise struggle to obtain, and it forces global firms into dependence on local infrastructure and contracts. What appears as a technical requirement is, in fact, a geopolitical move—a form of digital protectionism dressed in the language of security.

At the same time, the very architecture of the cloud undermines clean boundaries. Multi-region deployments, content delivery networks, and automated failover systems mean that data rarely sits in one place for long. A single request to stream a video might be handled in milliseconds by servers in three or four countries. The promise of redundancy and speed, the hallmarks of modern cloud design, is also a nightmare for regulators. To ask "where" a piece of data resides is increasingly to ask the wrong question. Data is not so much stored as it is *in motion*, perpetually mirrored, cached, and shifted according to algorithms that optimise for performance, not sovereignty.

Yet even this fluidity does not dissolve borders—it multiplies them. Each copy, each cache, each fragment is subject to the laws of the territory in which it happens to appear. What emerges is a patchwork sovereignty, where the same dataset may simultaneously fall under multiple, even conflicting, legal regimes. For firms, this creates staggering compliance complexity. For states, it creates opportunities for reach: if your adversary's data passes through your territory, even briefly, you may claim jurisdiction.

The strategic implications are profound. Just as control of sea lanes once conferred power over trade, control of data centres and cables now confers power over information flows. Countries that host major cloud infrastructure gain leverage, not only over their own citizens but over foreign firms and governments reliant on their servers. The United States has used this leverage for decades; China is building it rapidly; the European Union, through its General Data Protection Regulation (GDPR) and its push for "digital sovereignty," is seeking to carve out a third path. Smaller states must choose whether to align with one of these poles, to build regional coalitions, or to gamble on neutrality.

For the individual citizen, these debates often feel remote. Few think about where their emails are stored, or under which jurisdiction their photos fall. Yet the consequences are intimate. A journalist's sources, a patient's records, a voter's data profile—all can be exposed or protected depending on how cloud sovereignty is resolved. To be a citizen of the digital age is to live with the knowledge that your most personal information may be bound by the laws of a country you have never set foot in.

This raises unsettling questions. Should sovereignty follow the individual, wherever their data travels? Should it follow the company, whose servers store it? Or should it follow the state, within whose borders the servers sit? Each answer empowers one actor and disempowers another. Each creates new incentives for control, conflict, or evasion. The debate is far from settled.

Cloud sovereignty, then, is not an abstract problem for technologists. It is a frontier where law, power, and technology collide. It determines who may see what, under what conditions, and with whose consent. As firms continue to arbitrage jurisdictions, as states demand localisation, as treaties lag and enforcement falters, the central question remains unresolved: in a world where data flows freely but laws do not, who truly governs the cloud?

The Consent Trap

One evening in 2008, the London-based gamemaker Gamestation pulled an elaborate April Fools' prank. Buried within its online terms of service was a clause granting the company ownership of the customer's immortal soul. Ninety per cent of users clicked *I agree.* Only a handful spotted the joke and opted out. The story has since become folklore in digital rights circles, but its lesson remains uncomfortably sharp: consent, as currently practised online, is little more than a ritualised click.

Every day, billions of people around the world scroll past dense privacy policies and press a button that signifies nothing of the careful deliberation the law imagines. The modern internet rests on this fragile fiction: that citizens freely weigh the trade-offs of surveillance and tracking, that their "choice" is meaningful, and that they are therefore complicit in whatever follows. In reality, the act of consent has been hollowed out, reduced to a compliance exercise. The more serious the stakes—the collection of medical records, location data, children's educational histories—the more absurd the ritual appears.

The paradox is stark. Consent is meant to empower the individual, yet in practice it overwhelms and misleads. No one has the time to parse the endless legalese. No one can reasonably predict the long-term consequences of agreeing to let an app monitor their heartbeat, or a platform sell their browsing habits to brokers. By design or neglect, the burden of safeguarding the collective has been shifted onto the individual—whose only weapon is a checkbox.

At the heart of this failure lies what behavioural economists call *bounded rationality*. Humans make decisions under conditions of limited time, knowledge, and attention. We satisfice rather than optimise. Faced with a wall of text, we click because the alternative is paralysis: without acceptance, we cannot access the service, complete the transaction, or join the conversation. Consent, in this framing, is not an expression of autonomy but of coercion. It is the toll gate we must pass to live a modern life.

Technology companies understand this dynamic well and exploit it with what design researchers call *dark patterns*. Buttons are coloured to nudge acceptance, alternatives are buried, and choices are framed in ways that make refusal feel punitive. The famous cookie banner, ostensibly created to empower users, became a masterclass in manipulation: "accept all" glowing in bright blue, "manage preferences" hidden in grey. Over time, a generation of users has been trained to consent reflexively, like pressing a pedestrian crossing button that may or may not control the lights.

The deeper trap, however, is structural. Even if every citizen read every privacy policy in full, their choices would not add up to meaningful protection. Consider location tracking on smartphones. A single person declining consent does little if everyone else in their social circle accepts. The patterns of their movements—where they live, whom they meet, when they travel—can still be inferred. Privacy, in other words, is not an individual commodity but a collective condition. Yet the regulatory framework treats it otherwise, converting a shared social dilemma into billions of isolated, unmakeable decisions.

Case after case illustrates this collective vulnerability. Fitness trackers that aggregate "anonymous" jogging routes end up exposing military bases. Contact-tracing apps deployed during the pandemic demonstrated how even anonymised datasets can be recombined to identify individuals. Data brokers assemble profiles that follow people across elections, insurance markets, and job applications. Each profile is composed from countless small acts of "consent", none of which individually seemed dangerous. Only in the aggregate does the harm emerge.

The persistence of the consent model reveals a telling asymmetry. For companies, it is convenient: liability is deflected, responsibility outsourced, while data continues to flow. For regulators, it offers a veneer of protection without confronting the harder questions of power and structure. For citizens, it is an exhausting theatre. Clicking "agree" does not mean we agree. It means we surrender because the system gives us no workable alternative.

To break free of this trap requires shifting the frame from *performative consent* to *structural protections*. Imagine food safety regulated not by inspectors but by consumers carefully reading every label, weighing every risk, and rejecting unsafe products one by one. It would be absurd. Yet this is exactly how we treat data. We expect individuals to compensate for systemic failures in design, enforcement, and governance. Real protection would mean safe defaults, meaningful limits on data collection, and accountability built into the infrastructure itself. Consent should be the last line of defence, not the first.

Philosophically, this raises a profound question about what it means to be a citizen in the digital age. Are we merely consumers of platforms, bound to the terms of service they draft? Or are we members of polities, entitled to rights and protections that cannot be waived away with a click? The answer will shape not only the future of privacy but the texture of democracy itself.

And so the problem endures. Every day we click, scroll, and surrender, participating in a ritual we know is empty. The system depends on our compliance fatigue, on the quiet hope that the risks will remain invisible until it is too late. But what happens when the first great scandal emerges not from a breach or a hack but from the ordinary, lawful use of data we all “consented” to share? That question hangs unanswered, waiting for a reckoning that will redraw the line between autonomy and protection in the digital age.

Chapter 3

The Anatomy of a State Hacker

On a frosty morning in December 2015, the lights went out across western Ukraine. More than 200,000 people were left without electricity in the depths of winter. Power substations had been methodically disabled not by bombs or sabotage teams but by keystrokes. Investigators later traced the operation to a group with ties to Russian intelligence. What shocked observers was not only the disruption itself, but the sophistication of the tradecraft: coordinated intrusion into multiple utilities, malware designed to lock operators out of their own control panels, and even the wiping of systems to hinder recovery. This was not the work of lone hackers in basements. It was the manifestation of a state apparatus, organised, funded, and disciplined, operating with intent.

Such episodes force us to confront an uncomfortable truth: behind many of the most consequential cyber operations are not individuals but institutions. These institutions—sometimes hidden in military units, sometimes disguised as private contractors, sometimes tolerated in the form of semi-criminal proxies—are the modern heirs to espionage bureaux and covert services of old. But unlike their predecessors, they operate on a terrain where the line between peace and war is deliberately blurred. Their actions can disable hospitals, steal trade secrets, or sow disinformation, all without a single soldier crossing a border.

To understand state hackers is therefore to understand not only the code they write but the bureaucracies and cultures that produce them. An Advanced Persistent Threat (APT) is not just a technical label. It is an organisational form. It includes access brokers who sell footholds into corporate networks, operators who carry out missions, and managers who prioritise targets according to strategic goals. Budgets, doctrines, and internal rivalries all shape how these units move. Tempo is not random; it reflects whether an operation is experimental, opportunistic, or part of a longer campaign. By studying the anatomy of these entities, we gain a lens through which to read signals from the noise.

The infrastructure that sustains them is equally revealing. Behind every breach lie toolchains, and behind those toolchains lie economies. Zero-day exploits—the crown jewels of cyber offence—are discovered, brokered, and priced in markets that hover between the legitimate and the illicit. States participate in these markets, sometimes openly, sometimes through cut-outs. Price signals reflect rarity and risk, and procurement decisions in turn shape restraint. A government with a stockpile of unpatched vulnerabilities may feel emboldened, while one that invests in disclosure may strengthen collective defence. Thus the marketplace for code becomes a theatre of strategy, no less consequential than arms bazaars of the past.

Nor can we ignore the human dimension. Talent must be recruited, trained, and retained. Some states draw directly from universities, embedding cyber operations within their military academies. Others lean on patriotic hackers or criminal groups, offering protection in exchange for services. These arrangements create deniability but at a cost: proxies are unreliable, their interests divergent, their discipline uneven. When governments crack down selectively, it is rarely about law and order. It is a signal—an assertion of control, a warning to adversaries, or a recalibration of relationships. Every arrest, every tolerated gang, is part of the geopolitical script.

Around these structures swirls the constant dance of plausible deniability. False flags, rented servers, time-zone tricks: all are deployed to obscure attribution. Yet analysts are rarely fooled for long. Patterns of behaviour, linguistic slips, operational sloppiness—all leave traces that pierce the mask. Still, the ambiguity serves its purpose. In a crisis, leaders cannot act with the certainty they crave. Did this attack truly come from a rival state, or from opportunistic criminals? Was it authorised by the top, or a rogue contractor? These uncertainties complicate public communication, test alliances, and shape legitimacy itself.

At the core of the chapter lies a challenge: how do we read intent in the digital shadows? Not every intrusion is preparation for war. Some are probes, some are rehearsals, some are demonstrations meant to be seen. By mapping depth of access against political risk, by distinguishing practice from provocation, we sharpen the art of response. Without such discernment, governments risk either overreaction that escalates conflict, or paralysis that invites further aggression.

This chapter, then, invites the reader into the inner architecture of state hacking. It unpacks the organisations, the markets, the proxies, the misdirections, and the analytical tools that together define the field. To see a breach headline is one thing; to read it as a symptom of budgetary choices, cultural norms, or geopolitical gambits is quite another. By the time we step through its anatomy, we will be better equipped to answer the question that haunts every incident: not merely *what happened*, but *who made it happen, why, and what it portends for what comes next.*

Inside an APT

In 2014, the cybersecurity world was rocked when a group of analysts revealed a sprawling network of intrusions across governments, defence contractors, and energy firms. The fingerprints pointed not to a lone actor but to an organisation later dubbed "APT1"—a unit believed to be part of China's People's Liberation Army. The report mapped not only malicious code but working hours, language preferences, and even the rhythm of tea breaks mirrored in the log files. What emerged was less the shadow of an anonymous hacker and more the silhouette of a bureaucracy: regimented, resourced, and operating on a schedule. The incident forced a realisation that state-backed hacking was not just about keystrokes but about institutions, cultures, and chains of command.

The paradox is striking. The myth of the hacker has long been one of individual brilliance, a lone genius exploiting systems with flair and audacity. Yet the most persistent and effective intrusions come not from isolated savants but from teams organised much like any modern workplace. There are managers and junior staff, budget lines and performance metrics, standard operating procedures and improvisational flourishes. The acronym *APT*—Advanced Persistent Threat—captures this truth. What makes such groups formidable is not merely the sophistication of their tools, but their persistence, discipline, and organisational depth. To see them clearly, one must look not only at their malware but at their structure.

An APT is best understood as an ecosystem with distinct roles. At the perimeter lie *access brokers*—specialists or affiliates whose task is to secure the initial foothold into a target system. They might exploit phishing campaigns, unpatched servers, or insider contacts, often operating in a grey zone between crime and espionage. Once inside, operators—akin to field agents—take over. They move laterally across networks, exfiltrating data, escalating privileges, or planting backdoors for future use. Behind them sit analysts, who sort stolen material, filter intelligence value, and align findings with the demands of their superiors. Overseeing this machinery are managers and political masters, whose decisions shape target lists and prioritise sectors. The architecture is hierarchical but flexible, mirroring the bureaucratic cultures of the states that sponsor them.

Budgetary resources are a quiet but decisive factor. Well-funded units can afford to retain elite talent, commission bespoke malware, and even build internal research and development labs. Cash-strapped teams, by contrast, lean heavily on off-the-shelf tools, reusing publicly available exploits and open-source frameworks. These differences are not merely cosmetic. They show up in the tempo of operations. A wealthy unit may launch multi-pronged campaigns with patience, holding back undisclosed vulnerabilities until they can be deployed with maximum effect. A leaner group might strike opportunistically, using whatever tools are at hand, risking exposure for short-term gain. Observers who track tempo and tool choice can often infer resource levels, just as archaeologists deduce the wealth of ancient societies from the artefacts they leave behind.

Doctrine and culture add further texture. A unit steeped in military hierarchy may adopt rigid chains of command, with little room for improvisation by junior staff. Another, nurtured in a culture of entrepreneurial hacking, may prize initiative and experimentation, tolerating errors in pursuit of breakthroughs. These cultural signatures are visible in operational behaviour: one group may favour stealthy, multi-year infiltrations with elaborate compartmentalisation, while another may opt for smash-and-grab raids that accept detection as an acceptable cost. The doctrine that shapes a unit reflects the strategic worldview of its sponsors—whether they see cyberspace primarily as an arena for intelligence collection, coercion, or sabotage.

The interplay of doctrine and organisation also shapes *target selection*. Some groups show a narrow, laser-like focus: defence ministries, aerospace firms, critical infrastructure. Others roam more widely, scooping up data from universities, NGOs, and local governments. The breadth or precision of these campaigns speaks volumes about their mandate. A sprawling portfolio may suggest a doctrine of comprehensive situational awareness, while a sharper focus indicates preparation for specific contingencies. By comparing observed targeting with declared national strategies, analysts can reverse-engineer the priorities of a state.

Case studies abound. APT28, often linked to Russian military intelligence, has demonstrated a taste for disruptive operations: leaking stolen documents to sway elections, probing energy grids, and timing leaks for maximum political effect. Its tempo is rapid, its style aggressive, consistent with a doctrine of information confrontation. By contrast, groups tied to other states have shown a preference for quiet espionage, siphoning industrial secrets over years without detection. The signatures differ, but the organisational scaffolding is visible in each case.

Culture extends even to mundane details. Analysts pore over compilation times of malware samples to deduce working hours. They examine keyboard layouts embedded in code to infer language backgrounds. From these fragments emerges the profile of a workforce: professionals who log in at nine, take lunch at noon, and stop at five; contractors juggling multiple gigs; night owls compensated with bonuses for after-hours work. These glimpses humanise the machinery, reminding us that behind the abstractions are individuals embedded in systems, their behaviour constrained by pay scales, office politics, and performance reviews.

Understanding these structures equips defenders with predictive power. If one knows that a particular unit typically relies on access brokers, then unusual spikes in broker activity may presage a campaign. If one knows that a group values long-term persistence, then an unexpected, noisy intrusion may be a feint. Analysts can map capability not only by technical artefacts but by organisational logic. Just as military historians study the logistics of armies to understand battles, so too must cyber strategists study the bureaucracies behind the code.

Yet much remains opaque. States adapt, contractors switch allegiances, doctrines evolve. The boundaries between crime and espionage blur, with operators moonlighting in ransomware while fulfilling state contracts. What looks from the outside like a monolithic adversary may in fact be a loose coalition of units, subcontractors, and tolerated freelancers. To study an APT is to study a moving target, its shape shifting even as we trace it.

The task, then, is not to reduce an APT to a static organogram but to read it as a dynamic institution—alive, adaptive, and embedded in its political context. To observe its tempo is to glimpse its budget; to map its targets is to infer its doctrine; to decode its culture is to anticipate its next move. But how much can we ever truly know? And when states deliberately cultivate ambiguity, how should defenders and policymakers act upon partial knowledge? These questions linger at the edge of every analysis, reminding us that to understand the anatomy of an APT is not to achieve certainty, but to equip ourselves for decisions under uncertainty.

Toolchains and zero-day markets

In July 2021, a revelation from Amnesty International shook the political class: Pegasus, a spyware suite developed by the Israeli company NSO Group, had been used to compromise the phones of journalists, dissidents, and heads of state. The story was not merely about surveillance; it exposed the hidden economy of software flaws. Every successful intrusion depended on so-called *zero-days*—previously unknown vulnerabilities that no patch could defend against. Their scarcity, secrecy, and destructive potential gave them extraordinary market value. Behind the headlines lay a question that still troubles policymakers: when a flaw can be sold for millions, should it be treated as property, as a weapon, or as contraband?

The paradox of zero-days is sharp. They are intangible—lines of code, quirks of logic, or overlooked conditions in complex software—yet they command prices that rival fine art or rare diamonds. A single iOS remote code execution exploit, once valued at $2 million on grey markets, could grant near-total access to a target's device. Unlike art, however, its value lies not in being admired but in being unseen. The worth of a zero-day evaporates the moment it becomes public. This fleeting nature drives an entire ecosystem of discovery, brokerage, and operational use. It also explains why states, criminals, and corporations alike vie to control the supply.

The process begins with discovery. Vulnerabilities can be found by meticulous code auditing, fuzzing tools that bombard applications with random input, or serendipitous accidents. Some are unearthed by academic researchers seeking recognition, others by freelance hackers chasing profit. In many cases, governments cultivate in-house teams whose sole job is to probe widely used software—Windows, Android, industrial control systems—for cracks invisible to ordinary eyes. The skills required straddle disciplines: part reverse engineering, part mathematics, part artistry. A small handful of individuals, often young and self-taught, may wield knowledge worth more than the budget of an entire security agency.

Once a vulnerability is discovered, it enters a grey marketplace. Here, brokers act as intermediaries between finders and buyers. Some operate openly, such as Zerodium or Crowdfense, advertising bounties for certain classes of bugs. Others remain opaque, cultivating relationships with state agencies, defence contractors, or less savoury buyers. Prices fluctuate with rarity and potential effect. A flaw that requires physical access might fetch little; a remotely exploitable, reliable bug in a ubiquitous platform can command millions. These markets resemble commodities exchanges, except the assets are fragile, non-renewable, and capable of transforming geopolitics.

For states, the procurement of zero-days becomes an exercise in balancing secrecy and security. On one hand, hoarding flaws grants offensive power: the ability to penetrate adversary systems, spy on rivals, or prepare sabotage. On the other, stockpiling vulnerabilities exposes one's own citizens and infrastructure to the same unpatched risks. This tension is encapsulated in the debate over vulnerability equities processes—frameworks designed to decide whether to disclose a discovered flaw to the vendor (thereby strengthening defence) or to retain it for operations (preserving offence). Few states manage this balance transparently. The secrecy that cloaks such decisions only heightens suspicion among allies and adversaries alike.

Operational use adds another layer of complexity. A zero-day is not a tool in isolation but part of a *toolchain*: a sequence of exploits and payloads designed to bypass protections, escalate privileges, and maintain persistence. Crafting and deploying a toolchain requires extensive operational security. Once an exploit is used, it risks exposure; forensic analysts may capture samples, vendors may issue patches, and the asset's value plummets. Savvy operators therefore ration their zero-days, deploying them only for high-value targets or time-sensitive missions. Some are never used at all, kept as deterrents or bargaining chips. The lifecycle of a zero-day thus mirrors that of traditional weaponry: acquisition, stockpiling, deployment, and eventual obsolescence.

Case studies illustrate the stakes. Stuxnet, the worm that sabotaged Iran's nuclear centrifuges, relied on at least four zero-day exploits in Windows systems—an arsenal so expensive and rare that its deployment revealed the strategic priority of the mission. By contrast, less sophisticated campaigns, such as those by criminal ransomware groups, often repurpose publicly known vulnerabilities or borrow from leaks of state-developed tools. The disparity reflects the economics: few groups outside major powers can afford fresh zero-days, but many can recycle cast-offs. Leaks such as the Shadow Brokers' dump of NSA tools in 2017 democratised access to powerful exploits, sparking waves of ransomware outbreaks like WannaCry. The episode highlighted how fragile the line is between controlled state use and uncontrolled proliferation.

The philosophical stakes are no less profound. If data is the lifeblood of modern societies, then vulnerabilities are its fractures. To buy and sell them is to commodify insecurity itself. The moral question looms: should knowledge of a flaw that could endanger millions ever be privately owned? Advocates of disclosure argue that vendors must be informed so they can patch and protect users. Opponents counter that disclosure neutralises valuable intelligence capabilities and rewards adversaries who disclose less. Between these poles lies a murky reality: states pursue their own advantage, firms weigh profit against ethics, and users are left exposed to choices they neither see nor influence.

Bounded rationality and misaligned incentives complicate matters further. Governments may invest millions in hoarding vulnerabilities while underfunding basic cyber hygiene for hospitals or schools. Corporations may patch slowly, leaving systems vulnerable even after flaws are revealed. Hackers may chase the highest bidder, regardless of geopolitical consequences. In this fractured environment, the zero-day market functions not merely as a technical arena but as a stage where questions of sovereignty, ethics, and trust collide.

And so we arrive at the tension that drives policy debates: how should societies regulate tools that can both defend and destroy? Bug bounty programmes and responsible disclosure channels offer one path, channelling discovery into constructive repair. Yet these coexist uneasily with clandestine procurement and offensive stockpiling. Transparency is limited, oversight weaker still. The result is a shadow economy that influences diplomacy, commerce, and national security, all without the visibility accorded to conventional arms.

Perhaps the most unsettling aspect of this world is its fragility. A single leak, a disgruntled insider, or a vendor patch can collapse the value of assets worth millions. States and firms invest heavily in secrecy, but secrecy is brittle. The next breach could release tools into the wild, reshaping the balance of power overnight. How, then, should governments and citizens alike think about security in a world where the very discovery of a flaw can become a tradable weapon? That question remains unanswered, hanging over the digital landscape like a storm cloud—its eventual break both inevitable and unpredictable.

Recruitment and proxies

In 2016, the world awoke to headlines linking the Democratic National Committee hack to Russian operatives. What caught many observers off guard was not just the scale of the intrusion but the messy mixture of actors behind it. Some appeared to be formal intelligence officers, others freelancers, and still others criminal groups with histories of ransomware campaigns. The lines blurred: was this a state-directed operation, or a loose coalition of opportunists whose actions aligned with Moscow's interests? That ambiguity was not incidental—it was the point. The genius, and the peril, of cyber power lies in the ease with which states can cultivate deniable auxiliaries while never quite holding the reins.

Unlike the clean hierarchies of Cold War espionage, today's digital campaigns are built from a patchwork of contractors, academics, criminals, and volunteers. States are often less interested in direct employment than in influence—ensuring talent is nearby, loyal enough, and capable of producing results. Recruitment can be overt, with official advertisements for "cybersecurity researchers" inside military or intelligence agencies. It can also be subtle: fellowships in university labs that double as training pipelines, hackathons that identify gifted coders, or scholarships that tie bright graduates to government contracts. The pool of technical talent is too wide and too fluid for states to monopolise outright, but they can shape its flow.

Universities occupy a peculiar position in this ecosystem. In China, for example, institutions like PLA Unit 61398's affiliations with regional universities have provided a steady stream of graduates versed in computer science and network engineering, already socialised into the patriotic narratives of "cyber sovereignty." In the United States, the National Security Agency's partnerships with research universities have performed a similar role, albeit framed in the language of national service and career advancement. In both cases, the message is clear: your skills are not just personal assets, they are instruments of state power. Students are not merely educated; they are cultivated.

Yet recruitment alone is insufficient. States also rely on proxies—actors outside the formal chain of command, tolerated or even quietly encouraged because they provide capabilities at low cost and high deniability. Russia's posture toward ransomware gangs illustrates this logic. Groups like REvil or Conti operated from Russian soil with apparent impunity, targeting Western firms and critical infrastructure. Moscow could plausibly deny responsibility while reaping the benefits of pressure applied to its adversaries. When political conditions shifted—such as after US demands for action in 2021—Russian authorities suddenly cracked down, arresting figures who had long been visible to anyone paying attention. The timing was not about law enforcement capacity; it was diplomatic signalling.

This timing underscores the duality of proxies. They are useful because they can act where states cannot, taking risks too politically costly for official agencies. Yet they are dangerous because they can spiral beyond control. Criminal groups, once tolerated, may pursue profit in ways that embarrass or destabilise their patrons. Militias and volunteers may escalate conflicts in directions leaders never intended. The balance between utility and liability is delicate. Crackdowns are therefore rarely about eliminating proxies altogether; they are about recalibrating the leash. Arrests, purges, or sudden disappearances serve as reminders: independence is tolerated only within bounds.

Consider Iran's use of so-called "patriotic hackers." After the Stuxnet attack on its nuclear programme, Tehran encouraged a generation of technically skilled youth to engage in retaliatory attacks on Western targets. Over time, some were incorporated into more formal units, while others continued as loosely connected actors, blurring the line between state defence and vigilante action. The advantage for Iran was clear: a pool of motivated operators who could act unpredictably, signalling resilience and defiance without the state formally crossing red lines. The disadvantage was equally clear: operations occasionally revealed amateurism, attracting retaliation disproportionate to their strategic value.

Cultural context matters here. A state's doctrine shapes whether it sees proxies as assets or threats. Western democracies, concerned about legal accountability and reputational costs, tend to centralise operations within state agencies or contractors under close oversight. Autocracies, more comfortable with ambiguity, often embrace the chaos of proxy networks as a feature, not a flaw. Yet even within democracies, the temptation to outsource persists. Private military contractors in physical conflicts have their digital analogues: firms that sell intrusion services under contract, operating in a grey zone between defence consultancy and offensive capability provider.

The philosophical tension is striking. Recruitment and proxy use reveal that cyber power is not only about technology but about trust. Who does a state trust to wield tools that could trigger diplomatic crises? How much deniability is worth the risk of losing control? In practice, the answer lies in a shifting equilibrium: states tolerate more autonomy when strategic gains outweigh potential blowback, and they tighten control when the risks begin to outweigh the benefits. For outside observers, this equilibrium is revealing. A sudden crackdown on criminal hackers may not signify a moral awakening but a recalibration of interests.

This pattern places analysts, policymakers, and citizens in a difficult position. Every arrest, every leak, every exposé of a hacker group must be read as a signal. Was it genuine law enforcement, or was it a diplomatic gesture? Was the group truly independent, or was it operating with tacit blessing until it became inconvenient? The answers are rarely straightforward. The ambiguity is the strategy.

Recruitment pipelines and proxy networks remind us that state hacking is less a monolith than a mosaic. It is a living system of relationships, incentives, and bargains—formal and informal, stable and precarious. To study it is to accept uncertainty, to read between lines, to infer intent from half-steps. And perhaps that is the lesson: the greatest power of proxies is not in the attacks they launch but in the questions they leave hanging. When a hospital is paralysed by ransomware or an election database is breached, the question that echoes is not only *how* but *who*. And when the "who" remains unclear, every government action, every crackdown, every silence becomes part of the theatre of digital statecraft.

Plausible deniability

When a malware campaign cripples a power grid, or when a flood of disinformation suddenly tilts an election conversation, the first instinct of officials is to ask the simplest of questions: *who did this?* Yet in cyberspace, that question rarely finds a clean answer. Attackers understand that attribution is often more consequential than the attack itself. To obscure their hand is to blunt retaliation, to delay consensus, and to exploit divisions among adversaries. Plausible deniability is not an afterthought—it is strategy.

The 2007 cyberattacks on Estonia remain a formative example. Following the relocation of a Soviet war memorial, Estonian networks were battered by waves of distributed denial-of-service traffic, overwhelming banks, ministries, and media outlets. The Kremlin denied involvement, pointing instead to patriotic Russian youth enraged by the perceived slight. The evidence was murky enough that NATO hesitated. For Estonia, the message was unmistakable: Moscow could inflict pain without tripping the thresholds of collective defence. For Russia, the beauty of the operation was precisely in its ambiguity—damage delivered without a return address.

Plausible deniability operates through many tools. One is the use of *cut-outs*—intermediaries who handle operational details, providing insulation between the state and the act. These may be front companies contracted to provide "penetration testing services," freelance hackers hired via encrypted chat rooms, or third-party suppliers already embedded deep within global supply chains. Each additional layer obscures the true author, ensuring that if the thread is pulled, it frays into nothing more than circumstantial suggestion.

Another device is the so-called *bulletproof host*. These are servers deliberately located in jurisdictions with weak or complicit regulation, where takedown requests vanish into bureaucratic fog. Attackers can route malicious traffic through them, mixing it with ordinary activity, making attribution feel like unravelling a knot of identical threads. Even if investigators trace the path, they arrive at an unhelpful conclusion: a rented server in a country unwilling or unable to cooperate. The trail grows cold, not because the technology is impregnable, but because the politics are.

Time-zone games are subtler but no less effective. Malware may be compiled to mimic the working hours of one country while actually being developed in another. Linguistic quirks are deliberately planted—Cyrillic variables in code written by English speakers, Chinese-language comments embedded by Russian developers. These details serve as breadcrumbs, left precisely so that investigators following standard forensic procedures arrive at a misleading destination. In this sense, attribution becomes a hall of mirrors: every reflection plausible, none definitive.

Yet denial is rarely airtight. Analysts have learnt to pierce misdirection by layering methods: code comparison, infrastructure analysis, behavioural patterns, even geopolitical timing. No single piece of evidence proves attribution, but the accumulation of indicators can shift probabilities enough to generate confidence. When the United States and United Kingdom publicly attributed the NotPetya attack to the Russian military, they did so not on the basis of a single "smoking gun," but through a mosaic of technical signatures, intelligence intercepts, and contextual reasoning. This is why public communication is fraught: officials must strike a delicate balance between revealing enough to build legitimacy and holding back sources and methods to avoid burning capabilities.

The stakes extend beyond forensic neatness. In crises, attribution determines coalition-building. If an attack on a hospital can be credibly tied to a hostile state, allies may rally behind sanctions or collective defence measures. If attribution is muddled, consensus frays. The very act of casting doubt—claiming, for instance, that a ransomware group acted independently when it in fact operated with state blessing—can paralyse decision-making among allies who demand higher thresholds of proof. Ambiguity becomes a weapon to sow division.

This dynamic reveals the paradox of plausible deniability: it thrives not only on deception but also on the cautious habits of democratic governance. Open societies demand evidence before action; adversaries exploit this demand by ensuring evidence is forever contested. The result is strategic hesitation. Some policymakers, fearing escalation, prefer to accept deniability rather than risk miscalculation. Others argue that failing to call out state-backed activity invites further aggression. Both responses, in different ways, are conditioned by the fog deliberately manufactured by attackers.

For analysts and decision-makers, the challenge is to navigate this terrain without succumbing to paralysis. Attribution must be communicated with transparency about confidence levels—phrased in probabilities, not absolutes. This requires a cultural shift: to acknowledge uncertainty not as weakness but as realism. For publics accustomed to courtroom standards of proof, this can be uncomfortable. Yet in the domain of cyber conflict, the choice is rarely between certainty and doubt; it is between acting under imperfect knowledge or allowing ambiguity to become impunity.

The deeper lesson is that plausible deniability is not simply a technical puzzle to be solved. It is a political performance, staged for multiple audiences: the adversary, the allies, the domestic public. Every false flag, every cut-out, every carefully timed crackdown on proxy hackers is designed to shape perceptions as much as to shape outcomes. Analysts must therefore read these signals with the eye of a detective and the sensibility of a historian, aware that every trace left behind may have been planted for effect.

But how much ambiguity can the international system tolerate before deterrence breaks down entirely? If every hospital outage, every blackout, every electoral hack is wrapped in layers of denial, how long before publics stop believing their governments' attributions altogether? In that erosion of trust lies the deeper danger: plausible deniability may buy states tactical room to manoeuvre, but it risks corroding the very legitimacy on which collective security depends. And if legitimacy dissolves, what remains to hold back the flood of unseen, unclaimed, and unpunished acts that shape our digital age?

Capability and intent

When the SolarWinds breach came to light in 2020, investigators confronted a puzzle that reverberates through every conversation on cyber conflict. Was this sprawling intrusion—spanning thousands of organisations, including U.S. government departments—an act of espionage, a rehearsal for sabotage, or the prelude to something graver? The attackers had gained extraordinary access. Yet intent was less clear. Was the depth of penetration a show of force, a tool for gathering intelligence, or preparation for disruption in a future crisis? The answers mattered, not just for technical remediation but for geopolitical response. A quiet counterintelligence operation invites one kind of retaliation. A preparation for disabling critical systems might demand another. This uncertainty captures the essence of the challenge: separating capability from intent.

In cyberspace, capability can be dazzlingly deceptive. Malware may burrow deep into networks, but depth alone does not prove imminent attack. Some intrusions are scaffolding—access built and left dormant, a way of keeping options open. Others are demonstrations, their purpose not to cripple but to signal: *we can reach you; we can touch the systems you prize most.* The Stuxnet worm, for instance, revealed not just a specific capability to damage Iranian centrifuges, but an entirely new category of statecraft—digital sabotage at the heart of strategic infrastructure. Once revealed, it reshaped calculations across the globe, as much by its existence as by its immediate effect.

Intent, by contrast, is slippery, inferred through context and risk appetite. Analysts must ask: what political conditions surround the intrusion? Who stands to benefit from the act being public, or from it remaining covert? A ransomware gang holding hospitals hostage during a pandemic may be motivated by profit, but the tolerance of the state that shelters them reveals political calculation. Similarly, probing electoral systems months before an election may not signal an intention to disable them outright but to hold leverage: a sword suspended above the democratic process, to be lowered—or not—depending on shifting strategy.

This is why analysts increasingly turn to matrices to interpret operations. One axis maps the *depth of access*—how entrenched the adversary is in a system, whether they control an email account or entire industrial processes. The other plots *political risk*—the level of escalation an attack would provoke if uncovered. An intrusion into a small firm's invoicing system sits low on both scales: shallow and low-risk. Embedding malware inside a nuclear plant's control software, by contrast, is high on depth and high on risk. Where an incident sits on this matrix tells us whether it is likely probing, practice, or preparation.

Probing operations test defences. They are like scouts in military campaigns, mapping terrain and measuring vigilance. Chinese operators, for example, have been observed scanning utility companies' networks across multiple continents, not causing immediate damage but building a cartography of vulnerabilities. Practice operations are different—they exercise tools in live environments, refining craft against real-world defences. Demonstration operations, meanwhile, are overt by design. The Shamoon attack that wiped tens of thousands of computers in Saudi Aramco was not subtle. It was theatre: a performance of capability meant to resonate politically. Finally, preparation operations plant the seeds for later disruption—quietly embedding code, establishing persistence, and waiting for the moment when leverage is most useful.

Distinguishing between these categories is more than academic. Misreading practice as preparation can drive premature escalation; mistaking preparation for mere probing can invite disaster. Here lies the policy conundrum: leaders must make decisions under radical uncertainty, often with incomplete intelligence. Should they treat an intrusion as a warning or as a weapon? The decision is never neutral, for inaction communicates as much as action. A restrained response may signal prudence—or weakness. A forceful counterpunch may deter—or needlessly inflame.

Case studies illuminate the stakes. The Russian infiltration of U.S. power companies in 2018 prompted fierce debate: was it espionage, aimed at gathering information, or was it a latent capability, to be activated in the event of geopolitical crisis? Analysts noted the depth of access—control over industrial control systems—suggesting preparation. Yet intent was contested. Moscow could argue, as it often does, that it was merely collecting intelligence. Washington, reading the matrix, saw something more menacing. The response was calibrated accordingly: not all-out retaliation, but quiet warnings and increased resilience measures, coupled with public attribution to signal awareness.

Philosophically, this tension speaks to the enduring problem of reading adversaries' minds. Clausewitz observed that war is a duel of wills, each side interpreting the other's actions through fog and friction. In cyberspace, this fog thickens: packets move faster than diplomats, code travels without flag or uniform, and intent is inferred rather than declared. The best that can be achieved is probabilistic reasoning—a recognition that cyber operations often sit in the liminal space between espionage and warfare, between practice and preparation.

Policymakers and strategists must therefore cultivate a form of disciplined imagination. They cannot assume that every intrusion signals an immediate attack, nor can they dismiss depth of access as harmless. They must learn to ask: if this capability were activated, what would it mean for national security, for public confidence, for escalation dynamics? And if the attacker intended only to signal, how should we interpret the message without rewarding the theatre?

This is why a matrix of capability and intent is more than an analytical tool. It is a framework for decision under uncertainty, a way of disciplining instinct with structured judgment. It does not eliminate ambiguity but manages it—by distinguishing between types of behaviour, it equips leaders to calibrate response rather than swing between paralysis and overreaction.

Yet an unresolved tension lingers. If cyber operations are left dormant for years, ready to be activated at a moment of crisis, can restraint still be assumed? Or does the mere presence of capability—like a hidden minefield—alter the strategic landscape, constraining choices and eroding trust? In the shadows of these unanswered questions lies the central challenge of our digital age: to govern escalation when the line between probing and preparation is drawn not in craters, but in code.

Chapter 4

Espionage at Scale: The Supply-Chain Trap

When the SolarWinds breach was finally uncovered, investigators were struck not only by the scale of the compromise but by its elegance. A single trusted update, distributed to customers as routine maintenance, had become the Trojan horse through which some of the world's most secure networks were infiltrated. Ministries, defence contractors, global firms—all unwittingly installed the attacker's code. It was not brute force that opened the gates, but routine supply-chain trust. The very mechanism designed to maintain resilience became the channel of subversion. The story was not an outlier. It was a signal of a deeper structural truth: in a hyperconnected world, compromise often flows downstream from the suppliers, dependencies, and services we barely notice.

The paradox is stark. Modern systems are built on interdependence; efficiency demands it. Yet every layer of that interdependence, from obscure open-source libraries to proprietary chipsets, offers new points of exploitation. Espionage today no longer requires breaching the citadel wall. It requires corrupting the brick factory, the courier route, the inspector's seal. States and criminals alike have learned to strike not at the target itself, but at the trust relationships that sustain it. Espionage has always thrived on exploiting trust; at scale, it thrives on exploiting the trust embedded in supply chains.

This chapter explores how such traps are set and why they matter so profoundly for security, sovereignty, and strategy. We begin with the deceptively fragile ecosystem of open-source software, where countless applications depend on the unpaid labour of maintainers and the opaque webs of transitive dependencies. A single trivial package can ripple upwards into critical infrastructure, as demonstrated when compromised open-source modules disabled payment processors and logistics systems across multiple countries. Procurement officers and regulators must grasp this fragility, for the issue is not niche but systemic. Recognising software as infrastructure reframes responsibility: the failure of a library is no less consequential than the failure of a bridge.

From software we turn to hardware. Few tropes are as durable as the fear of hidden backdoors etched into silicon. Hollywood imagines rogue chips sending secrets home. Reality is subtler. Risks exist—from compromised firmware in consumer devices to vulnerabilities in baseband processors—but separating myth from plausible threat is vital. Excessive suspicion leads to costly theatre: endless inspections, bans driven more by politics than by evidence. Yet naivety invites real peril. The art lies in evidence-based assessment, reframing certification and inspection as diplomacy through standards. Decisions about what to trust and how to verify reverberate far beyond the laboratory. They shape alliances, supply chains, and ultimately the balance of power.

If hardware anchors trust in physical form, update channels anchor it in time. Every patch, every automatic update is a silent exercise of delegated trust. To accept an update is to accept that someone else, somewhere, has safeguarded the code, verified its provenance, and assured its integrity. Breaches of these channels—whether in SolarWinds, NotPetya, or the compromise of open-source package registries—show how devastating it can be when that trust is weaponised. Boards and executives, often distanced from technical detail, must recognise that update processes are not arcane rituals but board-level risk. Understanding code signing, continuous integration pipelines, and the architecture of trust is no longer optional. It is the difference between resilience and catastrophe.

The supply chain is not only technical but commercial. Vendor lock-in, long treated as a business inconvenience, emerges as a security risk. When switching costs are prohibitive, commercial leverage morphs into political leverage. A provider that dominates a market can be leaned on by its home state, willingly or otherwise, to shape outcomes far beyond commerce. Mapping these incentives, and designing exit ramps, becomes part of the sovereign toolkit. It is not enough to diversify energy sources; nations and firms must diversify their digital lifelines too.

Ultimately, the chapter turns to resilience. Not resilience as a slogan, but resilience as operational design. Minimal trust architectures, verifiable builds, staged rollouts, and continuous audits form the practical grammar of security at scale. These measures do not eliminate risk, but they transform it—from catastrophic systemic collapse to manageable, containable failure.

The lesson is simple but profound: resilience is cheaper than recovery, in money, time, and political stability.

The supply-chain trap is not new. Empires once rose and fell on the security of their grain routes, their shipyards, and their merchant guilds. Today's routes are digital, the cargo invisible, the dependencies hidden. Yet the stakes are no less existential. Espionage at scale turns the arteries of modern life into vectors of vulnerability. The question is no longer whether supply chains can be compromised—they already are—but how societies will adapt. Will trust remain fragile, dependent on the goodwill of unseen maintainers and opaque vendors? Or will a new architecture of resilience and accountability be built before the next SolarWinds-scale breach reshapes the landscape yet again?

Open-source dependency risk

In March 2016, a developer unpublished just eleven lines of code from the open-source package manager npm. The function, called *left-pad*, simply added padding characters to a string—trivial, unglamorous, barely worth notice. Yet within hours, major websites and applications across the globe broke. Banks, airlines, and social platforms scrambled. A single absent package, free to use and maintained by one unpaid individual, had revealed just how precarious the scaffolding of modern software had become.

The *left-pad* incident is not remembered because of its technical complexity; there was none. It is remembered because of its symbolism. Modern digital infrastructure rests on the labour of scattered volunteers, many unpaid, who maintain the small components on which vast systems depend. The paradox is that the smaller and more trivial the component, the less attention it receives—yet the greater the disruption when it fails. A hospital does not fall because of a spectacular exploit in its core systems, but because a dependency three layers deep is corrupted. Software collapses not at the fortress walls but through the overlooked cracks in its foundations.

This is the essence of open-source dependency risk. Today's applications are less *written* than *assembled*. A single service may depend on hundreds or thousands of external packages, each of which relies on others. These are called transitive dependencies: the hidden inheritance of software development. Few engineers know all of them, fewer still review them, and virtually no one can guarantee their integrity across the stack. Attackers understand this perfectly. By compromising one neglected library or manipulating an abandoned account, they can plant malicious code that propagates through global systems like a contagion. The efficiency of modern development becomes a weapon against itself.

The risk is not abstract. In 2021, attackers compromised the package manager PyPI with malicious uploads disguised as legitimate updates. Earlier, the event-stream package in npm, downloaded millions of times, was found to contain code designed to steal cryptocurrency wallets. Each incident followed the same pattern: attackers targeted packages so obscure that no corporate security budget had ever touched them, yet whose compromise cascaded into critical systems. The lesson is brutal: strategic exposure often lies not in the crown jewels, but in the overlooked pebbles at the gate.

At the heart of the problem lies economics. Open-source software has delivered extraordinary innovation and efficiency. But the incentive structures are skewed. A few giant firms capture immense value by building upon free codebases, while the individuals who maintain those codebases often do so in their spare time, without funding or institutional support. It is the equivalent of global shipping companies depending on bridges maintained by hobbyists. As with infrastructure, neglect is not sustainable. The system invites fragility, and fragility invites exploitation.

Procurement officers and regulators face a conundrum. Traditional models of supply-chain risk management assume that suppliers are known entities with contracts and accountability. In open-source, dependencies may be maintained by anonymous individuals scattered across jurisdictions, with no contractual obligations, no service-level agreements, and sometimes no ongoing attention at all. Yet the software they produce becomes embedded in life-critical systems—from pacemakers to aircraft. To regulate without suffocating innovation, to support without stifling openness, requires new models of governance.

Concrete reforms are beginning to emerge. Some argue for software bills of materials (SBOMs), inventories that document every dependency within a product, akin to ingredient lists in food. Others propose funding mechanisms to support critical maintainers, treating them as public infrastructure. A more radical approach is to embed security requirements directly into package repositories, enforcing signing, verification, and audit before publication. Each idea grapples with the same tension: how to preserve the openness and creativity of open-source ecosystems while addressing the systemic risks they generate.

The cultural element cannot be ignored. Many maintainers resist external oversight, fearing it would erode the ethos of volunteer collaboration. Governments, for their part, worry about liability: to fund a maintainer is, in some eyes, to assume responsibility for their failures. Meanwhile, large corporations continue to externalise risk, relying on unpaid communities while treating them as inexhaustible resources. The misalignment of incentives creates fertile ground for attackers and ensures that the problem will not vanish through goodwill alone.

Seen philosophically, the open-source dependency crisis reframes the concept of privacy and sovereignty in digital life. If nations cannot secure their infrastructure without depending on code maintained by anonymous strangers, then sovereignty itself is diluted. If individuals cannot trust that the software running their hospital or bank has been verified, then consent becomes meaningless. Dependency chains thus become not only technical constructs but political and ethical ones. The question is not whether to use open-source software, but how to build collective responsibility around it.

The dependency problem teaches us that digital interdependence, once celebrated as the height of efficiency, can easily shade into fragility. The smallest package may determine the security of the largest state. Every reform idea—from SBOMs to funding maintainers—confronts the same paradox: openness is both the source of resilience and the source of risk. The tension will not be resolved easily. What matters is whether institutions, from companies to governments, can recognise that the health of the digital commons is not peripheral but central to national security.

The next breach will not arrive at the front door of a government data centre. It will creep through a forgotten dependency, maintained by a tired developer working unpaid at midnight. The world has already seen what happens when that developer decides to walk away. The question now is whether we can learn to support, regulate, and redesign these fragile webs before attackers exploit them at scale. The clock is ticking, and the dependencies are multiplying.

Hardware backdoors: myth and reality

In 2018, a magazine cover story claimed that Chinese spies had planted rice-grain-sized chips on server motherboards bound for major American tech firms. The allegation was explosive: an invisible, mass-deployed hardware backdoor that could exfiltrate data from Fortune 500 companies and U.S. government agencies alike. Within days, markets wobbled, boards panicked, and governments demanded answers. Yet the story unravelled under scrutiny. Technical experts found no such implants. The supposed global breach seemed closer to fiction than fact. Still, the narrative lingered, fuelled by the simple, cinematic image of a rogue chip hiding in plain sight.

The episode captures a paradox of cybersecurity. Hardware backdoors inspire both the deepest fears and the wildest myths. They are terrifying because they are tangible, hidden in devices we hold in our hands or bolt into our data centres. Unlike software, which can be patched or rewritten, hardware feels immutable. If compromised at the factory, it seems beyond remedy. At the same time, the very invisibility of hardware exploits makes them fertile ground for conspiracy. Once suspicion is seeded, proof becomes secondary. Trust in supply chains, already fragile, erodes under the weight of speculation.

To separate myth from reality, we need to distinguish between what is theoretically possible, what has been demonstrated, and what is strategically likely. Yes, in controlled experiments, researchers have shown it is possible to insert malicious circuitry into a chip or to manipulate firmware during manufacture. Proof-of-concept implants can alter network traffic, bypass authentication, or open covert channels. But scaling such attacks across millions of devices, undetected, is another matter. The complexity of global hardware production, involving hundreds of suppliers and stringent testing, makes mass deployment highly improbable without leaks or anomalies. The real-world risk lies not in blockbuster implants but in more mundane, less cinematic avenues.

Firmware is the first layer where myth shades into reality. Baseband processors in smartphones, responsible for handling communications with mobile networks, operate largely unseen by users and even operating systems. Exploits here have been documented and weaponised. The NSA's leaked ANT catalogue revealed tools capable of modifying firmware in hard drives and routers to persist through reboots and reinstallations. Unlike mythical microchips hidden in circuit boards, these exploits are invisible to inspection yet achievable with targeted effort. Firmware backdoors do not require smuggling contraband into factories; they exploit the opacity of code already shipped.

The supply chain remains the stage for plausible threats. During production, firmware updates can be altered, testing processes can be bypassed, or trusted third-party components can be compromised. These are subtle, opportunistic attacks, not the sweeping espionage of Hollywood thrillers. Evidence exists: the 2008 discovery of compromised chips in counterfeit military hardware, or later revelations of tampered networking equipment seized in transit. Each case involved manipulation at choke points—points where oversight was weakest, not where visibility was highest. The lesson is not that every motherboard hides a spy chip, but that critical junctures in globalised production are attractive targets.

Here is where evidence-based risk management matters. If policymakers succumb to every whisper of sabotage, they risk costly theatre: tearing out equipment en masse, imposing protectionist bans, or mandating inspections that cannot meaningfully detect what they fear. Conversely, dismissing the possibility invites complacency. The challenge is calibration. Distinguish between plausible, demonstrated vectors—firmware manipulation, insecure update channels, compromised testing regimes—and the spectacular but improbable fears of ubiquitous physical implants. By anchoring analysis in evidence, governments and firms avoid being trapped by paranoia while still protecting against genuine exposures.

Certification regimes play a pivotal role. Hardware inspection is limited by physics; sophisticated implants can be smaller than the wavelength of visible light. No customs officer can spot a manipulated transistor. Instead, trust must be embedded in process: rigorous auditing of design, secure update architectures, and transparent manufacturing pipelines. Standards bodies, from ISO committees to telecom alliances, quietly decide how much scrutiny is applied, and how trust is distributed across global suppliers. Here the politics of standards become indistinguishable from the politics of security. If one nation insists on certification mechanisms that embed its own vendors, it shapes the market as surely as if it had imposed tariffs.

This is why hardware backdoors cannot be treated as a purely technical issue. They are diplomatic, economic, and strategic instruments. Accusations of hidden implants are as much weapons of narrative as they are of espionage. To brand a rival's products as untrustworthy is to weaken their export markets and strengthen domestic alternatives. This is not to say the threats are fictional, but that fear of them can be leveraged with or without evidence. The boundary between genuine risk and geopolitical theatre is porous, and it is often in that ambiguity that decisions are made.

The reality, then, is less cinematic but more insidious. Hardware backdoors exist, but rarely in the form imagined by sensational headlines. They are more likely to reside in invisible firmware routines, opaque update mechanisms, or tolerated weaknesses in supply-chain practices. They persist not because they are undetectable but because institutions fail to demand verification. They spread not because spies smuggle chips into factories, but because firms outsource trust without scrutiny.

The unresolved question is how much paranoia is rational. Can a nation afford to trust equipment manufactured abroad, or is mistrust itself a form of resilience? At what point does fear of hardware backdoors become a self-fulfilling prophecy, fragmenting supply chains into mutually suspicious blocs? Between myth and reality lies a space where evidence, governance, and diplomacy must meet. Whether we fill that space with careful calibration or costly theatre will determine whether hardware remains a foundation of trust—or a stage for endless suspicion.

The update channel as a weapon

For years, security officers drilled the same advice into employees: keep your software updated. Patching was the cure to vulnerabilities, the digital equivalent of hand-washing against infection. Yet in 2020, the very mechanism designed to protect became the weapon. The SolarWinds breach, one of the most consequential in history, unfolded not through exotic zero-days or cinematic hardware implants, but through poisoned software updates. Thousands of organisations—from U.S. government agencies to Fortune 500 corporations—downloaded what they believed were trusted improvements. Hidden inside was a backdoor, painstakingly crafted to evade detection. The paradox was stark: the guardians of security had unwittingly ushered in compromise.

This inversion of trust illustrates a deeper truth. Update channels are golden routes for intrusion precisely because they are invisible. No one scrutinises the medicine meant to heal. When an organisation downloads an update, it implicitly delegates trust: to the developer who wrote the patch, to the build system that compiled it, to the distribution mechanism that delivered it, and to the cryptographic signature that verifies it. Each step is a potential chokepoint. Compromise any link, and the whole edifice of trust collapses. The very efficiency of modern development pipelines—the automation of continuous integration and delivery—creates fertile ground for attackers who can slip malicious code into the bloodstream of global IT.

The mechanics matter. Digital signatures are supposed to safeguard authenticity. A software update arrives signed with a developer's private key, and the recipient's system verifies it against the corresponding public key. In theory, this cryptography should be unassailable. In practice, attackers rarely break the mathematics; they go after the humans and machines that wield it. If a build server is compromised, the attacker can sign their poisoned update with legitimate keys. If the key management system itself is breached, signatures become endorsements of betrayal. Trust, once delegated to machines, still depends on fragile human processes around them.

SolarWinds was not an anomaly. Earlier incidents revealed the same structural weakness. In 2017, the NotPetya attack weaponised the update mechanism of a Ukrainian tax software product, unleashing the most damaging cyberattack to date, crippling logistics networks and multinational firms. In 2013, Adobe disclosed that its build systems had been infiltrated, allowing malicious versions of software to be distributed. Each case demonstrated the asymmetry of cost: attackers needed only to compromise a single choke point in the update pipeline, while defenders had to safeguard an entire labyrinth of processes and personnel.

The allure of the update channel lies not only in its stealth but also in its scale. Unlike targeted phishing or bespoke zero-day exploits, compromised updates spread virally. Every client that dutifully installs the patch becomes a vector. This transforms the economics of espionage. Instead of painstakingly hacking one organisation at a time, attackers piggyback on trust to breach thousands simultaneously. Updates are the supply chain of digital life; corrupting them is equivalent to slipping poison into a city's water supply.

The governance challenge is acute. Boards and policymakers, conditioned to think in terms of firewalls and endpoint security, struggle to grasp the fragility of software delivery pipelines. Procurement contracts rarely audit build security. Regulators focus on privacy policies but neglect code signing practices. The very language of corporate risk disclosures tends to obscure systemic dependencies behind bland assurances. Yet as the breaches show, the locus of vulnerability is not at the outer walls of organisations but at the arteries of trust that connect them to their vendors.

Mitigation requires architectural fixes, not platitudes. Verifiable builds, where compiled binaries can be matched to audited source code, help shrink the space for hidden alterations. Multi-party signing, where updates require independent endorsements, reduces the risk of a single compromised key. Segregated build environments, continuous monitoring, and staged rollouts can catch anomalies before they propagate globally. None of these are glamorous, but all of them shift trust from blind delegation to verifiable process. Resilience in update channels is less about clever cryptography and more about disciplined engineering.

Yet the political dimension is equally inescapable. Nations scrutinise foreign vendors not only for technical weaknesses but for potential coercion. A compromised update mechanism becomes a tool of state power, whether wielded overtly or suspected covertly. The line between genuine security measures and protectionist theatre blurs. Banning foreign products may assuage domestic anxieties, but unless local update channels are hardened, the underlying risk remains. Trust, once shaken, is not easily rebuilt—especially in a geopolitical climate where accusations of backdoors double as trade policy.

The lesson, then, is unsettling. The update channel, once considered a safeguard, is now a contested battlefield. Every time we accept a patch, we are making a political as much as a technical choice: placing trust in developers, vendors, and the global infrastructure of software distribution. The breaches of the past decade reveal how easily that trust can be subverted.

And so the open question persists. Can the software ecosystem rebuild update mechanisms that are truly worthy of trust, or will every new patch carry the shadow of suspicion? If resilience does not catch up with dependence, the very process meant to heal may remain the most elegant weapon in the attacker's arsenal.

Vendor lock-in

In the 1970s, multinational corporations discovered a strange paradox. The more dependent they became on IBM's mainframes, the harder it was to imagine leaving. Competitors offered cheaper machines, sometimes even superior performance, yet the migration costs—rewriting applications, retraining staff, rebuilding workflows—were so great that "Nobody Ever Got Fired for Buying IBM" became both a punchline and a rule of survival. Half a century later, the same dynamic plays out not in the glass-walled data centres of the Cold War but in the cloud platforms, software ecosystems, and digital infrastructure that underpin today's economies. The more deeply a system is woven into daily operations, the more invisible the chains become.

Vendor lock-in is rarely imposed by force; it is cultivated through design. High switching costs—whether technical, financial, or psychological—become barriers to exit, ensuring customers remain tethered even when rivals beckon. The tools of lock-in are subtle: proprietary file formats, tightly integrated feature sets, exclusive APIs, and licensing terms that penalise departure. Once entrenched, these measures shift leverage from the customer to the supplier, allowing commercial power to mutate into political influence. When the vendor sits in a jurisdiction with its own strategic interests, dependence becomes a matter not just of procurement but of sovereignty.

Consider the cloud. Hyperscale providers such as Amazon Web Services, Microsoft Azure, and Google Cloud have built platforms that offer extraordinary convenience and capability. But customers who architect their systems around a particular provider's proprietary services—serverless computing frameworks, AI toolkits, or data pipelines—find migration daunting. The financial cost of moving workloads is compounded by the risk of downtime, the need for retraining staff, and the inertia of institutional habit. A decision that once appeared reversible hardens into a structural dependency. For governments, this creates vulnerabilities: a single vendor's pricing changes, outages, or compliance disputes can ripple across entire public sectors.

Lock-in is not confined to the cloud. In enterprise software, productivity suites, or industrial control systems, the same logic recurs. Hospitals reliant on a particular vendor's electronic health record platform may discover that extracting patient data for migration is technically possible but prohibitively costly. Municipalities tied to proprietary voting technologies may find reform blocked by the very companies whose systems they wish to replace. Defence contractors often require bespoke parts or proprietary software, creating captive markets that persist for decades. In each case, what begins as a pragmatic choice calcifies into a long-term constraint.

The incentives behind lock-in are rational. For vendors, it secures predictable revenue streams and erects barriers against competitors. For customers, the promise of integrated solutions can outweigh abstract concerns about future constraints. Short-term efficiency seduces decision-makers, even as long-term dependence grows. But the risks compound over time. The very factors that make lock-in commercially attractive—centralisation, exclusivity, and scale—also make it politically consequential. A supplier facing pressure from its home government may find itself compelled to restrict services or disclose data. At that point, the technical architecture of dependency intersects with the geopolitics of power.

There is also a cultural dimension. Organisations habituated to a particular vendor often develop skill sets, governance structures, and procurement practices that reinforce dependence. Engineers trained on one provider's tools may resist migration not because alternatives are inferior but because they are unfamiliar. Executives may rationalise lock-in as a form of "strategic partnership," mistaking a contractual relationship for an alignment of interests. The subtle psychology of sunk costs—what economists call path dependence—ensures that each additional investment strengthens the vendor's grip.

Examples of lock-in's political leverage are mounting. In 2019, U.S. sanctions against Huawei reverberated through European telecom operators who had become reliant on the firm's equipment. The decision to exclude Huawei from critical networks was not purely a technical assessment of security risk; it was also an exercise in untangling dependencies that had been quietly built over a decade. Similarly, when Russia invaded Ukraine, software vendors faced pressure to suspend operations in Russia. Companies that complied found themselves accused of politicising commerce; those that hesitated faced reputational damage. In both cases, the mere act of choosing whether to continue service had geopolitical consequences.

Exit ramps are therefore not luxuries but necessities. Strategies to mitigate lock-in include adopting open standards, mandating data portability, diversifying vendors, and designing modular architectures. These measures shift the balance of power, ensuring that customers retain agency. But they require foresight. Once dependence is entrenched, reforms face resistance not only from vendors but from the organisations themselves, whose incentives and investments have become aligned with the status quo.

The ethics of lock-in deserve scrutiny as well. At what point does a vendor's pursuit of legitimate commercial advantage become exploitation? When hospitals cannot afford to change electronic record providers without jeopardising patient care, or when schools remain bound to a single digital learning platform despite better options, the line between fair competition and coercion blurs. Lock-in magnifies inequality: wealthier organisations can absorb the costs of exit, while poorer ones remain trapped.

The paradox of vendor lock-in is that it often masquerades as freedom of choice. Customers sign contracts voluntarily, install software willingly, and architect systems knowingly. Yet the cumulative effect of these decisions is a narrowing of options, until the cost of change feels insurmountable. What begins as convenience ends as constraint.

The political stakes are rising. As digital systems become infrastructure—shaping elections, healthcare, finance, and defence—the dependencies baked into vendor relationships acquire national significance. Lock-in is no longer just a matter of procurement efficiency; it is a question of resilience and sovereignty. Recognising the incentives that keep customers captive is the first step. Designing credible exit ramps is the second. The unanswered question, and the one this chapter presses upon policymakers and executives alike, is whether societies can act before dependence hardens into inevitability—or whether future crises will force change at the worst possible moment.

Resilience by design

When the SolarWinds breach came to light in 2020, executives and policymakers were horrified by the scale of compromise: thousands of organisations, from Fortune 500 companies to U.S. federal agencies, had unwittingly installed backdoored software through a trusted update channel. But what made the incident devastating was not only the attacker's ingenuity—it was that resilience had been treated as optional. No systematic checks, no staged rollouts, no continuous auditing of what was delivered and deployed. Once the poisoned update slipped through, it cascaded unchecked across the globe. The lesson was brutal yet clarifying: in digital infrastructure, prevention alone is never enough. Recovery costs can be astronomical, reputational damage irreparable. Resilience, by contrast, is far cheaper to build than to retrofit.

Designing for resilience is not a matter of slogans or corporate platitudes. It demands operational practices grounded in scepticism and verification. To speak of *minimal trust* is not to indulge in cynicism but to recognise that every assumption—about suppliers, developers, even cryptographic signatures—can be broken. A resilient system presumes compromise and asks: how can damage be contained, discovered quickly, and recovered from at manageable cost? In this sense, resilience shifts the paradigm from fortress-building to risk choreography, a posture less about perfect defence than about graceful degradation under stress.

Take verifiable builds. In the traditional software pipeline, compiled binaries are black boxes: customers must trust that what emerges from the build server corresponds to the source code. But initiatives like reproducible builds change the equation, allowing independent parties to confirm that identical inputs yield identical outputs. This seemingly technical safeguard undermines entire classes of supply-chain attacks by making tampering visible. The principle is simple—*do not trust what you cannot verify*—but its consequences are profound. By embedding verification into development, organisations transform opacity into accountability.

Staged rollouts offer another pillar. The logic mirrors public health: exposure in small doses before mass deployment limits systemic harm.

Critical updates can first be released to a subset of systems, monitored for anomalies, and only then propagated more widely. This reduces the blast radius of malicious or defective updates, ensuring that no single compromise metastasises unchecked. Companies like Google and Microsoft have long employed phased release strategies, not only for stability but as implicit resilience mechanisms. What matters is not speed alone but measured speed, tuned to balance urgency with prudence.

Continuous audit closes the loop. Without constant inspection—of code provenance, dependency graphs, and runtime behaviour—resilience remains a theory. The most sophisticated attackers count on defenders' inattention, hiding in overlooked logs or dormant modules. Automated auditing, combined with anomaly detection and human oversight, converts raw visibility into actionable vigilance. Audits must be iterative rather than ceremonial: not annual checkboxes but living processes woven into operations. Just as financial audits deter fraud by raising the cost of concealment, digital audits deter compromise by collapsing the shadows in which it thrives.

Critically, resilience by design is not the enemy of efficiency but its safeguard. The argument that safeguards slow innovation misunderstands the cost curve. Every dollar not spent on proactive resilience multiplies into ten spent on crisis response, regulatory fines, or reputational recovery. The banking sector learned this decades ago with capital buffers and stress testing: resilience is not dead weight but the price of continuity. The digital sector, with far less margin for error, is catching up to this truth.

There are philosophical dimensions, too. Resilience recognises human fallibility—not only that attackers will succeed, but that defenders will err, updates will break, maintainers will overlook vulnerabilities. Designing with that humility creates systems that forgive mistakes instead of collapsing under them. The alternative is brittle perfectionism, which delivers an illusion of security until its first fracture shatters everything. In this way, resilience is less a technical property than an ethical orientation: a commitment to transparency, to distributed responsibility, and to preparing for the worst without paralysing fear.

The practical playbook grows from these principles. Minimal trust forces organisations to map dependencies and demand proof rather than promises. Verifiable builds institutionalise scepticism at the point of creation. Staged rollouts discipline the tempo of change, reducing the likelihood of systemic contagion. Continuous audit ensures that compromises, once seeded, cannot lie undisturbed. Each principle reinforces the others, forming a fabric strong not because it is untearable but because it tears in controlled, recoverable ways.

Resilience by design demands a cultural shift as much as a technical one. It asks boards to see cyber risk not as a peripheral IT matter but as a central strategic concern. It asks engineers to balance velocity with vigilance. It asks regulators to reward structural safeguards rather than box-ticking compliance. Most of all, it asks societies to embrace resilience as a public good, not a private afterthought.

And yet, the hardest question remains unresolved: can resilience be built before the next crisis, or will each breach only jolt organisations into belated reform? The temptation to economise on invisible safeguards is strong, especially when budgets are tight and competitors race ahead. But the choice is not between spending and saving; it is between paying upfront for resilience or paying later in catastrophe. Whether institutions will recognise this in time—or whether resilience will remain the lesson always learned too late—remains the open challenge.

Chapter 5

Algorithms with Teeth: AI in Conflict

In the winter of 2019, a crudely faked video of a senior politician stumbling through an incoherent speech began circulating online. Within hours, it had been shared hundreds of thousands of times, picked up by sympathetic outlets, and seeded into foreign-language forums that stripped away any context hinting at fabrication. The artefact itself was technically unsophisticated—its glitches obvious to any trained eye. Yet the damage was done: doubt had been planted, trust eroded, and narratives weaponised before fact-checkers could mount a response. This was not an attack on servers or satellites. It was an attack on perception, exploiting the very cognitive shortcuts that make human communication efficient. It was a glimpse into a future where the most decisive battlefield is not physical territory, but the contested terrain of belief.

The paradox is striking. Artificial intelligence promises precision, speed, and efficiency—qualities long celebrated in fields from logistics to medicine. But in conflict, those same qualities acquire a sharper edge. Algorithms that optimise advertising campaigns can just as easily optimise disinformation. Neural networks designed to recognise speech can be trained to synthesise it, with uncanny fidelity. Systems built to defend networks can be repurposed to probe and exploit them. The question is no longer whether AI will play a role in conflict, but how deeply its logics of automation and scale will reshape the very nature of power and persuasion.

What makes this transformation so urgent is its compression of time and accountability. A human analyst can sift through data streams, but a machine can parse billions of signals in real time, adjusting narratives and targeting individuals with surgical precision. A pilot can weigh the risks of firing, but an autonomous agent can act faster than deliberation allows, potentially triggering escalation before anyone has grasped what is happening. The logic of deterrence, painstakingly built during the Cold War, assumed time for human reflection. AI disrupts that premise, raising uncomfortable questions: where should humans remain in the loop, and where is control illusory?

Yet AI's role in conflict is not limited to offence. Machine learning also underpins new defensive paradigms: detecting anomalous patterns, training deception systems that lure adversaries into honeypots, generating diversity that makes attacks harder to scale. But here lies a second paradox—defensive AI often shares the same brittleness as its offensive counterparts. Classifiers trained on historical data may be easily fooled by adversarial tweaks. Deception systems risk entangling allies and civilians alongside attackers. The very speed and opacity that give AI its potency can also turn it into a liability, creating false comfort where vigilance is needed most.

Consider, too, the vulnerability of AI to poisoning. If data is the fuel of these systems, then tampering with that fuel is sabotage of the most insidious kind. Poisoned training sets can implant hidden biases or backdoors, enabling attackers to tilt outcomes while leaving few visible traces. Scraped datasets may already carry toxic artefacts; supply-side attacks may inject malicious examples directly into repositories. The effect is to corrode trust at its root, shifting the contest from the battlefield to the pipeline itself. Here, the old metaphor of territory resurfaces: control of data provenance is control of the high ground.

All of this converges on a political dilemma: how to govern algorithms with teeth. Rules of engagement must do more than echo slogans about "responsible AI." They must be operationalisable, testable, and enforceable across borders. Verification mechanisms, audit trails, and proportionality thresholds are not abstractions but necessities, if states and corporations alike are to avoid spirals of mistrust and retaliation. Without such norms, every innovation risks becoming a provocation, every deployment a potential escalator.

The coming pages dissect these dynamics. They move from cognitive operations that rewire attention, through the murky markets for poisoned data, to the sobering prospect of autonomous escalation. They explore the promise and perils of defensive AI, and the painstaking work of defining rules that bind machines and their makers alike. What unites these threads is a single truth: artificial intelligence does not float above politics. It embeds itself in doctrine, in markets, in the ethics of decision and the rhythms of conflict.

The deeper question—the one that threads through every section of this chapter—is not merely how AI can be used in conflict, but what it does to the human condition of war itself. Does it narrow the space for reflection, or expand the arsenal of deception beyond recognition? Does it stabilise by deterring, or destabilise by accelerating? The answers will shape elections, crises, and perhaps the very possibility of peace. The reader should be prepared for more than technical lessons. What follows is a reckoning with the future of conflict when intelligence itself, human and artificial, becomes weaponised at scale.

Cognitive operations

In the summer of 2020, as the world grappled with a pandemic, a video appeared online showing soldiers in hazmat suits loading body bags into unmarked trucks. The clip spread at speed, tagged and subtitled in multiple languages, feeding a narrative of governments hiding mass casualties. Within days, journalists traced the footage back to an old news segment from an unrelated accident years before. The uniforms, the bags, even the trucks were authentic—but repurposed. For millions who had already shared or seen the video, the correction came too late. Doubt had been sown. In the attention economy of conflict, plausibility mattered more than proof.

This is the paradox of cognitive operations: the targets are not servers or satellites, but the neural pathways of citizens. Where conventional cyber-attacks aim to disrupt infrastructure, these campaigns aim to disrupt attention, trust, and judgement. Artificial intelligence does not invent this form of influence—it accelerates it. By scaling persuasion, distraction, and fabrication, AI enables adversaries to mount operations at a speed, reach, and precision that human propagandists could never achieve alone.

The mechanics are both simple and devastating. Machine learning systems monitor engagement in real time, measuring not just what people click but how long their eyes linger, which phrasing makes them pause, which images stir anger or fear. These systems transform the act of persuasion from an art into an iterative experiment: millions of micro-tests conducted simultaneously, refined by feedback loops that reward emotional resonance over accuracy. The infrastructure of advertising—once aimed at selling shoes or shampoo—becomes a weapon of political warfare.

Micro-targeting extends this logic further. Instead of broadcasting one message to all, AI can tailor narratives to the anxieties of each audience segment, sometimes each individual. To a pensioner, a message about healthcare costs; to a student, one about job scarcity; to a parent, one about safety in schools. Each message is plausible in isolation, but collectively they fracture the shared space of debate. Citizens begin to occupy parallel realities, their perception of public life mediated by unseen algorithms optimising for persuasion.

Narrative laundering gives these efforts legitimacy. A falsehood seeded in an obscure forum may be picked up by fringe influencers, amplified by partisan blogs, cited by sympathetic media outlets, and finally debated on mainstream platforms. By the time it reaches the centre, the original fabrication has been stripped of its provenance. What remains appears to be a legitimate controversy—something reasonable people might disagree about. AI assists in this laundering by identifying the optimal channels, voices, and moments to propel stories through this chain, invisibly choreographing the cascade from lie to debate.

The stakes are highest in elections and crises, where the cognitive environment shapes not just perception but action. Disinformation campaigns can suppress turnout, inflame polarisation, or corrode faith in the process itself. During emergencies—natural disasters, terrorist incidents, pandemics—the injection of false narratives can delay responses, undermine trust in authorities, or provoke panic. In both cases, the objective is less to persuade than to destabilise: to leave citizens unsure of what is true, paralysed between competing claims, or simply exhausted by the noise.

Yet cognitive operations are not only offensive. They exploit vulnerabilities in the human condition itself. People are not rational processors of information but social animals, attuned to cues of identity and belonging. We share not what is most accurate but what is most resonant. The same heuristics that sustain community in normal times can be turned against us in moments of manipulation. AI does not override human psychology—it maps and magnifies it. The battlefield is as much within the mind as across the network.

For defenders, the challenge is formidable. Fact-checking is too slow. Content moderation at scale risks collateral damage to legitimate speech. Banning or labelling sources may even strengthen the perception of censorship. The question becomes: how can societies build resilience without suppressing dissent? How can they distinguish between genuine contestation—a hallmark of democracy—and orchestrated campaigns designed to mimic it?

Here, philosophy meets practice. If the essence of sovereignty is control over territory, then cognitive operations suggest a new kind of sovereignty: the defence of shared epistemic space. The integrity of elections, the capacity for collective action in crises, depends not only on physical security but on the protection of attention and trust. This reframes information defence not as a luxury, but as a prerequisite of democracy.

And yet the dilemma remains unresolved. Every defensive measure carries risks of overreach. Every act of regulation risks being cast as censorship. Every attempt to harden public discourse risks narrowing it. The same AI that detects disinformation can be deployed to monitor dissent. The line between defence and suppression is perilously thin.

The unsettling question lingers: in an age when algorithms can tailor reality itself, can open societies defend attention without closing themselves? Or will the very values they seek to preserve become the vulnerabilities that adversaries exploit most effectively? The answers will define not only the security of states but the texture of citizenship in the digital age.

Autonomy and escalation

On a quiet morning in 1983, Soviet officer Stanislav Petrov sat in a bunker outside Moscow watching screens designed to warn of incoming nuclear strikes. Suddenly, alarms blared. The system reported that five American missiles were on their way. Protocol demanded an immediate report up the chain of command, triggering a likely retaliatory strike. Petrov hesitated. His instincts told him the warning was false. He disobeyed procedure, reported a malfunction, and prevented what might have been the start of nuclear war. History remembers his human judgement as the decisive barrier between error and catastrophe.

Replace Petrov with an autonomous agent, and the story looks different. An AI system designed to compress response times would have acted without hesitation, executing escalation logic before doubt could intervene. No hesitation, no pause, no gut instinct—just execution. The world might have ended not in fire and fury, but in milliseconds of machine-validated certainty.

This is the core danger of autonomy in conflict: decision time shrinks while consequences expand. Autonomous systems are often justified on grounds of speed—cyber operations unfold faster than human reaction times, hypersonic missiles compress detection-to-impact windows to minutes, and information campaigns move in viral bursts that defy manual intervention. But the same compression erodes the buffer of deliberation that has historically prevented miscalculation from spiralling into disaster.

What deterrence once relied upon—time for leaders to absorb, question, and verify—is stripped away by systems optimised for immediacy.

Failure modes multiply under such compression. Autonomous targeting may misclassify a civilian radar as a military installation. Automated escalation logic may interpret a decoy as an attack. Swarms of drones may behave unpredictably when communication links falter. In each case, accountability blurs: was it the programmer, the commander, or the machine that erred? Responsibility, once traceable through human orders, dissolves into technical ambiguity.

Arms-race dynamics compound the risk. If one side deploys autonomous systems to gain speed, adversaries feel compelled to match or exceed them, lest they operate at a permanent disadvantage. Restraint becomes costly. This spiral recalls nuclear competition during the Cold War, but with a crucial difference: while nuclear escalation was constrained by the fear of mutual annihilation, autonomous escalation may be driven by fear of missing an opportunity. Speed itself becomes the battleground, with states racing not just for weapons, but for the fastest decision cycles.

Examples are already visible. The United States and China pour resources into autonomous systems for cyber defence and offence, drone warfare, and information operations. Israel has tested AI-assisted targeting in live combat. Russia has experimented with autonomous underwater vehicles capable of carrying nuclear payloads. Each test advances capability, but also sets precedent. What begins as a demonstration for deterrence may normalise deployment, pushing others to follow. In such an environment, the boundary between controlled use and runaway escalation thins alarmingly.

Philosophically, autonomy poses questions that law and ethics struggle to answer. The principle of distinction—separating combatants from civilians—depends on human judgement contextualised by experience, empathy, and doubt. Can an algorithm replicate that? Proportionality, the demand that force be balanced against anticipated harm, requires moral reasoning, not probabilistic optimisation. When responsibility fragments across coders, commanders, and machines, accountability risks vanishing altogether. The temptation to delegate decision-making to systems is strong, but the erosion of human agency in war erodes the very foundation of ethical constraint.

This is why thresholds for human-in-the-loop decision-making matter. The debate is not whether AI should assist—assistance is inevitable—

but where to draw the line between support and delegation. Should machines recommend targets, but humans approve strikes? Should automated escalation be capped at defensive countermeasures, never offensive retaliation? These thresholds are not merely technical—they are normative boundaries that express what humanity is willing, or unwilling, to surrender to code.

There is, however, a sobering tension. Human intervention slows the cycle. In contexts where milliseconds matter, inserting a human may mean losing advantage. Militaries face a cruel trade-off: preserve ethical oversight and risk defeat, or sacrifice oversight for speed. The more adversaries choose the latter, the more pressure others feel to follow. Thus, what begins as a principled stand risks becoming a strategic liability.

Lawyers, ethicists, and diplomats argue over how to regulate this space, but the practical dilemmas arrive first on the screens of commanders. In a live engagement, under pressure, the temptation to let the machine decide can overwhelm doctrine. Petrov's restraint is a reminder of what humans can save. The question is whether systems optimised for speed will allow space for that kind of saving act.

Autonomy promises efficiency, but it carries escalation risk that no state fully controls. In the rush to outpace adversaries, are we building arsenals of precision—or engines of miscalculation? The answer will depend less on what machines can do, and more on what we insist humans must still decide. The unresolved tension remains: can restraint survive in a race where hesitation itself is treated as weakness?

Defensive AI and deception

In 2013, a group of researchers demonstrated a striking trick: they showed a computer vision system a photo of a panda, then added imperceptible noise to the image. To the human eye, it remained clearly a panda. To the machine, however, it became a gibbon with near-total confidence. This was not just a laboratory curiosity—it revealed a vulnerability at the heart of machine learning. Systems designed to classify and defend can be bent, misled, or even weaponised through carefully crafted manipulations. Defence, when delegated blindly to algorithms, can create the illusion of safety precisely where danger lurks.

This paradox—that the very tools promising resilience may create new fragilities—lies at the centre of defensive AI. On one side are powerful opportunities: systems that can sift through oceans of network traffic, spot anomalies in real time, or maintain a shifting digital terrain that frustrates attackers. On the other side are brittle classifiers, vulnerable to adversarial inputs that exploit their rigid assumptions. Practitioners face a critical challenge: distinguishing genuine robustness from false comfort, and understanding where deception can be turned from enemy tactic into defensive strength.

Machine learning has already reshaped intrusion detection. Traditional systems relied on static rules—if a packet matched a known signature, it was flagged. But as attackers mutated tactics faster than rules could be written, those defences faltered. AI-driven detection, by contrast, learns patterns of normal behaviour and alerts when deviations appear. A spike in login attempts at 3 a.m., an unusual configuration change, or an odd sequence of system calls: all can trigger alarms. Yet these alarms are only as trustworthy as the models behind them. Feed a model skewed or poisoned training data, and it may normalise the very behaviour it is meant to detect. Attackers, aware of these weaknesses, actively probe and manipulate such systems, turning defence into a new attack surface.

Here deception enters the defensive playbook. Honeypots—deliberately vulnerable systems designed to attract and study attackers—have long been a staple of cyber defence. With AI, honeypots can become adaptive: presenting different apparent vulnerabilities depending on the attacker's behaviour, learning from probes in real time, and feeding disinformation back into the offensive ecosystem. A misdirected adversary wastes time and resources chasing false signals, while defenders gather intelligence to harden real assets. Similarly, moving-target defence leverages machine learning to continuously shift configurations—IP addresses, memory layouts, even file structures—so that an attacker's reconnaissance rapidly decays into obsolescence. The battlefield becomes unstable terrain, where knowledge degrades before it can be exploited.

Yet every adaptation invites counter-adaptation. Just as adversaries develop techniques to poison training data, they also craft strategies to identify honeypots or predict shifting patterns. Defence becomes less about erecting a perfect barrier and more about sustaining an advantage in the rhythm of adaptation. Here, the brittleness of simple classifiers is especially dangerous. A model that claims 99 per cent accuracy may crumble under adversarial pressure if its design lacks resilience. Building robustness requires not just more data or deeper networks, but systematic approaches to adversarial training, ensemble methods, and layered oversight.

For practitioners, the temptation to treat AI as a silver bullet is strong. Dashboards light up with anomalies, detection rates rise, and procurement officers can report measurable gains. But beneath the surface, if resilience is not tested against adversarial conditions, those numbers are little more than theatre. False comfort is perhaps the most insidious threat of all: it lulls organisations into believing they are secure while leaving blind spots wide open. This is why the most sophisticated defenders increasingly emphasise *red teaming*—continuous exercises where attackers, internal or external, attempt to deceive AI systems to expose weaknesses. In such rehearsals, deception is not just tolerated but institutionalised, sharpening defences through confrontation with failure.

The philosophical dimension is equally striking. Defence is traditionally conceived as passive—walls, shields, barriers. But in cyberspace, defence must often be active, fluid, and deceptive. This unsettles long-standing assumptions about the ethics of security. Is it legitimate for a defender to plant false data in an attacker's path? To manipulate perception in ways that resemble the very disinformation tactics it opposes? In practice, states and firms alike are moving in this direction, seeing deception not as dishonourable but as prudent. Yet this blurring of boundaries raises questions about proportionality, transparency, and the long-term stability of digital ecosystems.

For small teams, these questions are not abstract. A university security group defending research infrastructure, or a start-up protecting intellectual property, may lack resources for large-scale AI deployments. But exercises rooted in deception—mock attacks, controlled data poisoning, adversarial input testing—can teach resilience with modest means. The lesson is not that AI alone can secure systems, but that security emerges from a dialogue between defenders and attackers, mediated by adaptive tools. In this sense, defensive AI is not a product to be bought but a practice to be cultivated.

The trajectory of defensive AI suggests both promise and peril. Machine learning can illuminate patterns invisible to human analysts and empower defenders to outmanoeuvre sophisticated adversaries. Yet it can also entrench fragility if treated as unquestioned authority. The crucial shift lies in recognising that deception is not merely an offensive weapon but a defensive resource, and that resilience grows from stress-testing rather than comfort-seeking. The unresolved question remains: as attackers grow more adept at exploiting the very intelligence we deploy against them, can defenders sustain trust in systems that may themselves be the next point of failure?

Data poisoning

In September 2020, a group of researchers quietly unveiled a proof-of-concept attack they called "BadNets." They showed that by inserting a handful of malicious images into a training dataset—just a few out of tens of thousands—they could force a state-of-the-art image recognition model to misclassify objects on command. A stop sign with a carefully placed sticker could suddenly be read as a speed limit marker. The implications were sobering: the more powerful machine learning became, the more fragile it seemed, because its strength—learning from vast troves of data—was also its greatest vulnerability. If data is the fuel, then poisoning is not an inconvenience but sabotage at the root of trust.

This is the paradox that defines modern AI security. Models are no longer hand-coded by engineers; they are shaped by data scraped from the web, harvested from sensors, or purchased from third-party vendors. Each stage in this pipeline offers an opportunity for manipulation. An adversary does not need to break into a server or plant malware on a device; they need only nudge the data in subtle ways so that the machine "learns" the wrong lessons. A poisoned dataset is not noisy—it is corrupted in ways that remain invisible until the system is deployed, when failures occur not randomly but by design.

The most basic form of poisoning comes from the open web. Publicly available datasets—images, text, code—are scraped en masse to train large models. Here, attackers can seed malicious content in online repositories, forums, or code libraries, knowing that automated crawlers will scoop it up. What seems like a stray meme or an innocuous function call may end up embedded in a model's representation of the world. When that model is later deployed—in content moderation, autonomous driving, or medical diagnosis—the taint surfaces, not as a glitch but as an engineered outcome. The invisibility of this pathway is precisely what makes it so attractive.

A more advanced route is supply-side poisoning. Instead of waiting for data to be scraped, attackers target the providers of curated datasets or the contractors hired to annotate them. Annotation—deciding what an image contains or what sentiment a phrase conveys—creates ground truth for supervised learning. By subtly biasing these labels, adversaries can embed vulnerabilities that later manifest as skewed classifications. Imagine a facial recognition system trained on a dataset where certain features are deliberately mislabelled; the resulting model may fail spectacularly in predictable, exploitable ways.

These tactics are not hypothetical. Security researchers have repeatedly demonstrated that poisoning a fraction of a dataset—sometimes as little as 0.1 per cent—can induce highly specific misclassifications. The fragility arises from the sheer scale of machine learning: models interpolate patterns from millions of examples, meaning even a tiny proportion of malicious inputs can tip the balance. Unlike traditional exploits, which rely on zero-days or vulnerabilities in code, poisoning exploits the learning process itself. It is sabotage baked into the very logic of generalisation.

What makes this particularly dangerous is that poisoned models often perform normally under most conditions. Accuracy remains high, benchmarks are met, and procurement officers sign off on deployment. Only under targeted triggers—an image with a sticker, a phrase with a keyword—does the hidden vulnerability emerge. This gives poisoning a dual advantage: it avoids detection during testing while guaranteeing payoff when conditions are right. For adversaries, it is the perfect long game. For defenders, it is a nightmare of invisible compromise.

The strategic implications stretch far beyond the technical. In a world where AI governs critical infrastructure, elections, and military systems, data poisoning becomes a form of pre-positioning. A state adversary might poison datasets today, not for immediate disruption, but to guarantee exploitable weaknesses years down the line. This echoes the logic of espionage more than sabotage: lying dormant, awaiting activation. The blurred line between data and territory, between training corpus and national asset, reframes how states must think about sovereignty. Control over data provenance and integrity becomes as essential as control over borders or supply chains.

Responses to this threat are beginning to take shape, though unevenly. Technical countermeasures include robust training techniques that downweight suspicious data points, differential privacy that reduces overfitting to poisoned inputs, and auditing tools that flag anomalies in datasets. Yet these solutions are partial at best, because they assume defenders can access and scrutinise the entire training pipeline. In practice, organisations rely heavily on opaque third-party models or pre-trained systems, inheriting both their capabilities and their compromises. The supply chain of AI itself becomes a vulnerability.

Here lies the real challenge: investment has historically focused on model performance, not data provenance. The glamour lies in larger architectures, faster inference, and dazzling benchmarks. Provenance and curation—

painstaking, resource-intensive, unglamorous—have been neglected. Poisoning forces a rebalancing. Just as food safety relies on traceability from farm to fork, AI security demands traceability from dataset to deployment. Provenance is not a bureaucratic hurdle but the foundation of trust. Without it, every benchmark and every certification is potentially a mirage.

The philosophical dimension is equally sharp. Machine learning has been celebrated as a way to transcend human bias by relying on empirical data. Poisoning exposes a darker truth: data is not neutral, and reliance on it introduces not just human bias but adversarial intent. A poisoned dataset encodes malice into the statistical heart of AI, making manipulation indistinguishable from knowledge. This raises uncomfortable questions about the epistemology of machine learning. What does it mean to "know" when what is learned may be deliberately false? How do we calibrate trust in systems whose foundations are so easily corroded?

The policy implications are profound. Procurement guidelines must evolve to mandate dataset audits and disclosure of data sources. Regulation may require firms to demonstrate not just model accuracy but provenance integrity, much as pharmaceutical companies must prove not only efficacy but purity of ingredients. Internationally, standards diplomacy could help establish norms for dataset sharing, labelling practices, and verification mechanisms. Without such measures, poisoning risks becoming a silent arms race, where states and corporations alike attempt to seed vulnerabilities into rivals' AI pipelines.

The motif of sabotage is apt: poisoning does not break the machine, it makes the machine work *against* its owner. It is subversion rather than destruction. For defenders, the challenge is to shift mindset from detection after the fact to resilience by design: prioritising curation, building provenance chains, and assuming that adversaries are already probing for openings. The future of AI security may depend less on inventing new algorithms than on rediscovering an old truth—that trust is built not in performance alone, but in the integrity of inputs.

The unresolved question lingers: if every dataset can be seeded with falsehoods, every annotation manipulated, and every pipeline compromised, can we ever build AI that is truly trustworthy—or must we learn to live, permanently, with the possibility of hidden sabotage?

Rules of engagement

In October 1983, during NATO's Able Archer exercise, Soviet officials became convinced they were witnessing preparations for a nuclear first strike. Misread signals, compressed timelines, and brittle channels of communication nearly brought the world to catastrophe. What prevented escalation was not superior technology but human restraint—the refusal of individuals to act on incomplete or ambiguous information. The story lingers as a reminder that even in the nuclear age, rules of engagement mattered as much as weapons themselves. Today, as AI systems enter the field of security and governance, the same question resurfaces with new urgency: who sets the rules, and how do we ensure they are followed?

AI is not a missile to be counted or a tank to be inspected. It is software—adaptive, scalable, often inscrutable even to its designers. Its use in conflict and competition cannot be governed by the same treaties and verification tools that stabilised the Cold War. Yet the stakes are no less existential. Algorithms now mediate persuasion at election time, shape financial flows, and decide which signals rise to the attention of human operators in crises. Left without agreed constraints, their capacity to compress decision-making and blur accountability risks turning every flashpoint into a hair-trigger moment. To speak of "rules of engagement" for AI is therefore not an abstraction but a demand of prudence.

The first challenge is definitional. What counts as "engagement" in a world where cognitive operations may precede any physical confrontation? A disinformation campaign powered by synthetic personas may never fire a shot, but it can destabilise societies as effectively as a missile strike on infrastructure. Should its deployment by states be governed by the same principles of proportionality and discrimination that underpin the laws of armed conflict? To leave the question unanswered is to invite strategic ambiguity where restraint is most needed.

Verification presents a second problem. Nuclear treaties relied on satellites, sensors, and inspectors to confirm compliance. But how do you verify the absence of an algorithm? Unlike warheads, AI models are easy to duplicate, transport, or disguise as civilian applications. A facial recognition system for airports can, with minor modification, become a tool for mass surveillance. An autonomous drone for search and rescue can be refitted as a weapon. Auditability must therefore be built in at the design stage. That means logging decision processes, documenting training data, and subjecting algorithms to red-team testing before they are deployed. Verification in the AI age is not about counting assets but tracing provenance and intent.

Auditability, however, brings its own tensions. Too much transparency can empower adversaries, revealing how a defensive system might be gamed. Too little, and accountability vanishes. The balance is delicate. One promising approach lies in layered disclosure: high-level guarantees that can be verified internationally, coupled with deeper technical audits conducted by trusted intermediaries. This mirrors financial regulation, where firms disclose enough to assure markets of stability without handing competitors the keys to their internal models. The analogy is imperfect but instructive: AI oversight may need to borrow institutional forms from outside the military domain.

The principle of proportionality also demands re-examination. In traditional conflict, proportionality is judged by the scale of force relative to a military objective. In AI-driven operations, effects may be diffuse and delayed. A targeted disinformation campaign could erode democratic trust over years, making any assessment of "proportional" response nearly impossible. Yet abandoning proportionality is not an option; it remains the ethical core of restraint. The task, then, is to adapt proportionality into a cognitive register: measuring not just immediate casualties or damage, but longer-term impacts on legitimacy, cohesion, and rights. This reframing expands the horizon of engagement while grounding it in testable metrics.

What unites these themes is the need for language that travels. States and firms alike must negotiate rules across cultures, legal systems, and corporate strategies. A slogan—"responsible AI" or "ethical autonomy"—will not suffice. What negotiators require are terms that can be operationalised: thresholds for human oversight, protocols for escalation, standards for auditability. These must be simple enough to survive translation yet rigorous enough to bind behaviour. "Human-in-the-loop" is one such phrase, but it means different things in different contexts. Is the human a supervisor, an approver, or a fail-safe? Only testable definitions can prevent the phrase from collapsing into theatre.

The corporate dimension cannot be ignored. Firms develop many of the most powerful AI systems, yet they operate under commercial rather than geopolitical imperatives. Their rules of engagement are terms of service, compliance checklists, and shareholder pressures. Still, the line between corporate and state use is porous. Governments procure systems from firms, and firms operate in markets shaped by geopolitical rivalry. The

SolarWinds breach showed how software supply chains blur public and private interests. Rules of engagement must therefore extend beyond the battlefield to procurement offices, boardrooms, and standards bodies. Without this, firms risk becoming unwitting combatants in conflicts they never chose.

History offers both warnings and templates. The Geneva Conventions codified humanitarian principles not because states were suddenly altruistic, but because even in war, restraint was in their interest. Nuclear arms control treaties emerged from the recognition that unbounded escalation guaranteed mutual destruction. The parallel is not perfect—algorithms are not bombs—but the logic holds. Establishing rules of engagement for AI is less about lofty ideals than about survival: preserving trust, avoiding spirals of escalation, and maintaining a minimum of predictability in an unpredictable world.

Yet the path ahead remains uncertain. Every proposed rule encounters a counter-argument: transparency undermines secrecy, auditability burdens innovation, proportionality blurs in the digital realm. These tensions are real, but they are not fatal. They point to the deeper truth that AI is not merely a technical system but a political one. It forces us to confront perennial questions of power, legitimacy, and restraint in a new technological register.

The unresolved question hangs over every attempt at codification: can we design rules of engagement robust enough to restrain machines that act faster than human deliberation, yet flexible enough to accommodate the diversity of political systems and corporate incentives? Or will we, like those Soviet officers in 1983, find ourselves relying once again on human restraint in the face of imperfect signals—only this time, with algorithms accelerating the pace and narrowing the margin for error?

Chapter 6

The Surveillance Bargain

On a crowded street in Shenzhen, cameras hang like lanterns from lampposts, their lenses tracking the ebb and flow of pedestrians. A jaywalker is identified, their face matched against a database, their name and partial ID displayed on a nearby screen as a warning to others. Thousands of miles away, in Chicago, police commanders gather around a "heat map" generated by predictive algorithms, which claim to forecast where crimes are likely to occur. Both scenes are framed as innovations—tools for safety, efficiency, order. Yet both reveal the same underlying truth: surveillance has become a currency, traded between citizens, states, and corporations in exchange for convenience, protection, or simply compliance. The bargain is seldom explicit, but its consequences are inescapable.

The paradox is stark. Citizens are told that surveillance is the price of security, that liberty must be trimmed for safety to flourish. But history and design show otherwise. Well-constructed systems—transparent, proportionate, and accountable—can preserve both liberty and security, while poorly designed ones corrode trust, entrench inequality, and expand without end. The "trade-off" often presented to city leaders, policymakers, and technology firms is a false dichotomy born less of necessity than of imagination's failure. Once accepted, it enables what legal scholars call "emergency creep": temporary measures that calcify into permanent control. The story of modern governance is not just who collects data, but how design choices turn surveillance into either protection or domination.

Nowhere is this bargain more vivid than in the rise of smart cities. From Barcelona to Dubai, urban environments are being rewired with sensors, biometric checkpoints, and algorithmic dashboards. Vendors market these systems as engines of efficiency, but they are also instruments of power. Procurement contracts often favour speed and spectacle over accuracy and accountability, embedding biases into the very infrastructure of daily life. A facial recognition camera that misidentifies one demographic at a higher rate than another does not merely commit errors; it reshapes how communities are policed, who is trusted, and who is suspected. Once installed, such systems are hard to contest. The promise of seamless urban management becomes the justification for invisible, unrelenting scrutiny.

The commercial sector is no less implicated. Data brokers—operating largely out of sight—compile dossiers that rival the reach of any state intelligence agency. Every loyalty card purchase, mobile app permission, or website visit feeds into profiles that can be sold, merged, and resold. These dossiers do not just predict consumer preferences; they inform credit decisions, hiring practices, and even political targeting. When Cambridge Analytica used harvested data to manipulate electoral messaging, it exposed not an anomaly but a system whose scale already dwarfed traditional surveillance. In this market, citizens are not subjects of observation alone but commodities traded without their knowledge, their behavioural residues packaged into predictive assets.

Citizen scoring systems illustrate how these dynamics bleed into governance. China's social credit framework is the most infamous, but Western parallels—credit ratings, insurance risk scores, algorithmic eligibility checks—operate on the same principle: codifying trustworthiness into numbers that govern access to resources. These infrastructures nudge behaviour through subtle incentives and penalties, yet their cumulative effect is chilling. When every act can be scored, people adapt not to their conscience but to the system's expectations. What begins as soft control hardens into structure, shaping careers, communities, and futures with a veneer of objectivity. Here, the surveillance bargain reveals its sharpest edge: citizens are no longer just watched; they are moulded.

Yet resignation is not inevitable. Exit and voice remain possible, though their contours are constrained. Privacy-enhancing technologies—end-to-end encryption, decentralised identifiers, anonymisation protocols—offer individuals limited exits from data-hungry systems. Governance mechanisms—impact assessments, oversight boards, judicial challenges—amplify collective voice. Neither path is perfect; both demand realism rather than utopian hope. Encryption cannot shield against all metadata collection, and oversight boards can be neutered by political inertia. But together, tools and governance sketch out an architecture of agency, one that prevents surveillance from becoming destiny. To understand their limits is not to abandon them but to wield them wisely.

The surveillance bargain, then, is not a single negotiation but a recurring one, enacted across city councils, procurement offices, boardrooms, and living rooms. Each decision to deploy, accept, or resist surveillance tilts the balance between security, liberty, and power. For leaders, the test is whether systems can be designed to protect without eroding trust; for citizens, whether exits and voices can be made strong enough to matter. The stakes are more than technical—they touch dignity, autonomy, and democracy itself.

The unresolved question remains: can societies embed surveillance within structures that respect liberty, or will the bargain always tend towards coercion once the tools are in place? The answer lies not in technology alone but in political will, design discipline, and civic vigilance. The next sections will unpick this dilemma, tracing how smart cities, commercial markets, and citizen-scoring regimes entrench or resist control. What emerges is not a simple trade-off, but a contest over the very terms of freedom in a digitised world.

Security vs liberty

The weeks following the September 11th attacks saw governments across the world pass laws in haste, expanding surveillance powers in the name of preventing the next catastrophe. Few questioned the premise: that safety demanded a curtailment of liberty. Yet two decades on, many of those extraordinary measures remain in place, normalised far beyond their emergency origins. The promise was simple—sacrifice a measure of privacy for greater protection. The reality was more complex: liberties eroded, security gains uneven, and public trust diminished. The "trade-off" was not an iron law of governance but the consequence of choices, often poorly designed and rarely revisited.

The idea of liberty being pitted against security has a powerful rhetorical appeal. Leaders frame it as a zero-sum equation: every increment of safety requires a decrement of freedom. But this is a false dichotomy, born of shortcuts in institutional design. Systems that collapse rights in pursuit of control tend to backfire, eroding the very trust on which security depends. Conversely, systems that embed privacy and accountability often achieve both aims more effectively. Security and liberty are not natural enemies; they can be co-engineered. The challenge is recognising when "emergency logic" becomes a cover for lazy architecture or opportunistic power grabs.

Consider Estonia, a small country with outsized lessons. After enduring cyberattacks in 2007 that crippled its banks and ministries, Estonia responded not by concentrating authority in opaque agencies but by doubling down on transparency and decentralisation. Its e-governance model requires that every access to a citizen's record—by doctor, police officer, or bureaucrat—leaves an immutable log visible to the citizen themselves. Security is preserved through accountability, liberty through visibility. Rather than a trade-off, the two aims reinforce one another: citizens trust digital services precisely because misuse is traceable. The Estonian case shows how thoughtful design makes liberty a security asset, not a liability.

Contrast this with the growth of sprawling CCTV networks in major cities across the world. London, often called the most surveilled city in Europe, has invested heavily in cameras but without consistent oversight of how footage is accessed or retained. Independent evaluations suggest such systems deter little crime, yet they normalise a sense of being watched at all times. Security gains are marginal; liberty losses are structural. The lesson is not that surveillance technology is inherently illegitimate, but that poorly constrained use yields diminishing returns, both practically and politically. A design that embeds proportionality—targeted use, independent review, transparent deletion—can reconcile the tension. Without it, the "trade-off" narrative becomes a self-fulfilling trap.

Product design offers similar contrasts. In some jurisdictions, contact-tracing apps during the COVID-19 pandemic were built with centralised data collection, storing sensitive information on government servers. Others, such as Germany's Corona-Warn-App, chose a decentralised model developed jointly by Apple and Google, where contact events were logged locally on devices. Both aimed at public health security; only one preserved privacy by default. Uptake rates told the story: citizens were more willing to download and use the app when they trusted that their data was not being stockpiled. Here again, liberty proved instrumental to achieving the very security objective at hand.

The temptation to frame liberty as expendable stems not only from crises but from design shortcuts. When engineers or policymakers treat rights as afterthoughts, they create brittle systems vulnerable to abuse and mission creep. Emergency measures drafted quickly often lack sunset clauses; surveillance tools deployed for terrorism are repurposed for ordinary crime; databases built for immigration are cross-used by tax agencies. Each expansion is rationalised as necessary, but the cumulative effect is a ratchet: liberty yields ground, security gains plateau, and the system loses legitimacy. This dynamic—emergency creep—cannot be undone by rhetoric; it demands structural safeguards.

Guardrails exist. Rights-preserving systems can be deliberately engineered through techniques such as differential privacy, which allows statistical analysis without exposing individual records, or zero-knowledge proofs, which enable verification without disclosure. Procurement frameworks can mandate such design patterns, ensuring that city leaders and product teams are not locked into binary choices. Governance innovations like independent data protection authorities or citizen oversight boards provide another layer, turning abstract rights into operational constraints. These are not luxuries for stable times; they are prerequisites for resilience under stress.

The philosophical insight here is that liberty and security are both conditions of trust. A system that sacrifices one for the other corrodes the very social fabric it seeks to protect. Citizens who feel permanently surveilled with little recourse become less cooperative, less willing to share information or participate in collective projects. By contrast, systems that respect autonomy create legitimacy, making compliance voluntary rather than coerced. Liberty is not the opposite of security but its foundation: a society that feels free is more stable, more cohesive, and therefore more secure.

Yet the tension is never fully resolved. Policymakers will always face demands for decisive action in crises, and product teams will be pressured to privilege functionality over safeguards. The test lies not in eliminating the tension but in designing systems that resist its most corrosive tendencies. Can emergency powers be truly temporary? Can surveillance infrastructures be made transparent enough to earn trust? Can rights-preserving technologies become the default rather than the exception?

The answers will determine whether societies continue to stumble into false bargains or learn to engineer genuine security without liberty's sacrifice. What remains unresolved is whether political will can match technical possibility—whether leaders and designers will choose the harder path of building systems that do not force the trade-off at all. That open question shadows every debate on surveillance, every procurement decision, and every emergency law still on the books.

Smart cities and policing

On a spring morning in 2019, residents of San Diego awoke to discover their city's streetlights had been quietly upgraded—not only to provide efficient LED lighting but to house hidden cameras and microphones. The project had been marketed as a cost-saving measure to reduce energy consumption and improve traffic management. Few realised it was also delivering an unprecedented surveillance infrastructure, one that police could tap into at will. The lesson was clear: technologies sold under the banner of efficiency often arrive carrying a second payload—power.

This paradox defines the modern smart city. Sensors, cameras, and predictive algorithms are framed as neutral tools for urban optimisation, promising smoother commutes, cleaner air, and faster emergency response. Yet once installed, they become irresistible assets for policing, border enforcement, or political monitoring. Procurement contracts speak the language of efficiency, but the lived reality is one of asymmetrical control. What begins as infrastructure can quickly become infrastructure *for surveillance*, with consequences that ripple far beyond traffic flow or energy bills.

The seduction of smart-city technology lies in its surface rationality. Who could oppose more efficient waste collection, or predictive maintenance that prevents water main breaks? But in practice, the same data streams used to optimise city services often double as intelligence pipelines. A network of cameras designed for parking enforcement can be cross-applied to track protest movements. Microphones meant to detect gunshots can also capture conversations. Predictive policing software that claims to forecast burglaries can reinforce racial and socio-economic biases, mapping suspicion onto the same neighbourhoods again and again. Efficiency is the sales pitch; power is the purchase.

The procurement process itself is part of the problem. City leaders, under pressure to innovate, often rely on vendor promises rather than independent testing. Contracts may lock municipalities into proprietary systems, limiting transparency about how algorithms work or how data is handled. Vendors pitch "turnkey" solutions with glossy dashboards and futuristic demos, but obscure their training data, accuracy rates, or error margins. The result is public funds underwriting systems that are neither accountable nor easily audited. Procurement becomes less about democratically defined needs and more about technological persuasion.

Accuracy and bias compound these issues. Studies of facial recognition systems, for instance, consistently reveal disproportionate error rates for women and people with darker skin tones. When such systems are embedded into city surveillance, misidentification becomes not just a technical flaw but a civic injustice. Predictive policing amplifies the issue: because the software is trained on historical crime data, it reflects the biases of past policing decisions. Neighbourhoods with heavy police presence generate more arrest records, which then "teach" the system to predict more crime there, justifying further patrols—a feedback loop of suspicion. Efficiency here is not neutral optimisation but the automation of bias.

The problem is not simply one of flawed algorithms but of governance. When cities adopt surveillance tools without public debate or clear oversight, the democratic contract weakens. Citizens become subjects of opaque systems they cannot question, even as their daily lives are shaped by them. The technology may be operated by police or city agencies, but the underlying power lies with the vendors who control its design, updates, and data pipelines. A camera on every lamppost may look like municipal investment; in practice, it can amount to privatised surveillance outsourced to corporations.

Guardrails are possible, but they require deliberate design. Some cities have begun instituting procurement frameworks that mandate bias testing, independent audits, and public consultation before adopting new surveillance technologies. San Francisco and Boston, for example, introduced bans or restrictions on the use of facial recognition by city agencies, not as technophobic gestures but as democratic guardrails. Others have experimented with "sunset clauses" requiring reauthorisation of surveillance systems after a set period, ensuring that tools justified during emergencies do not become permanent by default. These measures show that oversight can be woven into smart-city governance, but only if leaders are willing to resist the seductions of vendor promises.

At a deeper level, the challenge is philosophical: what vision of citizenship underpins the smart city? Is the city conceived as a machine to be optimised, with residents reduced to data points and variables? Or is it a commons, where efficiency serves but never eclipses rights and dignity? The deployment of predictive policing tools illustrates the stakes. If efficiency alone governs decision-making, then reducing reported crime becomes the metric of success, even if achieved through disproportionate targeting of marginalised groups. But if dignity and accountability are built into the system, then legitimacy—not just numbers—becomes the test.

The motif of the "city as sensor" forces us to confront how power is distributed in urban space. Data-rich environments create asymmetries: those who control the sensors and algorithms wield disproportionate influence over those who merely pass under them. Without strong oversight, smart cities risk inverting democracy itself, concentrating power in municipal agencies and their corporate partners while leaving citizens with little recourse. The city ceases to be a place of shared belonging and becomes, instead, a grid of observation.

Yet the tension is unresolved. The very tools that can entrench bias and power can also be designed for accountability. Cameras can be configured to blur faces by default, with reversible de-anonymisation only under court order. Predictive tools can be built around community-defined priorities rather than arrest records. Sensors can collect aggregate rather than individual data, enabling efficiency without surveillance creep. These possibilities exist, but they depend on procurement choices, governance frameworks, and the political will to put liberty on equal footing with efficiency.

The open question is whether cities will take that harder path. Will procurement processes evolve from vendor seduction to democratic negotiation? Will oversight mechanisms keep pace with rapid technological change? Will citizens retain agency in shaping the digital architecture of their streets, or will efficiency's siren song continue to mask the quiet accretion of power? These questions hover over every contract signed, every camera installed, every algorithm deployed. The answers will define not only the future of policing, but the very character of urban democracy itself.

Surveillance capitalism

In 2018, a small data analytics firm most people had never heard of—Cambridge Analytica—was revealed to have harvested personal information on tens of millions of Facebook users without their consent. The scandal reverberated through parliaments, boardrooms, and dinner tables alike, but the real shock was not simply the misuse of data. It was the dawning recognition that an industry largely hidden from public view had grown powerful enough to rival state intelligence agencies. What Cambridge Analytica represented was not an outlier, but a symptom of something bigger: a world where personal data is not merely collected but relentlessly commodified, traded, and weaponised.

The paradox is stark. In democratic societies, intelligence services are hemmed in by laws, oversight committees, and budgetary constraints. Yet commercial data brokers operate with near impunity, aggregating and reselling information that often surpasses what governments can legally gather. They piece together dossiers from sources as disparate as shopping receipts, app location trails, loyalty cards, online searches, and leaked medical records. The result is a sprawling shadow economy of profiles so granular they can predict pregnancies, debts, or political leanings before individuals themselves have consciously registered them.

Follow the money and the scale becomes clearer. A mobile app offering a free weather forecast may sell location data to a broker, which in turn resells it to hedge funds, advertisers, or security contractors. A consumer's online shopping history is packaged into audience segments: "new parents," "diabetics," "gun enthusiasts." These segments can then be purchased by political campaigns, credit card companies, or even foreign actors probing societal divides. Each transaction is legal, lucrative, and largely invisible to those it concerns. The surveillance economy's invisibility is not accidental—it is designed into the flows of data, contracts, and mergers that keep citizens in the dark while investors and clients reap the benefits.

Mergers have turbocharged this ecosystem. When advertising giants consolidate, they integrate not only their media reach but also the behavioural data of billions of users. Telecommunications firms merge with media companies, blurring lines between infrastructure and surveillance. Even credit bureaus, historically tasked with financial reporting, now trade in lifestyle data and consumer analytics. The incentives are obvious: the more comprehensive the dossier, the more valuable the insights for advertisers, insurers, and political strategists. Over time, these conglomerates form data monopolies whose power exceeds that of many nation-states. Regulation has lagged hopelessly behind.

Leaks and breaches reveal the fragility of the system. In 2017, Equifax lost the personal data of 147 million Americans, including social security numbers and credit histories. In 2021, a scrape of Facebook data exposed information on over 500 million users, making phone numbers and personal details available to anyone with modest technical skills. Each breach underscores that the same systems designed to monetise attention and identity also create vast, unsecured stockpiles of sensitive data. Once leaked, this information flows into grey and black markets, fuelling fraud, identity theft, and manipulation. Surveillance capitalism is not only extractive; it is leaky by design.

The implications for governance are profound. Regulators cannot treat these firms as benign intermediaries; they must recognise them as de facto intelligence actors. The dossiers assembled by brokers can shape electoral campaigns, credit access, hiring decisions, and even immigration screenings. In some cases, governments themselves purchase data from brokers precisely because it sidesteps legal constraints on direct surveillance. The state becomes both customer and competitor in the market for behavioural insight. The citizen is left in an ambiguous position—simultaneously consumer, subject, and product.

Contrasting views highlight the tension. Proponents argue that personalised advertising and predictive analytics drive economic efficiency, offering consumers convenience and businesses growth. Critics counter that what is marketed as efficiency is in reality asymmetry: corporations know everything about individuals, while individuals know almost nothing about the corporations. The bargain is not freely entered into, because meaningful consent is impossible when privacy policies run to dozens of opaque pages and tracking occurs across thousands of invisible nodes. The result is not a contract but a capture.

Philosophically, surveillance capitalism forces us to confront an old question in a new guise: what does it mean to be free when one's choices are constantly anticipated, nudged, or constrained by unseen algorithms? Autonomy becomes conditional, filtered through probabilistic scores and behavioural predictions. Citizens risk becoming less like agents of their own futures and more like data points feeding a statistical model. The chilling effect is subtle but real—people moderate their speech, adjust their clicks, or avoid certain associations because they suspect, often correctly, that someone is watching.

Yet fatalism is unwarranted. Understanding how surveillance capitalism operates opens the door to reform. Procurement officers deciding whether to buy analytics tools can demand transparency about data provenance. Legislators can insist on limits to data retention, portability rights, and meaningful consent mechanisms. Citizens can push for bans on the sale of certain categories of sensitive data, such as health or geolocation, to commercial brokers. Companies can be required to prove not only that their datasets are valuable but that they are legitimate, curated, and secure. These are not radical interventions—they are overdue corrections in a market that has grown without guardrails.

Still, tension lingers. Surveillance capitalism thrives precisely because it is profitable, scalable, and adaptable. Even as new regulations appear, firms innovate around them, devising fresh techniques for capture and monetisation. The question, then, is whether democratic societies can evolve governance structures nimble enough to keep pace with an industry whose core product is opacity. If dossiers built in secret rival the reach of state intelligence, what mechanisms of accountability will ensure that citizens remain more than raw material in someone else's ledger? The answer remains uncertain—but the stakes could not be clearer.

Citizen scoring

In 2013, a Shanghai resident discovered he had been blacklisted from booking high-speed train tickets. The reason was not a court ruling, nor a criminal charge. It was his low social credit score, derived from a web of opaque assessments that included unpaid debts and alleged "untrustworthy" behaviour. The punishment was not prison, but exclusion—from travel, from services, from opportunities. A single metric had quietly reshaped his life.

This story is often invoked as a glimpse of a dystopian future, yet the logic of scoring is neither exotic nor confined to China. In Western democracies, credit scores already determine whether someone can secure a mortgage, lease a car, or even land a job. Employers increasingly consult reputational metrics scraped from social media. Ride-hailing apps assign star ratings that influence a driver's livelihood. Universities consider algorithmic assessments in admissions. What differs across contexts is not the presence of scoring, but the breadth of its reach and the degree of transparency.

The paradox is unsettling: societies that claim to value individuality increasingly reduce people to numbers. The justification is efficiency—scores promise to simplify complex decisions, to make risk legible at scale. Yet efficiency conceals a deeper transformation. Scoring infrastructures are not neutral tools; they are behavioural feedback loops. By rewarding certain actions and penalising others, they nudge populations towards conformity. A citizen may not fear jail, but she may think twice before attending a protest if she suspects her insurance premium or job prospects could be affected. This is how soft control hardens into systemic discipline.

Consider the example of credit scoring in the United States. Originally confined to financial risk, the FICO score has seeped into domains ranging from rental agreements to insurance pricing. This expansion has a chilling effect: those who fall behind financially are not only punished with higher borrowing costs but also with curtailed access to the very opportunities that could help them recover. The score does not merely measure risk—it amplifies it, creating a self-reinforcing cycle that entrenches inequality.

Elsewhere, scoring infrastructures operate under the guise of consumer convenience. Loyalty cards and shopping apps compile detailed purchase histories, translating habits into scores that shape personalised pricing or promotional access. The consumer, unaware of the underlying algorithmic logic, may experience a subtle narrowing of choice. What began as a tool for marketing becomes a mechanism of stratification. The danger is not only exclusion but also a normalisation of surveillance as a prerequisite for participation.

The philosophical stakes are profound. At the heart of scoring lies a redefinition of dignity. To be treated with dignity is to be seen as more than the sum of one's transactions, affiliations, or digital traces. Scoring systems invert this principle, rendering dignity contingent on compliance with behavioural expectations. This is not only a technical issue but a political one: whose values are encoded into the metrics, and who has the power to redefine them?

Feedback loops make the problem more insidious. A low score can limit access to jobs, which in turn prevents score improvement, locking individuals into downward spirals. Conversely, high scores consolidate privilege, rewarding those who already enjoy structural advantages. The chilling effects are collective as well as individual: entire communities may moderate their behaviour to avoid penalties, leading to a society that is outwardly compliant but inwardly constrained.

Guardrails do exist. Some jurisdictions impose limits on how scores can be used—for instance, restricting employers from factoring credit scores into hiring decisions. Transparency mandates, such as the European Union's General Data Protection Regulation, require individuals to be informed about algorithmic decisions that affect them. Yet enforcement is uneven, and the opacity of many scoring systems makes meaningful accountability elusive. More radical reform might involve shifting from punitive to restorative scoring models, where indicators of risk are balanced by opportunities for redemption.

The tension remains unresolved. On one hand, scoring promises order in complex societies; on the other, it risks eroding the foundations of dignity and autonomy. What begins as a tool of convenience or efficiency can, if unchecked, evolve into a scaffold for authoritarian governance. The critical question is whether societies can harness the utility of scoring without succumbing to its coercive potential. Can metrics be made to serve dignity rather than diminish it—or is the very act of scoring citizens destined to erode the freedoms it claims to organise? The answer will shape not only markets and institutions, but the lived texture of citizenship itself.

Exit, voice, and privacy tech

When WhatsApp announced in 2021 that it would share more metadata with its parent company, Facebook, millions of users declared their intent to quit. Telegram and Signal downloads spiked. Commentators speculated about a mass migration. Yet months later, most people were still using WhatsApp. The episode revealed a hard truth: exits from dominant platforms are rarely clean or complete. Network effects, habit, and convenience bind users even when trust is broken.

This difficulty of exit is mirrored in politics as much as technology. Citizens dissatisfied with government surveillance cannot easily opt out of state systems. Choosing another jurisdiction is impractical for most, and disengagement carries penalties. The challenge, then, is to find meaningful ways of exercising both *exit*—through tools and practices that reduce exposure—and *voice*—through governance and advocacy that reshape the environment. Neither path is sufficient alone. Tools without politics become fragile refuges; politics without tools leaves individuals exposed in the meantime.

Exits: practical but partial

The marketplace of privacy-enhancing technologies offers some real, if imperfect, exit ramps. End-to-end encrypted messaging, once niche, is now mainstream in apps like Signal and WhatsApp. Virtual private networks (VPNs) allow users to tunnel through restrictive regimes, while privacy-focused browsers such as Brave or extensions like uBlock Origin reduce data capture. More advanced options—such as onion routing through Tor or decentralised identity frameworks—provide stronger protections but often at the cost of usability and speed.

Yet every tool carries trade-offs. VPNs can be blocked or compromised by states. Encrypted platforms are only as safe as their implementation and the metadata they still reveal. Privacy coins promise anonymous transactions but attract regulatory pushback. The paradox of exit is that the more robust the tool, the higher the barriers to widespread adoption. In practice, most people tolerate convenience-driven compromises, leaving privacy tech as an elite rather than a mass shield.

Voice: governance as leverage

If exits protect the individual, voice seeks to reshape the system. Regulation can compel platforms to build privacy by default, as Europe's General Data Protection Regulation did by making consent meaningful and data portability a right. Civil society campaigns, from the Electronic Frontier Foundation in the United States to Access Now globally, use voice to expose overreach and shift norms. Even corporate actors deploy voice when lobbying for clear rules of the road that prevent surveillance capitalism from becoming a competitive necessity.

Voice has its limits. Governments often invoke national security to override privacy concerns, and lobbying power tilts towards incumbents. Still, voice matters because it alters the cost-benefit calculus of both states and firms. It makes certain practices reputationally toxic or legally untenable. When regulators in multiple jurisdictions align, as in efforts to restrict facial recognition in public spaces, the combined weight of their voice forces adaptation even by reluctant actors.

Privacy tech as scaffolding for agency

The relationship between exit and voice is not a binary but a feedback loop. Tools can empower voice: encrypted communication enables activists to organise without fear, while open-source audit tools provide evidence for advocacy. Likewise, voice can amplify exits: procurement rules that mandate open standards make it easier for citizens and cities to adopt privacy-protecting alternatives. The interplay creates scaffolding for agency—not immunity from surveillance, but leverage against its excesses.

Crucially, privacy tech is not a panacea. No encryption scheme can protect against a data broker quietly selling your location trail to advertisers or police. No VPN prevents your social graph from revealing itself through shared connections. The danger lies in treating tools as silver bullets, slipping into techno-utopian promises that obscure systemic reform. What matters is realistic deployment, with limits stated plainly. A Signal account is powerful for secure chats but irrelevant for financial data flows; Tor protects browsing anonymity but not against device-level compromise. A mature privacy culture is one that matches tool to context without illusions.

The larger question is whether societies can design exits and voices that scale. Can privacy tech evolve from niche adoption to infrastructural default? Can governance mechanisms balance innovation with dignity, ensuring that surveillance does not become the ambient condition of modern life? The answers are not fixed. They depend on whether individuals and institutions choose to see themselves as passive subjects of surveillance or as active shapers of its boundaries.

The tension endures: exits are never total, voices are never final. Both are contested, fragile, and necessary. The task is not to escape the surveillance bargain entirely—that is impossible—but to tilt its terms towards agency rather than acquiescence. Whether this is achievable depends less on the brilliance of new cryptographic tools or the eloquence of legislative preambles than on the everyday alignment of practice and principle. How far can citizens really bend the architecture of power without breaking the systems they rely on? The next chapter will press this question further, but the stakes are already clear: dignity in the digital age rests on whether exits and voices remain live options, or fade into comforting myths.

Chapter 7

Ransomware as Foreign Policy

On a spring morning in 2021, nurses at hospitals across Ireland arrived to find their computers locked by a ransom note. Patient records were encrypted, appointments cancelled, ambulances diverted. What appeared at first to be a straightforward case of extortion quickly revealed a deeper truth: the gangs behind the attack operated with impunity from jurisdictions where prosecution was unlikely. Their crime was not only theft—it was a pressure point against the very fabric of a nation's health system. The hospital corridors were quiet, but geopolitics was loud in the background.

Ransomware has travelled far from its origins as digital mugging. Today, its scripts and encryption tools are industrialised, its victims systemic, and its perpetrators less freelance than they appear. Criminal syndicates that once targeted individuals' laptops now paralyse oil pipelines and city halls. Their strikes often coincide with political currents, their safe havens aligned with national interests. What might look like cybercrime in isolation becomes, at scale, an instrument of statecraft. The line between crime and coercion blurs, and with it, the line between law enforcement and foreign policy.

This reframing matters. Treating ransomware purely as criminal activity risks underestimating its geopolitical function. The persistence of these gangs depends not only on their technical skill but on the tacit deals and blind eyes of host governments. A safe haven is a strategic asset: it channels Western security resources, raises insurance premiums, and sows doubt in civic institutions. To call it crime is accurate; to call it strategy is more honest. The chapter begins by tracing these patterns of complicity, reframing ransomware as a form of geopolitical leverage that demands more than police response.

From there, the focus shifts to the lifeblood of the ecosystem: money. Payment rails—whether cryptocurrency exchanges, mixers, or even traditional financial channels—determine the extent to which ransomware is profitable. The battleground is less about encryption algorithms than about liquidity and compliance. Policy-makers who grasp how funds are laundered through decentralised networks gain tools for real disruption. Here the question is not whether to sanction, but how to make sanctions bite in a system designed for opacity. International coordination, usually elusive, becomes indispensable.

But ransomware is not only a question of balance sheets and strategy papers; it is, above all, human. When a hospital cannot access records, lives are shortened. When a municipality's water treatment systems or payroll servers go dark, public trust fractures. The cases of cities and hospitals held hostage are not abstract—they are visceral reminders that *time kills.* The chapter retells these emblematic cases, highlighting how technical safeguards—segmentation, reliable backups, and rehearsed tabletop drills—translate into hours saved and lives preserved.

Beyond prevention lies the grim theatre of negotiation. Ransomware incidents follow a routine: initial contact, escalation, proof of decryption, and the agonising decision of whether to pay. The script is familiar to those who have lived it, yet shocking to outsiders. By laying out the negotiation playbooks—who speaks, what is demanded, how credibility is tested—leaders can approach crisis moments with clarity instead of panic. Awareness does not make the decision easier, but it makes it less blind.

Finally, there is the question of fighting back. Disruption operations—joint efforts by law enforcement, intelligence services, and sometimes private actors—have shown glimpses of success. Servers seized, decryption keys liberated, gangs briefly scattered. Yet the timing of these interventions is delicate: too early, and the deterrent effect is lost; too late, and victims are already scarred. Analysing both the successes and the limits of these operations reveals what can realistically be asked of authorities, and what still rests on the shoulders of institutions and companies themselves.

The story of ransomware is no longer just about shadowy hackers in basements. It is about the strategic use of digital crime as leverage, about the fragility of our civic infrastructure, and about the choices leaders must make under extreme pressure. To study ransomware is to study the weaponisation of dependency—on systems, on money, on time. And so the question lingers as the chapter unfolds: if ransomware has become a tool of foreign policy, how should nations, firms, and citizens recalibrate their defences—not only to survive the next attack, but to change the terms of this dark bargain altogether?

From crime to state leverage

On the surface, the ransomware groups that cripple hospitals or paralyse pipelines present themselves as ordinary criminals: calculating profit-seekers hiding behind anonymous chat handles and cryptocurrency wallets. Yet scratch the surface and a different pattern emerges. These gangs flourish most not in the world's lawless margins but in the shadows of strong states. They advertise openly, recruit with impunity, and launder their takings through banking systems that somehow never close their accounts. Their very visibility raises the question: how can so much "crime" persist in plain sight?

The paradox is telling. The most formidable ransomware and cyber-extortion groups operate from jurisdictions where state control is tight, yet enforcement is conspicuously absent. Police capable of cracking down on dissenters or street-level fraudsters somehow fail to act against those draining billions from foreign firms. This is no accident of bureaucracy. It is a tacit bargain. So long as the targets are Western corporations, hospitals, or municipalities—and not domestic entities—the gangs enjoy de facto immunity. They serve as instruments of pressure at arm's length, deniable assets in a geopolitical game.

Examples abound. After the 2021 Colonial Pipeline attack in the United States, investigators traced the perpetrators to DarkSide, a group based in Russia. The Kremlin disclaimed involvement, but the gang had long adhered to an informal rule: never target Russian entities. Similar patterns recur across Eastern Europe, where police raids on cybercriminals are rare unless they step on domestic toes. Safe havens thus function not only as protective shields but as strategic staging grounds. They allow governments to harness disruption without shouldering blame. The "non-state" label is convenient fiction.

This reframes how we think about cybercrime. It is not merely a law enforcement problem, but a geopolitical instrument. Just as Cold War intelligence agencies used proxies to extend their reach, today's states tolerate—or even quietly encourage—cybercriminal ecosystems to sap adversaries' resources, test defences, and generate leverage. Crime becomes a tool of statecraft, its ambiguity part of its appeal. A gang can be disavowed one day and quietly shielded the next, depending on diplomatic winds. For policymakers, the distinction between gangster and agent is less useful than recognising the continuum between them.

The economic logic reinforces the political one. Cyber gangs pump illicit revenue through exchanges and money-laundering networks that boost local financial centres. Their wealth circulates through real estate, luxury goods, and service industries. The state tolerates them not only for their geopolitical utility but for their economic contribution—small compared to national GDP, but significant enough to buy local protection. In some cases, the line blurs further: members of these groups have been rumoured to share information with security services or to perform tasks "off the books" in exchange for continued freedom.

For Western governments, the implications are profound. Sanctions or law enforcement actions aimed solely at individuals misdiagnose the problem. Arresting a handful of hackers or blacklisting a cryptocurrency wallet may disrupt operations temporarily but leaves intact the enabling environment of state tolerance. The strategic question is not "How do we stop the criminals?" but "How do we change the calculus of the states that protect them?" Pressure must be applied where impunity is manufactured, not just where the latest exploit lands.

This requires a shift in sanctions strategy. Instead of pursuing endless cat-and-mouse games with individual groups, policy-makers must focus on the infrastructures of protection—banks that launder proceeds, officials who turn a blind eye, regulators who decline to cooperate. The target is not just the gang but the web of tacit deals that sustain it. By framing ransomware as a tool of state leverage, sanctions can be reimagined not as moral rebukes but as instruments to reshape incentives. That is a harder, more politically delicate task, but also a more realistic one.

Yet the danger of escalation is real. If cybercriminals are functionally proxies, then pressure on their host states risks retaliation. The very ambiguity that shields governments also makes deterrence murky: how do you deter an adversary who claims the gang is beyond their control? How do you punish without overstepping into direct confrontation? These are not abstract puzzles but live questions in the corridors of diplomacy. They illustrate why seeing ransomware only as "crime" obscures the strategic stakes.

The broader lesson is that safe havens are not just permissive—they are deliberate instruments of policy. Tacit deals between criminals and states shape Western risk in ways subtle and profound. Hospitals delay surgeries, pipelines halt deliveries, city budgets are gutted—all while host governments posture as neutral bystanders. To see this dynamic clearly is to accept that cybercrime has outgrown the categories of policing and prosecution. It is now part of the repertoire of geopolitical competition.

And so the uncomfortable question lingers: if gangs are assets as much as adversaries, can the West ever expect their disappearance? Or must strategy shift towards managing their leverage, curbing their utility, and changing the incentives of the states that shelter them? The answers will determine not only the next phase of ransomware, but the rules of conflict in the digital age.

Payment rails and sanctions

When the United States cut Russian banks off from the SWIFT messaging system in early 2022, the effect was immediate and visible. Overnight, a vast economy found itself struggling to move money across borders. The sanctions were not merely symbolic: they struck at the arteries of global finance, where every transfer leaves a trace and every participant is bound by rules. The lesson was stark—control the payment rails, and you control the power to coerce.

Yet for every sanctioned account frozen, a workaround appears. The same year, ransomware gangs linked to Russian safe havens collected millions in cryptocurrency payments from Western victims, routing them through mixers and decentralised exchanges designed to obscure origin and destination. While the formal financial system was throttled, the shadow one thrived. It was a vivid demonstration of how states and criminals alike seek to exploit gaps in the plumbing of money. The battlefield is not only over territory or infrastructure, but over the invisible pathways through which value flows.

The paradox of the digital age is that money has never been more traceable, yet never more concealable. Traditional banking, bound by compliance regimes and know-your-customer rules, offers authorities unprecedented surveillance of transactions. At the same time, cryptocurrencies promise pseudonymity, mobility, and global reach. Their underlying ledgers are transparent, but with enough layering—through mixers, tumblers, and privacy coins—linking flows to identities becomes a game of probabilities rather than certainties. For those under sanctions, this duality is opportunity. For regulators, it is nightmare.

Consider mixers: services that take in cryptocurrency from multiple sources, shuffle it, and send it back out in unlinked fragments. To the user, it appears as though coins emerge cleansed of history. To authorities, they

represent a deliberate attack on the audit trail that underpins financial enforcement. When the United States sanctioned Tornado Cash in 2022, critics argued that it criminalised code rather than conduct. But the rationale was clear: without the ability to trace illicit payments, sanctions lose bite. Control over payment rails depends as much on undermining obfuscation tools as on regulating banks.

The compliance challenge is not limited to exotic cryptographic tools. Even legitimate exchanges and wallet providers, especially in loosely regulated jurisdictions, can serve as pressure valves for sanctioned entities. Some operate with wilful blindness, others with inadequate resources to screen users effectively. Here, geopolitics and finance converge: when one country's regulators enforce strict anti-money laundering standards while another's look away, the result is fragmentation that adversaries exploit. International coordination is not a luxury but a necessity.

Sanctions policy therefore lives and dies by coordination. Unilateral measures may score political points but often leak in practice. For every Western bank that blocks a transaction, another channel exists through an intermediary in a permissive jurisdiction. This is why the Financial Action Task Force (FATF) attempts to harmonise standards across borders, though enforcement varies widely. Without alignment, sanctioned entities arbitrage between regimes. Money, like water, flows where resistance is lowest.

But money does not only flow through banks and blockchains. Payment rails include correspondent networks, trade finance arrangements, even remittance companies serving diaspora populations. Each offers both resilience and vulnerability. For instance, informal hawala networks can move large sums with minimal digital footprint, complicating enforcement. In such contexts, coercive power is limited not by will but by visibility. To cut off an adversary's access to capital, you must first see it. And in many corners of the financial system, visibility is thin.

The ethical dilemmas run alongside the technical ones. Sanctions aimed at crippling a regime can end up crushing civilians who rely on remittances or access to basic goods. When compliance officers at global banks err on the side of overblocking, humanitarian aid stalls. Thus, the design of sanctions regimes requires calibration: broad enough to matter, targeted enough to preserve legitimacy. The infrastructure of money cannot be wielded as a blunt instrument without corroding trust in the very system it underpins.

Cryptocurrencies sit at the heart of the debate not because they have replaced the dollar, but because they reveal fragilities in enforcement logic. Blockchain analysis firms now work with governments to pierce the veil of pseudonymity, tracing flows from ransom payments to cash-out points. Yet this is a cat-and-mouse game. For every new analytic technique, adversaries develop countermeasures—layering transactions, exploiting decentralised protocols, or simply shifting into more opaque assets. Sanctions in the crypto era are not a solved problem but a contested frontier.

The deeper point is that coercion through money is only as strong as the system's weakest node. Global finance is not a monolith but a patchwork of rails—formal and informal, centralised and decentralised, licit and illicit. To coerce effectively requires not only freezing accounts but reshaping incentives: convincing intermediaries that the cost of compliance is less than the cost of being cut off themselves. This is why secondary sanctions—penalising those who do business with sanctioned entities—are so potent. They weaponise access itself, forcing firms and states to choose sides.

And yet, questions linger. As states harden control over payment rails, will adversaries accelerate the building of parallel systems—digital currencies, regional exchanges, barter arrangements—that dilute Western leverage? Is the future one of central bank digital currencies competing for transaction dominance, with compliance coded into their architecture? Or will money remain, as it has for centuries, an arena where control is always partial, contested, and temporary?

What is clear is that the movement of money is not a neutral backdrop but an active terrain of strategy. To treat payment rails as mere technical infrastructure is to miss their role as instruments of power. And in the age of ransomware, sanctions, and geopolitical rivalry, the question is no longer simply *who has the money*, but *who controls the rails on which it moves*.

Hospitals and municipalities

On a May morning in 2021, ambulances queued outside the emergency wards of Irish hospitals. Nurses carried paper charts through corridors, doctors scribbled drug doses on scraps of paper, and surgical teams delayed operations. The reason was not a strike, nor a natural disaster, but ransomware: the Health Service Executive's network had been crippled overnight, paralysing patient care across the country. The attackers demanded millions. For weeks, lives depended not on the availability of ventilators or blood supplies, but on whether IT teams could recover systems fast enough to restore diagnostics and prescriptions. Time, quite literally, was killing.

The Irish case was not unique. In Düsseldorf the year before, a woman suffering a life-threatening condition was turned away from her nearest hospital after ransomware had frozen its IT systems. She was rerouted to another facility nearly 20 miles away and died en route. Official investigations stopped short of blaming the attack for her death, but the symbolism was unmistakable: digital extortion could now exert the same life-or-death pressure as a blocked artery. In Baltimore, Atlanta, and Johannesburg, it was not operating theatres but city halls that ground to a halt. Residents could not pay bills, file permits, or in some cases even call emergency services. Ransomware had turned the most prosaic functions of civic life into points of vulnerability.

What ties these cases together is not their technical sophistication but their human cost. The malware deployed was rarely advanced; the attackers were often opportunists rather than elite state hackers. Yet the consequences were profound precisely because hospitals and municipalities embody services where downtime is intolerable. A payment processor can lose a day and recover; a patient cannot. A municipal payroll can be delayed; a fire brigade cannot. The asymmetry between attacker effort and societal impact makes these targets especially attractive.

The Irish health system learned that hard backups alone are not enough if they are poorly segmented. Attackers had reached into the very heart of operations, locking files across domains and crippling redundancies. Segmentation—the architectural separation of networks so that a breach in one does not collapse the whole—was absent or inadequate. In Baltimore, years of underinvestment in IT security had left civic services brittle. When ransomware hit, the city's recovery costs ballooned to over $18 million, dwarfing the original ransom demand. The common lesson is stark: resilience is rarely a question of budget size alone, but of where that budget is directed.

Tabletop drills—simulated crisis exercises—have emerged as one of the most effective tools for preparedness. Hospitals that had rehearsed going "paper cold" could switch to manual processes without chaos. Municipalities that had tested ransomware response knew who should make the call on whether to pay, how to engage insurers, and when to bring in law enforcement. Yet in many cases, these drills are treated as bureaucratic exercises rather than existential rehearsals. The pandemic taught governments the price of underpreparedness; ransomware teaches it in microcosm, with the added cruelty of adversaries watching and waiting.

There is also the delicate question of ransom payments. Hospitals, under pressure to preserve life, often have little choice but to pay. Municipalities, constrained by law and precedent, may refuse even at great cost to services. This divergence creates moral and strategic dilemmas. Paying fuels the business model, inviting further attacks; refusing risks prolonging harm to citizens. The calculus is not abstract: mayors weigh budgetary constraints against public fury, hospital directors weigh financial losses against the Hippocratic oath. No decision feels clean, and attackers know it. They design their targets and timing precisely to maximise leverage.

The broader tension is between local responsibility and national security. Hospitals and municipalities are often the least resourced but most essential units of governance. They lack the cyber teams of central governments or large corporations, yet their compromise reverberates most immediately in human suffering. When Irish hospitals went dark, it was not only a national issue but a European one, forcing the EU to reassess how solidarity mechanisms might apply in digital crises. Just as natural disasters prompt regional assistance, so too must ransomware. The idea of "civil defence" has to expand from physical shelters to digital scaffolds.

Some argue that ransomware against civic services is simply crime, to be treated like armed robbery. Yet the pattern of tolerated gangs operating from safe havens complicates this view. When municipalities in the United States are attacked by groups that law enforcement cannot touch because they reside under the protection of adversarial states, the line between crime and geopolitics blurs. For a local mayor struggling to restore city systems, this may feel remote. But the strategic reality is that hospitals and town halls have become pawns in larger games of leverage.

The motif that emerges is one of fragility exposed. Civic services, often invisible until they fail, have become prime targets precisely because of their importance. A society that cannot deliver emergency care or issue birth certificates is a society destabilised at its core. And unlike attacks on corporations, where losses can be absorbed, these strikes erode trust in public institutions themselves. Citizens do not distinguish between a hacker in Moscow and their local government's IT procurement choices; they see only that essential services failed when needed most.

The unresolved question is how societies will balance immediate fixes with structural resilience. Will cities invest in segmentation, tested backups, and drills, or will they rely on after-the-fact recovery funded by taxpayers? Will hospitals embed digital resilience into patient safety protocols, or treat it as an IT add-on until the next crisis? And above all, will governments treat ransomware against civic services as the national security threat it is, or continue to leave mayors and hospital directors alone on the frontline?

For now, what endures is a chilling certainty: the clock starts ticking the moment the ransom note appears, and in hospitals and municipalities, every tick of that clock can cost a life. The attackers know it. The question is whether we will build systems that acknowledge it too.

Negotiation playbooks

The first contact is almost always the same: a flashing message on a locked screen, or a text file dropped into critical folders. *Your files are encrypted. Pay or lose everything.* In that moment, panic is the natural response. Servers are dark, phones are ringing, staff are paralysed, and leaders are caught between the unbearable choice of surrender or collapse. Yet for the attackers, this is not chaos but choreography. They are following a script refined through hundreds of assaults. For the victims, survival depends on whether they too have rehearsed.

Consider the city of Atlanta in 2018. Its municipal systems were frozen by a ransomware attack that demanded just over $50,000 in Bitcoin. Officials hesitated. Should they pay? Could they recover? The delay stretched into days. Court proceedings halted, police files became inaccessible, and citizens could not pay bills. In the end, Atlanta refused the ransom, but the recovery cost ballooned to $17 million. The attackers had long since moved on, but the city remained trapped in their play. The lesson was brutal: hesitation without preparation is ruinously expensive.

Negotiation in the ransomware world is not improvisation; it is performance under duress. Attackers establish channels—often via anonymous chat portals—where they offer "customer service" to victims. They may provide a sample decryption to prove they hold the key. They apply pressure with countdown clocks or threats of data leaks. On the other side of the screen, victims must rapidly assemble a team: technical leads, legal advisers, communications staff, insurers, and—if foresight allows—specialised negotiators. Roles must be clear. Who speaks to the attackers? Who briefs the board? Who decides on payment? In the absence of such clarity, internal conflict can do more damage than the malware itself.

One of the most overlooked aspects of negotiation is timing. Attackers know that every hour offline compounds losses. Hospitals struggle to care for patients, factories stop production, cities face public outrage. Victims, in turn, are tempted to pay quickly, hoping to restore services before the damage becomes irreversible. But early payments invite overpayment or betrayal: some gangs take the money and vanish, others provide keys that fail to work. A structured playbook emphasises verification—testing decryption tools on a subset of files, demanding proof of life for stolen data—before any transfer is made.

Insurance complicates this dance. In many cases, cyber-insurers step in to negotiate or even to pay ransoms, reasoning that it is cheaper than prolonged disruption. Yet this has created perverse incentives. Attackers increasingly tailor their demands to known insurance thresholds, exploiting the very mechanisms designed to protect victims. The presence of insurance alters negotiation dynamics, sometimes emboldening attackers, sometimes constraining defenders. A playbook must anticipate this tension, ensuring that insurers support rather than dictate strategy.

The ethical dilemma is acute. Paying ransoms sustains a criminal economy that fuels further attacks. Refusing to pay risks prolonged suffering for employees, customers, or citizens. Leaders find themselves at the intersection of morality and pragmatism, with no easy exit. Here, philosophy meets the boardroom. What is the duty of a hospital director when a ransom demand is the only path to restoring cancer treatment systems? What is the obligation of a mayor when a refusal could keep police and emergency services offline for weeks? The playbook does not erase these dilemmas, but it forces them to be considered in advance, when time is still a luxury.

Beyond the ransom itself, negotiation playbooks must plan for messaging. Silence invites speculation; panic breeds mistrust. Staff need instructions, patients need reassurance, and the public needs honesty. Communication must strike a delicate balance: transparent enough to maintain trust, restrained enough not to embolden attackers or compromise investigations. In Atlanta, the city was criticised for opacity. In other cases, over-disclosure has given attackers leverage. The art lies in disciplined communication rehearsed alongside technical drills.

Pitfalls abound. One is assuming that decryption marks the end of crisis. In reality, restoration is often slow, partial, and fraught with data corruption. Attackers may have lingered in systems long before striking, exfiltrating sensitive information. Even after payment, leaks can follow. Another pitfall is treating negotiation as a purely technical exercise. It is as much about psychology as encryption: projecting calm, probing the adversary's incentives, and resisting the manipulation of artificial deadlines. Experienced negotiators know that gangs often extend timers if pushed, and that appeals to pragmatism sometimes temper greed.

The value of a playbook is not in removing uncertainty but in reducing panic. It transforms a paralysing crisis into a set of rehearsed steps. Identify the negotiating team. Verify the attacker's claims. Control communication. Assess options. Escalate to law enforcement where appropriate. Decide on payment or refusal with clarity. Each step does not simplify the dilemma but makes it navigable.

And yet, even the best playbook cannot erase the deeper problem: the asymmetry of power. Attackers need only a fraction of the victim's urgency. They can wait, watch, and tighten the screws, while defenders bleed money, trust, and time. The negotiation is always uneven, however polished the routine. What can shift that balance is preparation before the crisis—segmented networks, hardened backups, international coordination—so that negotiation is a last resort, not the only option.

Still, the uncomfortable truth lingers. Every ransom note opens a theatre in which both sides know their lines. The only uncertainty is whether the victim has studied their part in time. And in that darkened stage, one question remains unresolved: can societies ever hope to rewrite the script, or are we condemned to perform it again and again?

Disruption operations

In early 2021, a coalition of law enforcement agencies and private-sector researchers quietly executed one of the most ambitious cyber disruption operations to date. The target was Emotet, a sprawling botnet long regarded as the "Swiss Army knife" of cybercrime, used to deliver ransomware, steal banking credentials, and enable espionage. Instead of simply indicting perpetrators—many of whom lived in jurisdictions beyond reach—authorities seized servers, replaced malicious payloads with code that neutralised infections, and dismantled the infrastructure that criminals had cultivated for years. For a brief moment, defenders tasted what victory could look like: the lights on one of the most dangerous global cyberthreats went dark.

The triumph was striking, but its impermanence was equally sobering. Within months, fragments of Emotet reappeared, reconstituted by surviving operators or absorbed by rival groups. The episode revealed both the promise and the fragility of disruption operations. At their best, they puncture the aura of invincibility surrounding ransomware syndicates and force criminals to recalculate risks. At their weakest, they resemble mowing a field of weeds: temporary, symbolic, and ultimately unable to alter the soil that nourishes the problem.

Disruption, in this context, is about more than technical takedowns. It is a performance of power, one that requires timing, coordination, and precision. Seizing servers too early risks alerting criminals and scattering them into harder-to-trace fragments. Waiting too long risks further harm to victims. The decision of *when* to strike is as strategic as the act itself. Authorities must balance intelligence collection—watching how criminals operate—with the imperative to halt ongoing damage. The calculus mirrors dilemmas in counterterrorism and counterintelligence: how much do you observe before intervening, and how do you ensure the blow is decisive rather than symbolic?

The successes worth studying often involve international alliances. Botnets and ransomware groups operate across borders, renting servers in one jurisdiction, coding malware in another, and laundering money through yet another. No single nation can hope to dismantle them alone. Operations such as the takedown of Avalanche, a massive hosting platform for cybercriminals, were possible only because dozens of countries coordinated raids, arrests, and seizures simultaneously. This kind of orchestration sends a deterrent signal: that cybercriminals can no longer rely on safe havens indefinitely. But it also exposes fault lines. Some states shield groups for strategic reasons, others simply lack capacity or political will. The uneven geography of enforcement means that disruption is, by definition, partial.

Private companies often play a crucial role, providing the forensic insight, infrastructure access, or even operational muscle that governments lack. Microsoft, for instance, has repeatedly partnered with law enforcement to seize control of botnets exploiting its platforms. Yet these partnerships raise questions. Should corporations act as de facto cyber police? What are the limits of their legitimacy? And how do you prevent commercial interests from skewing the targets of disruption operations? The blending of public and private power is a hallmark of cyber conflict, but also a source of tension.

The limits of disruption must be faced squarely. Server seizures can cripple infrastructure, but they rarely dismantle the human networks behind it. Arrests, when possible, have more enduring impact, yet extradition remains a labyrinth of politics and law. Even when successful, prosecutions are often slow, visible only years after the damage is done. Worse still, some operations carry unintended consequences: disrupting one group may open opportunities for more ruthless competitors, or push criminals into deeper secrecy, complicating future intelligence efforts.

Nevertheless, disruption matters because it buys time. For a hospital in the middle of a ransomware crisis, the seizure of a criminal group's command servers could mean restored access to patient records. For a municipality under siege, it can prevent further extortion. At the macro level, disruption punctures the myth of inevitability. If gangs can be touched, even temporarily, their bargaining power erodes. The knowledge that their servers may be seized, their cryptocurrencies traced, or their keys confiscated forces a recalibration of risk.

Timing is everything. The most effective disruptions are not merely reactive but synchronised with broader strategy. A takedown that coincides with public indictments can amplify reputational costs. One that seizes decryption keys at a moment of peak criminal activity maximises deterrence. Conversely, a poorly timed operation may achieve little more than a press release. Victims and policymakers should learn to ask sharper questions: Was the disruption coordinated with allies? Were victims provided with tools to recover? Did the operation degrade capabilities in a way that criminals cannot easily rebuild? These questions separate tactical victories from strategic illusions.

There is a deeper lesson here: disruption is not an end state but a tool in a larger arsenal. It must complement sanctions, regulatory pressure, resilience-building, and diplomatic engagement. Alliances that can act together in disruption operations signal more than technical competence; they embody political resolve. When the FBI, Europol, and private firms coordinate to dismantle infrastructure across continents, they demonstrate that the international system, though often slow and fractured, can still muster collective defence.

And yet, the unresolved tension remains. Criminal ecosystems adapt faster than bureaucracies. Servers can be rebuilt, code rewritten, affiliates recruited. Disruption operations give us glimpses of what coordinated power can achieve, but also underline the resilience of illicit markets.

The real question is whether societies can make disruption more than a temporary reprieve—whether they can institutionalise it as part of an enduring deterrence framework. Until then, each takedown carries a paradox: it proves that we can act, but also reminds us how much remains beyond reach.

Chapter 8

Switches, Pipes, and Wires

One winter morning in Ukraine, power vanished for hundreds of thousands of people. Not because of a snowstorm, a broken transformer, or a routine fault—but because someone, somewhere, typed commands into a keyboard. The 2015 cyberattack on Ukraine's power grid was the first time digital sabotage cascaded into a national blackout. Lights went out in homes and hospitals. Trains stalled. Control rooms watched their systems obey instructions they had never given. What had once seemed like a theoretical possibility—code reaching into steel—was suddenly undeniable. The modern state, it turned out, could be shaken not only by bombs or blockades, but by unseen manipulations of switches, pipes, and wires.

This story, unsettling as it is, points to a deeper reality: our most physical infrastructures are increasingly governed by fragile digital threads. The electricity that hums through our cities, the fuel coursing through pipelines, the containers unloaded at ports, the planes guided through crowded skies—all depend on communications and control systems that blend human trust with machine logic. These systems were not designed with sabotage in mind. Many pre-date the internet altogether. Yet today they sit exposed to adversaries who understand that breaking infrastructure is a way of breaking societies themselves.

The premise of this chapter is that infrastructure is not background—it is the stage upon which power, safety, and legitimacy play out. When grids collapse, it is not just electrons that fail; it is the reliability of governments and markets. When pipelines choke, food and energy prices spike across continents. When navigation signals are spoofed, vessels veer off course, and geopolitical tempers flare. Each disruption is a reminder that steel and silicon are entwined, and that the boundary between the digital and physical is thinner than we once believed.

Energy grids form the most visceral example. Unlike corporate IT systems, industrial control systems (ICS) and supervisory control and data acquisition (SCADA) networks prioritise uptime and safety over secrecy. Operators cannot simply patch or reboot at will when a single misstep could plunge a city into darkness. Attacks on these systems teach us why cyber defence here cannot mimic conventional IT security. The logic of resilience is different: redundancy, segmentation, and safe failure matter more than perimeter firewalls. For regulators and corporate boards, this shift in perspective is not optional. It is the difference between treating outages as rare accidents and recognising them as predictable consequences of design choices.

But grids are only the beginning. Pipelines and ports reveal the connective tissue of globalisation itself. A single software compromise in a logistics hub can ripple across continents, delaying medical supplies, stranding exports, and distorting markets. The 2021 ransomware strike on Colonial Pipeline in the United States showed how swiftly digital intrusions can become national emergencies. Drivers queued for petrol not because pipelines were physically broken, but because the systems coordinating flows were paralysed. Ports, too, are choke points where a container's journey can hinge on a few lines of code. Case studies from Rotterdam to Singapore show that efficiency tools sold as neutral are, in practice, deeply geopolitical. Whoever controls the flows of goods controls leverage over nations.

Aviation and maritime communications add yet another layer of dependency. Aircraft today navigate not by sight, but by a constellation of signals that are vulnerable to jamming and spoofing. Ships crossing busy straits rely on automated identification systems (AIS) that can be manipulated to mask illicit activities or sow confusion. The vulnerabilities are not always maliciously exploited, but their very existence widens the horizon of risk. What happens when GPS becomes unreliable for days in a major conflict? How does a city function if timing signals—on which financial markets and transport systems depend—are subtly corrupted? The brittle nature of these invisible systems calls for layered mitigations, yet most remain underexamined outside specialist circles.

Above these terrestrial networks lies orbit itself. Satellites provide imaging for militaries, timing for finance, and connectivity for rural communities. Yet they are fragile in ways both expected and surprising. They can be jammed from the ground, hacked from afar, or even physically struck—creating debris that lingers for decades. A conflict in orbit is not science fiction but a scenario planners quietly model. The consequences spill over into agriculture, commerce, and disaster relief. Farmers rely on satellite weather data. Generals rely on reconnaissance. Citizens rely on broadband from above. Control of space infrastructure is not a technicality—it is sovereignty reframed.

And when failures occur, recovery is not merely about restoring service. Disasters end twice: once when power returns, and again when trust returns. A blackout may be fixed in hours, but the suspicion that it could happen again, or that authorities mishandled it, lingers far longer. That is why accountable narratives—rooted in forensic truth—are as important as technical remediation. Leaders who rebuild legitimacy after infrastructure shocks are those who confront not only the practicalities of backup and repair, but the psychology of reassurance.

What ties all these domains together is the recognition that the visible world of pipes and wires is inseparable from the invisible world of code and governance. The resilience of modern societies depends not only on engineers who design fail-safes, but on regulators who set priorities, and on publics who understand the stakes. To study switches, pipes, and wires is to study sovereignty itself, refracted through steel, silicon, and trust. The question that hovers over every page is deceptively simple: when the infrastructures that hold life together falter, who or what can still be relied upon?

That question will guide us through this chapter—across grids and ports, skies and orbits, outages and recoveries. Each system reveals vulnerabilities that are technical, political, and human. Each demands fresh thinking about resilience and responsibility. And each leaves us with the uneasy awareness that the infrastructures we take for granted are both our greatest strength and our most profound weakness.

Energy grids - Operational tech differs from IT; we decode ICS/SCADA realities. We show how outages cascade and why safety trumps secrecy. This matters to regulators and boards. It grounds the abstraction in steel.

In December 2015, operators at three Ukrainian power distribution companies watched their screens in disbelief. Mouse cursors moved without their control, circuit breakers opened, and substations went dark. Within hours, over 200,000 people were left without electricity in the depths of winter. This was not a software bug nor an errant command; it was a coordinated cyberattack that reached through the digital layer into the physical one, switching off the very lifeblood of modern society. For the first time in history, a hostile actor had taken down a national grid remotely—and in doing so, revealed a truth long ignored: the infrastructure that keeps our lights on, our hospitals running, and our economies functioning is as fragile as the code that now controls it.

The Ukrainian blackout marked a turning point, but it was not an isolated case. A few years later, malware known as *Industroyer2* again targeted critical substations, and in the United States, the Colonial Pipeline ransomware incident demonstrated how quickly operational paralysis could spiral into public panic, even without physical sabotage. Queues at petrol stations grew, prices spiked, and political leaders scrambled to reassure the public. These episodes highlight the paradox at the heart of energy security today: the machinery that powers our lives is vast, industrial, and built to last for decades, yet it now depends on software protocols that can be manipulated in seconds.

Understanding this paradox requires distinguishing between information technology (IT) and operational technology (OT). IT systems manage data, emails, and databases; their failures can be disruptive but are often recoverable. OT systems—industrial control systems (ICS) and supervisory control and data acquisition (SCADA) networks—manage flows of electricity, gas, and water. Their failures can cause cascading blackouts, physical damage, or even loss of life. While IT security often prioritises confidentiality and secrecy, OT security must prioritise safety and continuity. Shutting down a misbehaving server may be acceptable in an office; taking a substation offline can trigger instability across a grid serving millions.

The design logic of these systems reflects a different era. Many ICS/SCADA components predate the internet and were never intended to be connected to it. Protocols like Modbus and DNP3 were designed with reliability, not resilience against hostile actors, in mind. Air gaps once provided a degree of insulation, but digital convergence—remote monitoring, predictive maintenance, smart grid optimisation—has eroded those boundaries. What was once a closed circuit of trusted operators is now an ecosystem where suppliers, contractors, and cloud providers all connect into the heart of national infrastructure. With each link comes efficiency, but also vulnerability.

Outages in energy grids cascade in ways that can surprise even seasoned engineers. A trip in one region can overload lines elsewhere, triggering protective shutdowns that spread like falling dominos. The 2003 blackout across the north-eastern United States and Canada began with a single transmission line brushing against overgrown trees. What should have been a local fault cascaded into a massive outage affecting 50 million people. In today's context, deliberate manipulation of control systems can accelerate and magnify such cascades. Attackers need not destroy infrastructure outright; they can trigger instability that forces the system to harm itself.

For boards and regulators, this reframing is critical. Energy resilience is not only a matter of building higher digital walls. It is about acknowledging that the priorities of operational technology—*availability* and *safety*—often collide with traditional security practices. A patch that secures a vulnerability in theory may require a reboot that risks downtime in practice. As a result, vulnerabilities can remain unaddressed for years, creating what some call "technical debt" in the heart of critical systems. Regulators tasked with oversight cannot treat energy infrastructure as just another sector with cybersecurity needs. The stakes are different, and the timelines for failure are unforgiving.

There are models of resilience that go beyond secrecy. The aviation industry, for example, has long relied on transparent incident reporting, where near-misses are shared to improve collective safety. Energy grids could learn from this ethos. Instead of hiding attacks or faults for fear of reputational damage, operators can adopt frameworks that emphasise forensic truth and collective learning. Openness, paradoxically, can be a greater shield than silence. When attackers know that their methods will be swiftly analysed and shared across the sector, the value of their exploit declines. When regulators and boards can see patterns across incidents, they can direct investment towards systemic fixes rather than ad hoc patches.

The Ukrainian blackouts also underscored the human dimension. Operators in control rooms, under stress and often lacking playbooks for such scenarios, faced split-second decisions with national consequences. Training, tabletop exercises, and cross-border drills are therefore as vital as firewalls. Resilience lies not only in machines but in the humans who interpret alarms, override defaults, and maintain composure under pressure. For leaders, recognising this means investing in staff competence and mental readiness with the same seriousness as in hardware upgrades.

Philosophically, the challenge forces us to revisit what "security" really means. In IT, secrecy and confidentiality often dominate. In OT, secrecy is a brittle comfort. What matters is the preservation of life and function: that hospitals remain powered, that water continues to flow, that heating works on winter nights. This hierarchy of values should shape regulation and boardroom priorities. Investing in resilience is not about preventing every possible intrusion but about ensuring systems can absorb shocks, recover quickly, and maintain trust.

Yet a tension lingers. Efficiency drives—smart meters, remote optimisation, automated trading of energy flows—pull systems towards greater digital complexity. Each step promises cost savings and environmental gains, but also expands the attack surface. Can societies reap the benefits of smart grids while avoiding the brittleness of hyper-connectivity? Or will the pursuit of optimisation outpace the capacity for resilience?

The steel and concrete of energy grids are deceptively solid. What recent years have shown is that their true strength lies not in their mass but in the careful balance of flows they sustain. When that balance is disrupted—whether by accident, negligence, or malice—the consequences ripple far beyond kilowatts and substations. They touch confidence in governments, stability of markets, and the rhythms of daily life. The open question, which regulators and boards must grapple with, is not whether outages will occur, but how societies can live with the inevitability of shocks without surrendering trust. That tension will shape not only energy policy but the very legitimacy of modern governance.

Pipelines and ports - Logistics are networks of networks; small failures ripple globally. Case analyses illustrate choke-points. Understanding this guides national priority setting. It sharpens risk registers.

When a single ship, the *Ever Given*, lodged itself across the Suez Canal in March 2021, the world was reminded that global commerce rests on fragile arteries. For six days, the beached container vessel blocked one of the most critical maritime passages, holding up nearly 12% of global trade. Oil tankers, electronics, food, and medical goods all waited at anchor while billions of dollars of cargo accumulated in queues. Even when the channel was cleared, the ripple effects lasted for weeks: ports became congested, schedules collapsed, and costs surged. What began as a local mishap became a global shock, revealing that pipelines and ports are not simply infrastructure—they are the nervous system of globalisation, where a blockage in one node can paralyse the entire body.

The paradox is that these systems appear both robust and brittle. Robust, because they are vast, interconnected, and capable of moving staggering volumes of goods and energy across continents every day. Brittle, because their efficiency depends on precisely choreographed flows, where a failure in one segment can cascade through others. Modern logistics thrive on just-in-time precision, but precision is unforgiving: small disruptions amplify into systemic crises. Understanding pipelines and ports means understanding not just physical assets, but the choreography of dependencies, contracts, and signals that allow them to function.

Pipelines, though buried and unseen, are among the most geopolitically charged infrastructures in existence. They bind producers and consumers in long-term interdependence, sometimes uncomfortably so. Europe's reliance on Russian gas pipelines is the most obvious example. For decades, these steel conduits underpinned both economic growth and political vulnerability. When conflict erupted in Ukraine, the pipelines became both weapon and bargaining chip, shaping European policy and accelerating energy diversification. Sabotage of the Nord Stream pipelines in 2022 dramatised another lesson: energy arteries are not just economic tools but strategic targets, whose disruption can destabilise markets, alliances, and public confidence.

Ports are no less critical, and no less vulnerable. They are not singular facilities but layered ecosystems: cranes, warehouses, rail spurs, trucking fleets, customs systems, and digital platforms all must operate in synchrony. A cyberattack on the Port of Antwerp's IT systems in 2011, for instance, allowed traffickers to manipulate container records, redirecting illicit shipments undetected. This was not sabotage for destruction but exploitation for profit, revealing how digital infiltration can turn physical ports into gateways for criminal networks. In Los Angeles and Long Beach, the twin hubs handling over 40% of US containerised imports, even minor labour disputes or delays can ripple through supply chains, emptying shelves thousands of miles away.

What makes these infrastructures distinctive is that they are *networks of networks*. A pipeline is not merely a pipe; it depends on pumping stations, compressors, electricity supplies, monitoring systems, and sometimes satellite connectivity. Ports, likewise, depend not only on cranes and docks but on fuel supplies, digital manifests, inland transport, and global finance.

A failure in any one layer—whether through technical malfunction, cyber sabotage, labour strike, or natural disaster—can trigger failures across the others. Risk registers that treat each element in isolation fail to capture the systemic nature of the hazard.

Case studies make this point vivid. In 2017, a cyberattack on Maersk's IT systems via the NotPetya malware crippled operations across dozens of ports worldwide. Ships were left stranded, cargo untraceable, and terminals paralysed. Maersk later estimated its losses at $300 million, but the wider economic shock was harder to quantify. Unlike the Suez blockage, this was not visible in a single canal but distributed invisibly through digital networks. Here the chokepoint was not physical geography but the software backbone of a global shipping giant. For risk managers, the lesson is stark: digital single points of failure can be as consequential as physical ones.

The philosophy of resilience in these sectors cannot be limited to redundancy. Building additional pipelines or terminals is costly and politically fraught, and redundancy itself may create false confidence if vulnerabilities are systemic. Instead, resilience must also mean flexibility: the ability to reroute flows, adapt contracts, and coordinate internationally under pressure. During the Colonial Pipeline ransomware incident in 2021, fuel shortages across the US East Coast highlighted how much civilian life depends on continuity in these hidden networks. Queues at petrol stations and spikes in price were not mere inconveniences—they were reminders that disruption in a single pipeline could shake public trust and political stability.

For national security planners, this sharpens the task of priority setting. Not every port or pipeline is equally critical; some are chokepoints whose loss would reverberate globally, while others can be bypassed or substituted. Identifying these nodes requires a combination of technical mapping, economic analysis, and geopolitical foresight. It also requires confronting uncomfortable truths: dependence on foreign-controlled ports, reliance on single-source pipelines, or concentration of capacity in a handful of mega-terminals. Strategic autonomy in logistics may be impossible, but strategic clarity about vulnerabilities is indispensable.

Ethically, these infrastructures embody a tension between efficiency and resilience. The drive to cut costs, speed flows, and consolidate hubs makes economic sense in the short term but increases exposure to systemic risk. Decentralisation, diversity of routes, and investment in contingency planning may appear inefficient on spreadsheets, yet they represent insurance against cascading failure. Boards, regulators, and ministers who focus narrowly on quarterly costs risk overlooking the longer-term fragility of national lifelines.

The recurring motif across these stories is that logistics is not just about goods and fuel but about trust. When pipelines explode or ports stall, confidence in governments, companies, and alliances is shaken. Citizens who experience shortages of petrol, heating, or essential goods lose faith not only in infrastructure but in leadership. This is why resilience planning is not merely a technical exercise but a political one. It requires honest communication, accountability, and foresight—qualities that determine whether disruption becomes a crisis or a recoverable setback.

Yet the unresolved tension lingers: can globalised logistics, optimised for efficiency, ever be reconciled with the messy realities of resilience and sovereignty? Or are societies destined to live in cycles of crisis and patchwork repair, waiting for the next ship to run aground or the next pipeline to rupture? For those tasked with safeguarding the arteries of commerce and energy, the challenge is clear. The harder question—the one without easy answers—is whether political will can catch up with the vulnerabilities already laid bare.

Aviation and maritime comms - Navigation, timing, and communications are brittle in unexpected ways. We map dependencies and spoofing risks. This widens the reader's threat horizon. It leads to layered mitigations.

On a calm morning in 2019, dozens of ships anchored near Shanghai began reporting their positions kilometres inland, as though they were moored in farmers' fields rather than the world's busiest port. The vessels had not drifted; their GPS receivers had been spoofed. Around the same time, pilots landing in the Middle East reported losing satellite signals during approaches, forcing them to switch to older systems. What might appear to passengers as minor glitches were, in fact, symptoms of a deeper fragility. The modern systems that guide planes and ships across oceans—navigation, timing, and communications—rest on invisible signals vulnerable to interference, error, or manipulation. The infrastructure that makes global travel routine is far more brittle than most assume.

The paradox is striking: aviation and maritime operations, industries built on precision and reliability, depend on signals that can be jammed by cheap transmitters or subtly corrupted by clever adversaries. While air traffic controllers and captains still train for compass-and-chart scenarios, the reality is that both sectors have become deeply dependent on satellite-based navigation and digital communications. The more invisible and seamless these systems appear, the less visible their fragility becomes.

Take navigation first. Global Navigation Satellite Systems (GNSS), of which GPS is the most widely known, provide not only position but timing—critical for synchronising everything from cockpit instruments to port cranes. But GNSS signals are weak by the time they reach Earth, easily drowned out by deliberate jamming or even accidental interference. In aviation, loss of satellite signals can force diversions or increase workload at exactly the moments when margins for error are narrowest, such as in crowded airspace or adverse weather. In maritime contexts, spoofed signals can mislead crews into hazardous waters or mask the movements of vessels engaged in illicit activity. Off the coast of Crimea and in the Black Sea, spoofing has been used to cloak naval manoeuvres, creating uncertainty about who is where—an uncertainty that is itself a weapon.

Communications are no less exposed. In aviation, air-to-ground radio remains the backbone of air traffic management, but digital datalink systems have been layered on top, transmitting flight plans and clearances. Both can be intercepted or mimicked. In 2020, researchers demonstrated that unauthenticated Automatic Dependent Surveillance–Broadcast (ADS-B) signals, used for aircraft tracking, could be spoofed to create ghost planes on controllers' screens. In maritime settings, the equivalent Automatic Identification System (AIS) is similarly vulnerable, allowing the creation of phantom ships or the erasure of real ones. These are not theoretical risks: manipulation of AIS has been documented in smuggling operations and geopolitical flashpoints alike.

The problem is compounded by hidden dependencies. Aviation relies on satellite timing not only for navigation but for coordinating airport operations, synchronising radar sweeps, and aligning communications networks. Maritime logistics depends on accurate positioning to choreograph docking schedules, crane movements, and customs flows. An outage in navigation signals cascades beyond individual aircraft or vessels into systemic disruption. What looks like a single point of failure is in reality a web of interdependencies waiting to unravel.

This fragility is exacerbated by the economics of efficiency. Airlines and shipping firms optimise for cost and speed, not resilience. Redundancy—maintaining backup systems, training crews for manual navigation, or investing in hardened signals—carries costs that are hard to justify until disaster strikes. Regulators face a similar dilemma: mandating resilience can be politically difficult when the benefits are invisible in peacetime. As a result, layered mitigations—such as eLoran terrestrial navigation, encrypted satellite services, or resilient multi-sensor fusion—remain patchy and underfunded.

The risks are not symmetrical. Commercial actors are often most exposed, while military operators invest in hardened systems and anti-jam technologies. Yet civilian infrastructures, from global supply chains to passenger travel, depend heavily on commercial aviation and shipping. A disruption in these sectors can cascade into political crises, as stranded travellers, empty shelves, or delayed energy shipments test public patience and governmental competence. In this sense, spoofing and jamming are not just technical nuisances but tools of strategic leverage.

The philosophical tension lies in the balance between invisibility and trust. Navigation and communications systems work best when they fade into the background, allowing pilots and captains to focus on their tasks. Yet their very invisibility blinds societies to how easily they can be undermined. Trust is built on the assumption of reliability, but that trust becomes brittle when shocks expose the underlying vulnerabilities. The question is not whether disruptions will occur but how societies prepare for and absorb them.

Aviation and maritime communications remind us that resilience cannot be retrofitted after the fact. It requires conscious investment in layered mitigations—multiple sources of timing, cross-checks between independent systems, human training, and international standards that acknowledge rather than hide fragility. It also requires a cultural shift: recognising that efficiency without redundancy is fragility disguised.

Still, the unresolved question remains: can global industries built on razor-thin margins and just-in-time efficiency truly afford the redundancy and diversity that resilience demands? Or will societies continue to fly and sail on trust in signals that can be bent or broken by anyone with motive and means? The answers will determine not only the safety of travel but the stability of the global economy itself.

Space and satellites - Orbit is infrastructure: imaging, timing, and internet from above. We assess jamming and kinetic spill-overs. This matters for both farmers and generals. It connects to sovereignty debates.

When Russian troops crossed into Ukraine in early 2022, their advance was mapped not only by soldiers and spies but by commercial satellites available to anyone with a subscription. Images of convoys, craters, and scorched fields raced around the world, shaping diplomacy and public opinion in real time. At the same moment, Ukrainian commanders leaned on SpaceX's Starlink network to coordinate defences and keep government communications alive. For farmers in the countryside, those same satellites offered precision navigation for spring planting. The same constellation that helped generals plan offensives guided tractors through muddy fields. Orbit, once the preserve of superpowers, had become a shared nervous system for warfighters and civilians alike.

This duality is the paradox of modern space. Satellites are sold as commercial services, but they underpin military strategies and civilian livelihoods at once. Weather forecasting, crop monitoring, financial transactions, maritime logistics, missile warning—all depend on eyes, ears, and clocks in orbit. Strip them away and daily life would falter as surely as a blackout cripples a city. Yet their apparent omnipresence masks fragility: the signals are weak, the satellites exposed, the governance contested. What happens in orbit is no longer abstract science fiction but immediate geopolitics, shaping sovereignty and survival.

Consider timing. The nanosecond-precise signals from GPS and its counterparts coordinate power grids, synchronise stock exchanges, and keep mobile networks aligned. Farmers use them to optimise yields; container ships depend on them for routes. Interference, whether from deliberate jamming or accidental noise, can bring hidden dependencies crashing into view. A farmer's tractor drifting off course may seem trivial, but when entire harvests are affected, food security is at stake. When communications networks fall out of sync, emergency services falter. Timing from space is the quiet glue of modern societies.

Imaging, too, has shifted power. Once monopolised by national intelligence agencies, high-resolution satellite imagery is now sold commercially, enabling journalists, NGOs, and even individuals to verify state claims. In conflicts, this transparency constrains governments and shapes alliances. Yet it also makes satellites tempting targets, not only for espionage but for denial. States have tested anti-satellite missiles, scattering debris that endangers every orbital operator, civilian and military alike. A single destructive strike risks cascading into a debris field that threatens thousands of satellites—an accident that becomes permanent because fragments orbit for decades.

Jamming is cheaper and subtler. Truck drivers in Europe have used GPS jammers to hide from employers, sometimes inadvertently disrupting airport navigation systems. In theatres of conflict, more sophisticated systems blanket regions with noise, blinding aircraft or disrupting guided weapons. Unlike kinetic destruction, jamming leaves no debris, but it can neutralise satellites as effectively as a missile. Worse still is spoofing: creating false signals that deceive receivers. Ships have been lured onto false courses; aircraft have reported phantom positions. Trust in space signals, once assumed, now requires suspicion.

The economic stakes are as vast as the orbital horizon. Satellite internet constellations promise connectivity for remote communities, but they also shape strategic influence. Who controls the uplinks and downlinks? Who has the authority to cut or prioritise access during crises? In Ukraine, Starlink proved a lifeline, but its reliance on a single commercial provider raised questions about accountability. Should sovereignty depend on the goodwill of a corporation? The line between private infrastructure and national security asset blurs in orbit more than anywhere else.

Alliances matter, yet coordination lags. The United States, Europe, China, Russia, and emerging space powers each operate constellations of satellites. The rules for sharing, protecting, or retaliating remain thin. International law, drafted in the Cold War, prohibits the weaponisation of space but offers little clarity on grey-zone tactics like jamming, cyber intrusions, or commercial control. Meanwhile, the number of satellites grows exponentially, with mega-constellations altering orbital dynamics and intensifying competition. Space is no longer vast emptiness; it is crowded real estate with no agreed zoning plan.

The philosophical challenge is sovereignty itself. If a nation's communications ride on foreign-owned satellites, is that dependence a vulnerability or a pragmatic choice? If commercial images shape public diplomacy, who controls the narrative of war and peace? If a single adversary can deny navigation signals to an entire region, what becomes of autonomy? Orbit forces nations to rethink sovereignty not as control of land, sea, and air but as reliance on invisible infrastructure above.

What makes this debate urgent is not the distant prospect of futuristic battles in space but the immediacy of spillovers. A single missile test can pollute orbit for decades. A jamming campaign designed to blind a drone can inadvertently disrupt civilian flights. Farmers and generals, financiers and doctors, all share the same orbital environment whether they know it or not. The infrastructure is global, but the politics remain national, creating a gap that adversaries exploit.

The pressing question is whether societies will invest in resilience before fragility is exposed by crisis. Redundancy in timing, diversification of communications, norms for orbital conduct—all require foresight. Yet foresight is difficult when the infrastructure feels invisible and abstract, until it suddenly fails. Satellites remind us that sovereignty is no longer only about what lies beneath our feet. It is also about what floats silently overhead, vulnerable, contested, and indispensable.

How long can we sustain the illusion that orbit is a neutral commons, when it has become the most strategic terrain of all?

Recovery and memory - Disasters end twice: once when power returns; again when trust returns. We explain forensic truth and accountable narratives. This prepares leaders to rebuild legitimacy. It closes the infrastructure arc.

When the lights come back on after a blackout, relief is palpable. Families cook again, hospitals resume operations, businesses reopen. But the deeper wound lingers. People want to know *why* the systems they rely upon failed, and whether those entrusted with their protection were competent—or complicit. The immediate material recovery is not the end of the disaster. The second, often harder stage is the restoration of trust. Until explanations are offered, mistakes acknowledged, and lessons internalised, the outage or breach remains alive in collective memory. Infrastructure crises, it turns out, are as much about legitimacy as about kilowatts or bandwidth.

Consider the 2003 Northeast blackout in North America. Within hours, power was restored to most affected areas. Yet the reputational fallout lasted years. Confusion over accountability—was it a software bug, a lack of tree-trimming, or inadequate cross-border coordination?—fuelled public scepticism about whether the grid was truly reliable. Investigations dragged, narratives clashed, and regulators struggled to reassure. Citizens may have forgiven the darkness; they did not forgive the opacity. In the age of complex, interdependent systems, the demand for forensic truth is not merely technical. It is civic.

The first phase of disaster recovery is largely mechanical: engineers replace equipment, technicians reboot systems, data is restored from backups. The second phase—the one that shapes long-term resilience—is interpretive. Who investigates? What stories are told? Which institutions are believed? A cyberattack on a hospital may be solved with restored servers and patched software, but unless patients and staff are convinced that security has genuinely improved, the memory of vulnerability endures. Leaders who confuse repair with reassurance risk undermining the very authority they seek to preserve.

This dual ending exposes a philosophical truth about infrastructure. It is not only steel, wires, or code; it is also narrative. Systems are trusted because they are seen to be competently managed and transparently explained. The forensic investigation after a crisis, if independent and credible, becomes a ritual of re-legitimation. Think of the aviation industry: every crash is exhaustively examined, with findings publicly shared. That willingness to confront uncomfortable truths sustains passenger confidence in the skies. In sectors like energy, water, or digital services, the same transparency is too often absent.

The stakes are heightened when suspicion of cover-up arises. After the Fukushima nuclear disaster, Japanese authorities initially withheld or downplayed radiation data. The power plant operator's reputation never recovered, and public trust in nuclear energy eroded globally. The lesson was stark: concealment is costlier than candour. Truth may sting in the short term, but it inoculates against cynicism. Memory, left unmanaged, festers into myth and conspiracy, weakening democratic institutions. Leaders must learn that narratives, like power lines, require maintenance.

The question of *who controls memory* is therefore central. Governments may prefer official reports; communities may craft grassroots testimonies; journalists and NGOs may expose contradictions. The struggle over narrative can be as contentious as the disaster itself. In authoritarian systems, tightly managed storytelling may suppress dissent, but it rarely rebuilds genuine legitimacy. In democracies, open inquiry can be painful, but it strengthens resilience by teaching societies how to fail better. To prepare for future shocks, leaders must not only restore infrastructure but also embrace accountability as part of recovery.

Forensic truth is more than a technical autopsy. It must explain not just what failed, but why safeguards fell short, why warnings went unheeded, why the cascade was not contained. This demands institutions with both expertise and independence. Without them, the line between explanation and excuse blurs. The public does not want abstract jargon about "unexpected anomalies." They want plain language that links causes to reforms. When this link is missing, every subsequent outage reopens the wound of the previous one.

Memory also shapes regulation. Catastrophic events often act as political catalysts: the 2003 blackout spurred reforms in North American grid oversight; the Colonial Pipeline ransomware attack in 2021 accelerated U.S. efforts to strengthen pipeline cybersecurity. But reforms follow only if the memory is institutionalised. If the narrative is allowed to fade into obscurity or partisan blame games, lessons are lost. The paradox is that societies crave forgetting to move forward, but resilience requires remembrance. How much memory is enough, and how much becomes paralysing?

This tension extends beyond governance into personal and collective psychology. Communities hit by long outages or cyberattacks often experience a loss of confidence that exceeds the objective damage. A hospital may restore systems in days, yet staff continue to second-guess whether digital records can be trusted. Citizens in blackout zones keep emergency supplies for years afterwards, shaped by memory more than by present risk. Leaders must recognise these lingering scars not as irrational but as rational adaptations to perceived fragility. Addressing them requires empathy as well as engineering.

As we close this arc on critical infrastructure, one insight crystallises: disasters are never purely technical events. They are also crises of meaning. Recovery demands more than physical repair; it requires accountable narratives that bind fractured trust. Without them, societies stumble from one outage to the next, learning little, remembering much, but never integrating the lessons.

The open question for leaders is stark: will you manage not just the return of power, but the return of trust? For in the long shadow of memory, legitimacy is the infrastructure upon which all others rest.

Chapter 9

Quantum Gambits

In 1994, mathematician Peter Shor published an algorithm that seemed, at first, like an elegant theoretical curiosity. It showed that a sufficiently powerful quantum computer could break the cryptographic locks guarding global finance, diplomacy, and military communications. At the time, such a machine felt as distant as a perpetual-motion device: clever on paper, impossible in practice. Three decades later, Shor's insight no longer reads as science fiction. Laboratories in California, Shenzhen, and Delft hum with superconducting qubits and trapped ions. Progress is uneven, but undeniable. For the first time, a credible horizon looms in which mathematics that once guaranteed secrecy may be rendered brittle, even obsolete. The paradox is sharp: the very tools hailed as the next leap in science may also unravel the security scaffolding of the digital world.

This looming disruption does not arrive in a cinematic instant—no switch is flipped, no single morning announces the death of RSA or elliptic curve cryptography. Rather, it creeps through anticipation. Security agencies already warn of "harvest now, decrypt later" tactics, where adversaries quietly stockpile today's encrypted traffic in the expectation that tomorrow's quantum breakthroughs will unlock it. The uncertainty of timelines is its own form of risk. If quantum supremacy in codebreaking is five years away, unprepared nations face imminent exposure. If it is fifty, those who panic may squander resources chasing shadows. The challenge, then, is to navigate between complacency and alarm—investing wisely in resilience without succumbing to paralysis.

What emerges is less a single breakthrough than a strategic theatre. Cryptography is only the opening act. Quantum sensing promises to upend navigation and detection: ships and submarines locating themselves without GPS, militaries tracking stealth aircraft with unprecedented precision. Quantum timing could recalibrate financial markets and critical infrastructure, where nanoseconds determine flows of capital and power.

Each advance carries dual-use risks—civilian benefits twinned with military leverage. For decision-makers, the question is no longer whether quantum technology matters, but how its diffusion reshapes bargaining power between states, firms, and citizens.

The migration to post-quantum cryptography embodies this dilemma in miniature. It is not a software patch or a plug-in upgrade; it is a generational shift in organisational practice. Inventories must be taken, pilot deployments tested, and entire communication infrastructures retooled—while maintaining compatibility with partners and avoiding self-inflicted vulnerabilities. Financial institutions holding decades of sensitive records, healthcare providers guarding patient data for lifetimes, defence agencies archiving military secrets: for all, the horizon of quantum threat is not theoretical. The secret stolen today may be weaponised decades later. Investment decisions made in boardrooms and ministries now will determine whether archives remain shielded or laid bare.

Quantum's allure has also ignited a new kind of arms race. Billions in state funding, tightly controlled export rules, and talent wars between laboratories have transformed physics into geopolitics. The contest is not only about building the first general-purpose quantum computer but also about defining the standards, patents, and alliances that will govern its use. Science policy becomes strategy. The laboratories of Cambridge, Sydney, and Vienna are no longer just centres of research; they are nodes in a contest for economic and military advantage. Citizens scanning headlines about breakthroughs in "error correction" or "quantum volume" are, in fact, witnessing moves in a global gambit with profound political stakes.

And yet, this is not only a story of great powers. Small and mid-tier states face choices that will shape their sovereignty. Some may band together in consortia to pool resources; others may seek neutrality, keeping a foot in multiple camps; a few may specialise in niche areas such as quantum-safe communications or regional manufacturing hubs. The strategies chosen today will determine who remains dependent, who gains leverage, and who is left irrelevant in a future defined not only by classical power but also by qubits and entanglement.

To grapple with quantum is to confront a strange temporality: a threat both near and distant, a promise both exhilarating and unnerving. The chapter ahead will not deal in hype, nor in fatalism. It will sketch what breaks and what survives, trace the migrations already underway, and explore how quantum sensing, timing, and competition will ripple across security and society. The deeper question is whether we can approach this frontier with foresight rather than fear. For quantum gambits are already unfolding. The moves taken now—by governments, industries, and citizens—will decide whether the technology becomes a bridge to resilience or a lever of coercion. The pieces are on the board; the endgame is unwritten.

What breaks, what survives

In 2019, the U.S. National Security Agency quietly updated its public guidance on cryptographic standards. Algorithms that had served faithfully for decades—RSA, elliptic curve cryptography, Diffie–Hellman key exchange—were flagged for retirement. The reason was not that these methods had suddenly been broken, but that the clock had begun to tick on a different kind of threat: the quantum computer. At that moment, no machine existed with the power to crack a single RSA-encrypted email. Yet governments and companies were told to start planning for a world where that prospect was no longer unthinkable. The paradox was stark. Cryptosystems still secure enough to guard nuclear command and control were, in another sense, already obsolete.

The tension lies in the uneven march of time. Classical computing follows incremental, visible patterns: chips shrink, clock speeds rise, architectures evolve. Quantum computing does not move with such predictability. A laboratory breakthrough in error correction or qubit coherence could collapse timelines overnight. The result is a peculiar form of insecurity: systems are safe until suddenly they are not. This uncertainty complicates both strategic planning and public communication. Panic risks wasted investment and brittle solutions; complacency risks catastrophic exposure. The key is understanding which cryptographic pillars are most at risk, which are likely to endure, and how to navigate the grey zones between them.

The headline is simple, if sobering. Public-key cryptography, the backbone of digital trust, is fragile under quantum attack. RSA, the workhorse of secure web browsing, digital signatures, and financial transactions, falls to Shor's algorithm once a sufficiently powerful quantum computer exists. The same fate awaits elliptic curve cryptography, prized in recent years for its efficiency. Diffie–Hellman, the ingenious method of establishing shared keys across hostile channels, also crumbles. The vulnerability is structural: all rely on the difficulty of factoring large numbers or solving discrete logarithms—problems that quantum computation renders tractable.

What feels impregnable to classical machines becomes transparent under quantum light.

Yet not everything collapses. Symmetric cryptography—the family that includes AES—proves more robust. Grover's algorithm can accelerate brute-force search, but only quadratically. In practical terms, this halves the effective key length: a 256-bit key offers 128-bit security against a quantum adversary. That is still strong enough for most foreseeable uses. Message authentication codes and hash functions also survive with strengthened parameters. The picture that emerges is not of universal collapse but of selective vulnerability. Some systems break cleanly; others bend but do not shatter.

This uneven landscape matters because it reframes timelines. The "quantum apocalypse" is not an instant when all secrets fall. It is a differentiated process. Financial transactions that depend on digital signatures may become insecure years before bulk-encrypted archives are vulnerable. Military communications might be exposed sooner than consumer messaging apps, depending on the protocols in use. Planning must therefore be layered. Organisations cannot wait for a single migration date; they must prioritise according to exposure, longevity of secrets, and adversary intent.

Here lies another often-misunderstood point: *harvest now, decrypt later.* Adversaries do not need to wait for quantum machines to arrive before they act. They can intercept and store encrypted traffic today—diplomatic cables, defence blueprints, genomic datasets—with the intention of unlocking them when the tools become available. For any information with a long shelf life, the threat is immediate. This includes not only classified state material but also intellectual property, healthcare records, and critical infrastructure schematics. The past itself becomes a battlefield, its archives potentially weaponised.

The uncertainty of quantum timelines deepens the policy dilemma. Estimates vary wildly: some experts predict functional quantum computers capable of breaking RSA within a decade; others place the horizon half a century away. Each forecast is tethered to assumptions about error correction, qubit scaling, and investment flows. The risk is that debates about exact dates distract from the structural certainty: that the vulnerabilities exist, and that migration will take years. By the time a definitive breakthrough is announced, it will already be too late to adapt.

Against this backdrop, the instinct to panic is understandable but unhelpful. Not every system is equally threatened; not every investment makes sense. Strengthening symmetric key lengths and adopting quantum-resistant algorithms are prudent steps, but organisations must also manage interoperability, cost, and usability. A bank cannot simply swap out protocols without coordinating across partners, regulators, and customers. A defence ministry cannot migrate in isolation; alliances require aligned standards. The process is as much political and organisational as it is technical.

There is also a philosophical dimension. Cryptography is more than a tool; it is a social contract. It underpins trust in commerce, governance, and intimacy. The fragility revealed by quantum threats raises questions about how societies anchor confidence when technical certainties dissolve. Do we rely on a perpetual cycle of upgrading algorithms, always racing ahead of the next leap in computing? Or do we reconsider the balance between secrecy, transparency, and resilience? In this light, the quantum challenge is not only about mathematics but about the nature of trust in a digital age.

The truth is that quantum computing, whether it matures in ten years or fifty, will not neatly announce its arrival. Breakthroughs may be shrouded in secrecy, guarded by states that recognise the leverage of silence. The first successful quantum codebreaking may never be revealed; its power lies in remaining invisible. What breaks and what survives, therefore, is not just a technical classification but a strategic map. Those who understand the contours of fragility and endurance can invest wisely, prepare proportionately, and avoid both paralysis and waste.

And yet, a final uncertainty lingers. Even as post-quantum algorithms are being standardised, no one can guarantee their long-term safety. Just as classical systems once thought unassailable now stand exposed, so too may today's proposed defences prove brittle tomorrow. Security remains provisional, trust contingent. The question that follows is stark: if every cryptographic fortress is ultimately temporary, how do we design societies, markets, and alliances that can live with impermanence? The answer is unfinished—but the work of finding it cannot be deferred.

PQC migration

In 2022, the U.S. National Institute of Standards and Technology (NIST) announced the first set of algorithms selected for post-quantum cryptography (PQC). The choice was not merely academic. It signalled to governments, banks, and technology firms that the era of quantum resilience had begun. Yet the announcement did not instantly make systems safe. The lesson was plain: adopting these algorithms is not like downloading a patch or installing a new firewall. It is a multi-year organisational transformation, closer to replacing the foundations of a house while still living inside it.

The paradox is that the danger feels distant, yet the work must begin now. Most organisations remain dependent on cryptosystems vulnerable to quantum attack—RSA, elliptic curves, Diffie–Hellman key exchange—while adversaries are already harvesting data for decryption later. The challenge is not only technical but managerial. Boards and chief security officers must treat PQC migration as they would any major capital project: scoped, budgeted, staged, and governed. The question is not whether the transition will be painful, but whether it will be deliberate or chaotic.

Migration begins with something deceptively simple: *knowing what you have.* Most organisations cannot answer basic questions about the cryptography embedded in their systems. How many applications use vulnerable public-key algorithms? Which vendors supply them? Which contracts depend on them? Cryptography is often buried deep inside third-party products, legacy infrastructure, or undocumented code. Without a comprehensive inventory, migration is impossible. Just as financial auditors insist on a balance sheet before restructuring, security leaders must assemble a catalogue of cryptographic assets before designing their future.

Once the landscape is mapped, the next stage is prioritisation. Not all secrets are equal, and not all systems demand immediate change. A hospital may store decades of patient records; a bank may retain transaction data with regulatory retention periods; a defence agency may hold strategic intelligence that will matter long after today's adversaries have retired. These are *long-lived secrets*, the highest priority for quantum protection. By contrast, ephemeral communications—temporary messaging, short-lived transactions—may tolerate longer timelines. Organisations that fail to distinguish between these categories will waste resources and miss what matters most.

Pilot projects follow. No organisation can switch wholesale to post-quantum algorithms without first testing their effects on performance, interoperability, and usability. Lattice-based schemes, for example, may require larger key sizes and introduce latency. Code-based approaches may demand significant storage. Pilots reveal such frictions before they spread through the entire system. They also serve another function:

building confidence. Staff who have tested, measured, and refined PQC deployments are less likely to panic when full migration begins. Pilots turn uncertainty into experience, and experience into institutional knowledge.

Rollout, when it comes, must be staged and layered. Critical systems—payment rails, identity services, core communications—migrate first, followed by secondary infrastructure. Contracts with vendors should specify PQC compliance; procurement offices must learn to ask the right questions. Regulators will eventually demand reporting on progress, much as they already do with capital adequacy in finance or safety cases in aviation. The challenge is global. An email system is only as secure as the weakest node in its chain. Migration cannot stop at national borders; it requires international coordination on standards, timelines, and trust anchors.

The complexity of the task is magnified by legacy systems. Many industrial control systems, medical devices, and embedded technologies were designed with decades-long lifespans. Updating their cryptography is not as simple as a software patch; it may require replacing hardware still otherwise functional. Boards and policymakers must be prepared for the costs, and societies must decide how to allocate them. Do we subsidise upgrades for hospitals and utilities? Do we demand compliance from vendors at their own expense? These are not technical questions but political choices about who bears the burden of resilience.

Beyond the mechanics, PQC migration raises deeper questions about how institutions adapt to uncertainty. The temptation is to wait for certainty—for definitive proof of quantum timelines, for finalised standards, for others to move first. But certainty will never arrive. Cryptographic migration is not just a technical fix; it is an exercise in strategic humility. It requires acting under conditions of ambiguity, allocating resources without guarantees, and balancing present costs against future risks. In this sense, the PQC challenge is not unique but emblematic of a broader truth: resilience is built in the face of doubt, not in its absence.

The cultural challenge may be as great as the technical one. Cryptography is often invisible, taken for granted by executives and end-users alike. Migration requires making it visible—something boards discuss, budgets reflect, and governments oversee. It demands sustained collaboration between mathematicians, engineers, lawyers, and regulators, groups that rarely share vocabulary, let alone goals. Organisations that treat PQC as a purely technical upgrade will fail; those that recognise it as an organisational and cultural transformation stand a better chance of success.

And yet, even with planning and investment, no migration is ever final. Post-quantum algorithms themselves may one day fall to new mathematical insights or unforeseen advances. Today's lattice-based schemes may prove brittle tomorrow. Migration, then, is not a one-off project but the beginning of a perpetual process: anticipating the next break, preparing the next shift, and embedding agility into institutional DNA. The true lesson of quantum risk is not the fragility of today's cryptography but the impermanence of every defence.

So the question lingers: how do societies design migration pathways not as desperate scrambles but as disciplined routines? Can organisations make peace with the reality that security is never permanent, only provisional? The answers are unfinished. But the necessity is not. PQC migration is no longer optional. It is the price of trust in a world where the physics of information are being rewritten.

Quantum sensing and timing

In 2017, Chinese scientists made headlines by demonstrating satellite-based quantum communication between Beijing and Vienna. Less noticed, but equally significant, was a parallel advance: experiments showing how quantum entanglement could sharpen measurement beyond the reach of classical physics. While the headlines focused on unbreakable codes, the quiet revolution was in clocks and sensors. Codebreaking may dominate the popular imagination of quantum technology, but the first world-shaping applications may not be in cryptography at all. They may be in seeing further, navigating without satellites, and measuring the imperceptible.

Consider navigation. Modern economies depend on the Global Positioning System (GPS) and its equivalents—Galileo, GLONASS, BeiDou—not just for planes and ships, but for power grids, financial transactions, and smartphones. GPS signals are faint, vulnerable to jamming, and reliant on a handful of satellites in orbit. A nation capable of blinding GPS can paralyse civilian logistics and military operations alike. Quantum timing offers an alternative. Atomic clocks, refined with quantum coherence, could allow vehicles or critical infrastructure to maintain accurate positioning even when satellite signals are denied. The promise is autonomy from space—freedom from reliance on a fragile orbital architecture.

Detection follows a similar logic. Submarines, designed to hide in the depths, have long been central to nuclear deterrence. Yet quantum magnetometers and gravimeters, capable of detecting minute variations in magnetic and gravitational fields, may erode that invisibility. The same sensitivity that allows geologists to map underground resources or engineers to survey infrastructure could allow militaries to track submarines. What one side hails as transparency, the other fears as vulnerability. A technology designed to illuminate can destabilise by stripping away the very shadow in which strategic balance rests.

These are *dual-use* dilemmas at their sharpest. A quantum sensor can help a farmer monitor soil conditions with unprecedented precision. The same physics can help a navy locate a ballistic submarine. A quantum clock can ensure resilience for financial exchanges cut off from satellites. The same independence can permit missiles to guide themselves without reliance on GPS. As with nuclear fission, the boundary between civil and military is porous. Unlike fission, however, the barriers to entry are lower. Laboratories across Europe, North America, and Asia are racing to refine prototypes into deployable devices. The frontier is not hidden behind barbed wire; it is diffused through universities and start-ups.

Yet for all the promise, uncertainty remains. Quantum sensors are not magic devices that suddenly make all hidden things visible. They are susceptible to noise, difficult to calibrate, and costly to operate. Scaling from laboratory bench to battlefield or industrial field site is not trivial. Military planners must therefore distinguish between hype and reality, just as investors must. But even partial advances matter. The ability to map underground tunnels more reliably, or to maintain navigation for hours rather than minutes without satellites, can change calculations of risk. Incremental improvement, not science fiction breakthroughs, may define the early quantum decade.

The geopolitical implications are profound. Navigation independence reshapes alliance dynamics: countries less reliant on shared satellite constellations may feel freer to act alone. Detection tools may alter deterrence by undermining second-strike guarantees. Civilian sectors—aviation, shipping, agriculture—may find themselves both beneficiaries and hostages of the same technologies. Regulatory authorities will need to ask whether quantum sensors should be controlled like arms, exported like commodities, or shared like scientific instruments. Each choice carries risks: restrict too tightly, and innovation stifles; release too freely, and adversaries gain parity.

There is also a philosophical dimension. Human societies have always relied on uncertainty. Fog on the battlefield, the opacity of the sea, the limitations of clocks—all created margins of error that shaped strategy and politics. To pierce these limits is to redraw the conditions of human conflict and cooperation. A world in which submarines cannot hide, or in which no city is free from precise mapping, is a world of radical transparency. Transparency promises safety, but it also removes ambiguity—the ambiguity that sometimes prevents escalation by making intentions unknowable. The irony is sharp: technologies designed to reduce uncertainty may increase strategic instability.

For businesses, the questions are more immediate. How resilient are operations if GPS becomes unreliable? What value chains depend on timing signals without redundancy? How will quantum sensors affect industries from mining to insurance, where precise data alters competitive advantage? Boards cannot treat these as abstract curiosities. The rollout of quantum timing and sensing will shape procurement, regulatory compliance, and national strategy. The organisations that begin adapting now—auditing dependencies, testing alternatives, investing in pilot applications—will be better positioned when the transition moves from laboratory to market.

The shadow of quantum sensing, then, is not merely technological but societal. Who owns the data produced by hyper-sensitive sensors? Who is trusted to wield detection technologies that can reveal hidden infrastructure? Who controls the standards for timekeeping when time itself becomes a weaponised resource? These questions are not distant. They are emerging now, in research budgets, procurement policies, and diplomatic discussions.

The pace of quantum codebreaking remains uncertain, but the impact of quantum sensing and timing may arrive sooner, and in subtler ways. Less dramatic than a cryptographic collapse, but more pervasive. The stakes lie not only in who masters the science but in how societies choose to govern it. Will quantum sensing be treated as a tool of collective resilience, or as an instrument of unilateral power? The answer is not yet written. But one thing is certain: in a world built on fragile signals and hidden depths, the ability to see more clearly and measure more precisely will redraw the balance of trust and risk. And it will do so sooner than most expect.

Arms race in labs

In 2019, a Chinese laboratory claimed to have achieved "quantum supremacy," executing a specific calculation faster than the most powerful supercomputer. In the same year, Google's team announced a similar milestone, sparking a flurry of headlines that treated science as sport. But what looked like an esoteric contest between engineers was, in reality, something larger: a public glimpse of an intensifying geopolitical rivalry. Laboratories, once imagined as havens of open inquiry, had become frontlines of strategic competition. White coats and circuit boards had joined aircraft carriers and missile silos as symbols of power.

The paradox is stark. Quantum research thrives on openness—peer review, shared datasets, collaborative conferences—yet states increasingly treat it as a matter of national security. The very mechanisms that accelerate discovery clash with the instincts of strategic secrecy. When research papers are embargoed or conferences restricted, the signal is clear: science policy is no longer merely about innovation, but about sovereignty.

This contest is not only about machines, but about money. Public funding shapes the battlefield. The United States' National Quantum Initiative, Europe's Quantum Flagship, China's multi-billion yuan programmes—all pour resources into attracting talent and building infrastructure. Budgets are not neutral instruments of curiosity; they are wagers on the future. To underfund is to cede ground. To overfund is to distort priorities, pulling research towards politically favoured applications. In this way, allocations of grant money become strategic postures in their own right.

Talent, too, has become a weapon. Laboratories compete not just for breakthroughs but for people: physicists, cryptographers, materials scientists. Visa regimes, research fellowships, and cross-border hiring restrictions are deployed as tools of policy. For young scientists, the choice of where to pursue a doctorate can now feel like an act of allegiance. Brain drain is no longer just an academic worry; it is a geopolitical vulnerability. The "war for talent" is waged in job offers, but its consequences are written in national power.

Export controls reinforce this dynamic. Just as the United States restricted the flow of advanced semiconductors to rivals, so too have governments debated whether to limit exports of quantum technologies. The line between commercial and strategic is thin: a sensor designed for mineral exploration may also reveal submarine movements. A quantum key distribution system built for secure banking could secure military communications. Every licence granted—or denied—carries an implicit judgement about trust and rivalry. The laboratory is, once again, inseparable from the arsenal.

For citizens reading headlines about "quantum advantage" or "next-generation encryption," these dynamics are often invisible. Yet they matter profoundly. When a government invests in quantum research, it signals not only a bet on technology but also a conception of alliance and independence. Collaborative projects between European nations suggest one vision of shared resilience; unilateral national investments suggest another. Understanding the language of labs is therefore not a technical luxury but a civic necessity.

The consequences ripple outward. Standards bodies, once seen as dry technical committees, become arenas of contest. If China's cryptographic proposals shape international norms, global commerce may depend on protocols aligned with Beijing's preferences. If the United States and its allies dominate standards, the tilt goes the other way. Laboratories supply the science, but states shape the scaffolding of trust. Here, the arms race is not about who can publish first, but about whose protocols others are compelled to adopt.

There is also a deeper irony. Science has long been idealised as universal, a realm of shared truths beyond politics. Yet the current moment reveals a different story: knowledge as a scarce resource, guarded and leveraged. The very values of openness and replication that make science powerful also make it exploitable. To protect advantage, states may limit dissemination, eroding the collaborative culture that underpinned 20th-century progress. Citizens, then, must grasp not only the technical stakes but the cultural trade-offs. What happens to the spirit of science when its currency is national power?

The laboratory arms race is thus not reducible to who builds the first fault-tolerant quantum computer. It is about shaping ecosystems: funding pipelines, visa policies, intellectual property laws, export regimes, and international standards. Each element interacts with the others, forming a dense web in which discoveries are simultaneously scientific and strategic. In this environment, neutrality becomes a rare commodity. Even nations that aspire to remain outside the great-power competition—small states, non-aligned blocs, or scientific consortia—find themselves drawn in, forced to decide how to host talent, fund research, and regulate technology.

The outcome is uncertain. It is possible that quantum research becomes fragmented, with separate blocs developing divergent technologies, echoing the bifurcation of the internet. It is also possible that pragmatic cooperation persists, sustained by the sheer difficulty of the science and the mutual benefits of collaboration. Between these poles lies the messy reality of shifting alliances, contested standards, and laboratories that serve both discovery and deterrence.

For now, the image of the laboratory is ambiguous. It is at once a beacon of curiosity and a fortress of strategy. The same experiment can be read as a triumph of human ingenuity or as a move in a geopolitical game. The reader, informed of the funding flows, the talent migrations, and the export debates, gains the ability to interpret headlines not as isolated announcements but as signals in a wider struggle. The question is not whether the arms race in labs will shape geopolitics—it already does—but whether the culture of science can survive the weight of strategy. And that is a tension no laboratory, however advanced, can resolve alone.

Small-state hedges

In 1955, at the height of the Cold War, Austria signed the State Treaty that re-established its sovereignty on the explicit condition of permanent neutrality. It was a hedge, not a capitulation: a way for a small state, encircled by giants, to survive with autonomy. Today, the dilemmas faced by mid-tier nations navigating quantum and digital geopolitics are different in form but familiar in essence. The challenge is not whether to build nuclear stockpiles or host foreign troops, but whether to invest in quantum infrastructure, join technology consortia, or deliberately abstain from alignment. The stakes remain the same: bargaining power tomorrow depends on choices made under pressure today.

The paradox is that small states are often both marginal and pivotal. On one hand, they lack the resources to dominate research or production. On the other, they can tilt alliances, control critical standards votes, or occupy key niches in the global division of labour. Estonia's leadership in digital governance, Switzerland's centrality in finance, Singapore's role in logistics—all show how nations with limited size but sharp strategy can exert influence far beyond their demographic weight. When applied to quantum and emerging technologies, these lessons matter profoundly.

One obvious hedge is **consortium membership**. For states without the means to sustain billion-dollar laboratories alone, pooling resources through regional initiatives offers scale without surrendering sovereignty. The European Union's Quantum Flagship exemplifies this: individual members could not match US or Chinese budgets, but together they assemble enough critical mass to compete. Consortia also spread risk, insulating smaller players from the volatility of breakthroughs and failures.

Yet membership is not costless. It requires trust, compromise, and a willingness to let others set parts of the agenda. The art lies in negotiating seats at the table that ensure visibility without diluting national identity.

Another hedge is **neutrality**. Just as Austria carved a space between East and West, some states may opt to remain technologically unaligned, resisting pressure to join either American- or Chinese-led frameworks. Neutrality can offer insulation, but it demands discipline. Remaining outside great-power technology blocs means carefully balancing export controls, standards decisions, and diplomatic commitments. It also risks isolation: abstention may protect against entanglement, but it can also mean exclusion from the cutting edge. For smaller nations, neutrality is a hedge only if they simultaneously cultivate reputations as trusted mediators or safe harbours—roles that ensure others have an interest in their survival.

The third hedge is **niche excellence**. If a country cannot compete across the whole quantum spectrum, it may specialise in one area: cryptographic analysis, quantum materials, or high-precision sensing. Denmark's prominence in wind energy, Israel's in cybersecurity, and Finland's in telecommunications show how narrow focus can translate into disproportionate bargaining power. But niches are double-edged. They create dependence: if a nation excels in one domain, it becomes vulnerable to shifts in that field's relevance or to coercion targeting its comparative advantage. The strategy works best when paired with alliances that amplify the niche rather than expose it.

Case studies reveal the practical tensions. Take Singapore, which invests heavily in quantum communications and cryptography research. It cannot outspend the United States or China, but by positioning itself as a regional hub for secure communications, it anchors itself in global supply chains. Or look at Switzerland, whose financial neutrality translates into a role as a trusted custodian of sensitive data and a hub for cryptographic standards discussions. These are not accidents of geography; they are conscious hedges designed to future-proof sovereignty in a crowded landscape.

Yet hedges cannot eliminate risk; they only redistribute it. A consortium may collapse if larger members quarrel. Neutrality may be violated if one bloc perceives abstention as obstruction. A niche may evaporate if the field is leapfrogged by unexpected breakthroughs. For small states, the challenge is not to seek perfect safety but to craft resilience: enough options to avoid being trapped, enough credibility to make their choices respected.

Philosophically, this raises a deeper point about power itself. Great powers often conceive strategy as expansion: more allies, more bases, more technologies under control. Small states, by contrast, practise strategy as constraint: knowing when to align, when to abstain, and when to excel. Their art lies not in dominance but in calibration. This humility is not weakness. It is a recognition that in a world of volatile technological shifts, agility can outlast brute force.

For mid-tier nations, the horizon of quantum technologies crystallises these dilemmas with new intensity. A breakthrough in error correction, for instance, could suddenly privilege whichever bloc controls the first fault-tolerant machine. The ripple effects would extend beyond encryption to finance, logistics, and national defence. Small states cannot control that outcome, but they can decide whether they are positioned to absorb the shock, mediate between blocs, or leverage a specialised expertise. The hedge is not insurance against loss but preparation for opportunity.

These strategies also foreshadow a broader debate about the future of alliances. If small states coordinate their hedges—forming coalitions of neutrality, or clusters of niche excellence—they may exert collective influence greater than the sum of their parts. A group of digitally advanced mid-tier nations could, for instance, set standards that even great powers must respect. Conversely, if they hedge in isolation, they risk being picked off, co-opted, or ignored. The difference between agency and irrelevance will lie in whether they see themselves as solitary actors or as architects of new constellations.

The lesson for leaders is clear: hedges are not passive shelters but active investments. To delay is to drift into dependence. To act is to shape the bargaining position of tomorrow. Small states may never command the laboratories or budgets of the great powers, but they can decide how to map their vulnerabilities into leverage. The harder question—the one that cannot be deferred—is whether they will do so with imagination and resolve, or whether they will find themselves spectators in a game that nonetheless determines their fate.

Chapter 10

Shielding the Citizen

In October 2021, a single parent in Manchester opened an email that appeared to be from her child's school. Within minutes, her laptop froze, demanding payment in cryptocurrency to unlock her files. The ransom was not vast, but it was devastating: family photographs, work contracts, and tax records were all held hostage. She was neither a CEO nor a government official—just an ordinary citizen caught in the crossfire of global cybercrime. Her story is emblematic of a larger truth: digital insecurity is no longer an exotic concern reserved for intelligence agencies or multinational firms. It is a kitchen-table issue, as intimate as lost memories and as urgent as a disrupted hospital ward.

The paradox is stark. Citizens are at once the weakest link in the global digital chain and the first line of defence. Sophisticated nation-state hackers and opportunistic ransomware gangs alike exploit the same mundane vulnerabilities: weak passwords, unpatched software, inattentive clicks. Yet the same citizens, when equipped with clear frameworks and modest tools, can dramatically reduce both their personal exposure and the systemic risk that ripples outward from their homes, schools, and small businesses. Shielding the citizen is not only a matter of individual prudence; it is an act of collective resilience.

This chapter turns abstract geopolitics into lived practice. It begins with personal threat modelling—teaching individuals to ask: *What do I have that matters? Who might want it? How could they get it?* This simple triad of assets, adversaries, and attack paths replaces vague fear with concrete plans. The reader's first win is clarity, and clarity scales. Parents can extend the model to their children's online habits; families can use it to weigh trade-offs in privacy and convenience. Security ceases to be an endless, paralysing worry and becomes a structured, manageable discipline.

From there, we move to baselines for the home and device. Most harm arises not from cinematic hacks but from preventable lapses: unpatched operating systems, guessable passphrases, lost phones without backups. We will set out minimum viable postures—hardware keys for critical accounts, simple network hygiene, reliable backup routines. The focus is not perfection but durability: habits that stand the test of time and require little ongoing effort. Regulators and boards debate strategy at the national scale, but resilience begins in ordinary households.

Small businesses, often running on lean budgets and overextended staff, present another front line. They process payroll, handle invoices, and live by email—precisely the domains targeted by ransomware operators. For them, the goal is not building fortress walls but reducing the attack surface with a 90-day plan: lock down accounts, protect backups, segment networks. Insurance markets increasingly demand these controls, and when properly understood, insurance becomes more than a financial backstop. It is a lever for governance, nudging firms toward better hygiene by aligning private incentives with public safety.

The chapter also speaks to institutions with the least margin for error: schools and hospitals. These are mission-critical and chronically underfunded, yet they hold sensitive data and sustain daily life. Procurement choices and routine drills often provide more protection than glossy tools. A well-rehearsed tabletop exercise can save more lives than another brochure about "next-generation" firewalls. When civic infrastructure is hardened, it protects the vulnerable at scale—children, patients, and the elderly—anchoring the democratic promise that security is not only for the privileged.

What threads these domains together is a reorientation: from fear to agency, from reactive panic to proactive planning. Shielding the citizen is not about perfection, nor about expecting individuals to bear the weight of structural failures. It is about building habits, institutions, and incentives that distribute resilience across society. The citizen is not a helpless consumer of security but an active participant in shaping it.

As we enter this chapter, the stakes should feel both intimate and universal. The lesson is not that threats are everywhere, but that preparedness is possible. Digital life will never be risk-free, but it can be made livable, sustainable, and even empowering. The more ordinary people learn to shield themselves, the less oxygen is left for those who thrive on chaos. The task now is to map the paths by which that transformation becomes real.

Personal threat modelling

One winter evening in Oslo, a retired teacher discovered that her bank account had been emptied. She had not clicked on any suspicious link, nor installed unfamiliar software. Instead, her email—secured with a weak, recycled password—had been quietly breached months before. Criminals had studied her correspondence, waited for the moment her pension was deposited, and then drained it in a single transfer. She was shocked not only by the theft, but by its deliberateness: someone had modelled her life, her habits, her vulnerabilities, before she had ever thought to model them herself.

Here lies the paradox of digital life. Every person, whether they know it or not, already features in someone else's threat model. Marketers profile browsing habits, data brokers collate location histories, criminals scan for exploitable accounts, and in some cases, intelligence agencies catalogue patterns of travel and communication. Yet few individuals ever reverse the process—asking the basic but transformative questions: *What do I have that matters? Who might want it? How could they get it?* The act of answering reframes cyber security from an amorphous cloud of anxieties into a concrete plan. Fear dissipates once it is named and structured.

At its core, personal threat modelling is disarmingly simple. It begins with assets: the things worth protecting. These are not only bank balances or laptops, but also family photos, medical records, reputations, and even time itself. For a journalist, unpublished notes may be more valuable than cash. For a student, exam submissions and identity documents are critical. By naming assets, one makes implicit value explicit—and with it, a clearer sense of what must not be lost.

The second layer is adversaries. Not all threats are equal, nor all attackers equally capable. A teenager trying to guess a Wi-Fi password, a criminal gang launching phishing campaigns, or a state actor monitoring dissidents represent very different levels of intent and resource. Most people are not targets of espionage, but nearly everyone is a target of indiscriminate crime. Mapping adversaries forces an honest assessment: one cannot defend against every possible enemy, but one can calibrate defences to the most probable.

Finally, attack paths: the practical routes by which adversaries reach assets. These are often mundane rather than exotic. An email attachment bypasses complex firewalls because a finger clicks it. A phone is stolen from a café table, not cracked by quantum codebreakers. A poorly secured cloud account leaks photos because its password was reused across dozens of forgotten logins. Seeing attack paths clearly allows individuals to cut them off cheaply—strong passphrases, multi-factor authentication, offline backups—rather than chasing cinematic threats that may never arrive.

Consider the case of small families. Parents may worry about predators online or bullying through social media. A family threat model surfaces concrete assets—children's privacy, photos, location data—and the realistic adversaries: not faceless state actors but school peers, opportunistic scammers, or predatory adults. The attack paths might include gaming platforms, messaging apps, or overshared location services. From this model, rules emerge naturally: no sharing of geotagged images, device controls in bedrooms, rehearsed responses to suspicious messages. What could have been diffuse fear becomes a set of lived, teachable practices.

For professionals, the model scales further. A lawyer must protect client confidentiality across email, cloud drives, and mobile devices. An activist may confront the risk of surveillance, where even metadata—who called whom, when—becomes an asset of interest. In these cases, the modelling exercise clarifies trade-offs: perhaps a separate device is worth the inconvenience, or an encrypted messenger becomes not an affectation but a necessity. By surfacing choices, threat modelling restores agency.

Critics sometimes dismiss personal models as futile against determined adversaries. They argue that ordinary citizens cannot match the sophistication of attackers. Yet this overlooks a fundamental asymmetry: attackers tend to seek the path of least resistance. A household that patches devices, uses hardware keys, and maintains backups is an unattractive target compared to the millions who do not. The point is not invulnerability, but deterrence and resilience. Even when an incident occurs, a family that has rehearsed responses—who to call, how to restore files, how to limit damage—suffers far less dislocation than one improvising under pressure.

There is also a philosophical dimension. Threat modelling forces us to ask: *what do I value most in the digital sphere?* For some, it is privacy; for others, continuity of work; for others still, the preservation of memories. By ranking assets, one inadvertently ranks values. The exercise is not merely technical but ethical: it teaches individuals and families to decide consciously, rather than letting convenience or fear make the choice.

A final insight: models evolve. Assets shift as life changes, adversaries emerge or fade, attack paths adapt with technology. A new job, a new child, a new device—all alter the balance. The discipline, then, is not a one-time audit but a recurring habit, as ordinary as changing smoke alarm batteries. Institutions conduct risk registers annually; citizens can do the same in miniature.

Disasters, digital or otherwise, often feel overwhelming because they collapse our sense of control. Threat modelling offers its opposite: a simple, situational map that re-anchors agency. To ask the triad of assets, adversaries, and attack paths is to reclaim the initiative, to move from being modelled by others to modelling oneself.

The unresolved question is whether societies will normalise this practice beyond specialists. Will children learn to model digital threats alongside fire drills? Will families adopt it as routinely as they lock doors at night? The answer will shape not only individual safety, but the resilience of the wider networks we all inhabit.

Home and device baseline

The majority of digital disasters begin not with exotic state malware or cinematic cyber assaults, but with the small lapses of everyday life. A family in Manchester lost every photo from a decade when a ransomware strain encrypted their only laptop. A retired engineer in Barcelona found his pension siphoned away after a reused password gave intruders access to his email. A start-up founder in Nairobi spent weeks rebuilding operations after a simple software update had been ignored, leaving a server exposed to a trivial exploit. None of these cases required extraordinary skill from the attacker. They exploited ordinary neglect.

The paradox of digital security is that while headlines are dominated by quantum threats and AI-driven espionage, the bulk of harm flows from the mundane. The same mistakes repeat across continents: unpatched software, weak or reused passwords, absent backups, careless clicks, unsecured Wi-Fi. Each by itself may seem trivial, but together they form the fertile ground where most digital crime thrives. For individuals and households, the path to resilience is not paved with exotic tools but with a baseline: a minimum viable posture, established once and maintained as habit.

Backups are the first line of defence. Data is both fragile and irreplaceable: photos, documents, creative work, correspondence. Hard drives fail silently, ransomware locks indiscriminately, and cloud services can revoke access overnight. The remedy is redundancy—copies stored separately, in the cloud and offline. A simple rhythm—weekly incremental backups, monthly full backups—reduces the catastrophic to the inconvenient. Yet here, trade-offs matter. Cloud backups bring convenience but demand trust in providers and vigilance against account compromise. Offline drives provide autonomy but require discipline. The baseline is not perfection but *plurality*: at least two distinct backups, with one physically separated from the device.

Patching follows. Every device—phone, laptop, router, even doorbell—runs on software, and software decays as vulnerabilities are discovered. Attackers do not search for unknown flaws when known ones remain unpatched. The WannaCry outbreak of 2017 spread through a weakness for which a fix already existed; the problem was not the absence of knowledge but the absence of action. Automatic updates, long resisted for fear of disruption, have become essential. Still, there are trade-offs: updates can break legacy applications or disrupt workflows. The pragmatic baseline is layered—critical security patches apply automatically; non-critical updates can be scheduled. The guiding rule: *unpatched equals unsafe.*

Passwords remain the perennial weak point, despite decades of warnings. The baseline shift is clear: from passwords to passphrases, and from memory to managers. A long, unique passphrase is far stronger than a short, complex password. A password manager simplifies the burden, generating and storing credentials across devices. Yet convenience collides with risk: a compromised master password can expose the vault. This is where hardware keys—physical tokens for authentication—become decisive. Unlike codes sent via SMS, which can be intercepted, or apps, which can be phished, hardware keys resist remote compromise. The baseline is again layered: password managers for diversity, passphrases for resilience, hardware keys for critical accounts such as email, banking, and cloud storage.

Network hygiene anchors the environment. Home Wi-Fi routers are often left with default settings, outdated firmware, and weak credentials—making them soft entry points. A strong passphrase, regular firmware updates, and the separation of guest networks from primary devices mark a robust baseline. Beyond the home, vigilance continues: public Wi-Fi is assumed hostile unless mediated by encryption, and device sharing is treated as risk exposure rather than convenience. None of this is dramatic. All of it is effective.

What unites these measures is their banality. They require little technical expertise, only clarity of defaults and discipline of habit. Yet this banality is deceptive. When practised collectively—by households, schools, small businesses—they create a population-level shield. Cyber criminals thrive on predictability; if millions of users patch promptly, back up consistently, and authenticate securely, the economics of attacks shift. The easy prey diminish. Threat actors must invest more to succeed. At scale, the mundane becomes strategic.

There is also a deeper human insight. Establishing a baseline is not only about technology but about psychology. People are drawn to novel tools and dramatic fixes, yet security depends on routine. The repetition of backups, the reflex of checking updates, the discipline of using hardware keys—all cultivate a posture where protection is second nature. Security becomes less about constant vigilance and more about ingrained habit. Like washing hands or fastening seatbelts, these practices fade from attention precisely because they work.

And yet, one tension remains unresolved. Will individuals and families normalise such baselines before another wave of digital disasters forces them to? Governments and regulators can set standards, insurers can nudge with incentives, but durable security begins at home. The question is whether the everyday citizen will come to view backups, patching, and passphrases as ordinary hygiene—or continue to leave their digital lives perched on fragile foundations. The answer will determine whether the mundane remains the most dangerous frontier, or finally becomes its most effective defence.

Small-business controls

On a Tuesday morning in Coventry, a family-owned construction firm found itself locked out of its entire invoicing system. A routine click on what looked like a supplier's email unleashed ransomware that encrypted payroll records, tax filings, and every ongoing contract. The ransom note was blunt: pay in cryptocurrency within 72 hours or lose everything. The owners faced a cruel paradox. They were small enough to fly under the radar of regulators and law enforcement, but large enough that even a week's disruption could push them into insolvency. What nearly destroyed them was not exotic espionage—it was the absence of simple, affordable controls that could have been in place within months.

The paradox extends across economies. Small businesses represent more than 90% of enterprises worldwide, employing billions and forming the backbone of supply chains. Yet they are also disproportionately targeted by cybercriminals. Attackers know that these firms rarely have dedicated IT departments, let alone chief information security officers. They rely on

trust, speed, and lean budgets. That makes them vulnerable. Paradoxically, the very agility that allows small firms to thrive in markets also renders them brittle when criminals exploit the digital seams.

The remedy is not to transform these firms into miniaturised fortresses of cybersecurity. The baseline is more pragmatic: a 90-day plan that hardens the obvious points of entry—payroll, invoicing, and email. These are the arteries of small-business survival, and they are precisely where ransomware and fraudsters concentrate their strikes. The point is not perfection but resilience. A few well-chosen measures shift the balance of power, buying time and leverage.

Payroll is both sensitive and routine, which makes it a prime target. Attackers often use stolen credentials to reroute salaries to their own accounts or to inject fraudulent staff entries. Multi-factor authentication, ideally with hardware keys, drastically reduces this risk. For businesses that cannot afford tokens for every employee, a tiered model suffices: owners, finance officers, and system administrators receive the strongest protection, while others use app-based authentication. Regularly reconciling payroll with bank confirmations provides another safeguard. The cost is modest; the gain is existential.

Invoicing carries equal peril. Fake invoices are a persistent fraud tactic, often exploiting trusted relationships with suppliers. Training staff to verify unusual payment requests by phone—not by replying to the suspicious email—is an immediate defence. Segregating duties, where one employee initiates payments and another authorises them, reduces the chance of unilateral error or compromise. Free or low-cost invoicing platforms increasingly include fraud detection and anomaly alerts. Implementing such tools may appear minor, but for a small firm they are the equivalent of circuit breakers: they stop small sparks from becoming financial fires.

Email remains the universal gateway for compromise. A single careless click can unleash malware, steal credentials, or trigger ransomware. Here the baseline rests on three pillars: robust filtering, disciplined habits, and rapid containment. Cloud email providers now offer advanced filtering and quarantine features; businesses must enable them by default. Staff training is less about abstract awareness and more about rehearsed reflexes: hesitate before opening attachments, verify before clicking links, escalate if in doubt. Finally, containment demands preparation—ensuring that if one inbox is breached, it cannot cascade through shared drives and business systems. Segmenting access and enforcing least-privilege principles sound abstract but boil down to a simple rule: no employee should hold more digital keys than their role demands.

A 90-day plan begins with inventory: knowing which systems, accounts, and devices exist. This alone often reveals forgotten laptops, shadow accounts, and outdated software—each a doorway for attackers. From there, the rollout is staged. Month one secures email and mandates multi-factor authentication. Month two reinforces payroll and invoicing with verification steps and reconciliations. Month three strengthens backups and tests recovery. Each stage is small enough not to overwhelm, but cumulative enough to create a shield. Crucially, this process creates habits. Once controls are in place, staff become accustomed to the friction of verification and the rhythm of updates.

Insurance connects these measures to governance. Increasingly, insurers scrutinise whether small businesses have implemented baseline protections before offering cyber cover. Premiums rise for those that lag, while firms with robust controls benefit from lower costs and higher credibility. Insurance thus becomes less a bailout after disaster and more a lever for discipline. Well-designed policies do not merely transfer risk; they reshape behaviour, nudging firms toward resilience.

The philosophical lesson is clear: security at the small-business level is not about defeating every adversary. It is about denying criminals easy victories. Each hardened login, verified invoice, and rehearsed backup shifts the economics of crime, making attacks less profitable and therefore less frequent. At scale, when thousands of firms adopt such baselines, the ripple effect alters entire ecosystems.

And yet, the unresolved question lingers: will small firms embrace this discipline before catastrophe strikes? The tools exist, the costs are modest, and the steps are simple. But simplicity is not the same as inevitability. For many owners, cybersecurity still feels like an abstraction compared to the immediacy of cash flow and customer service. The true challenge is cultural—embedding the idea that in the digital age, the resilience of payroll, invoicing, and email is as vital as the resilience of the product itself. If that cultural shift takes root, small businesses will not only survive in the shadow of cyber threats but will form the front line of collective defence.

Schools and hospitals

When the Ryuk ransomware group crippled the largest public school district in Baltimore, thousands of students were abruptly cut off from

lessons, teachers lost access to grading systems, and parents faced weeks of uncertainty. The attackers did not need cutting-edge exploits; they simply exploited neglected systems in a chronically underfunded environment. In parallel, across the Atlantic, the 2017 WannaCry outbreak paralysed parts of the UK's National Health Service. Operations were cancelled, ambulances diverted, and digital records frozen—all because outdated Windows machines lacked a basic patch. The pattern is grim but consistent: the institutions most vital to public trust and human welfare are often the least prepared.

There is a cruel irony here. Schools and hospitals command enormous social importance, yet their cyber budgets are fragile, often subordinated to the urgency of hiring staff, repairing roofs, or buying medical equipment. The cyber threat they face is not abstract: ransomware gangs know that disruption here exerts maximum pressure, since leaders cannot easily "wait out" an outage when pupils or patients are at risk. Attackers understand that urgency equals leverage. That is why these institutions are disproportionately targeted—not despite their poverty, but because of it.

Glossy vendor tools promise salvation, but history shows that true resilience stems from fundamentals. For schools, the baseline is surprisingly prosaic: strong password management, timely patching of widely used platforms, and routine data backups. Many ransomware cases succeed not because defences are absent but because routine maintenance is inconsistent. For hospitals, the priorities extend to segmenting operational technology—the infusion pumps, MRI scanners, and monitoring devices that should never be exposed to the public internet. Segmentation is not glamorous, but it prevents an infection in one wing from cascading into intensive care.

Procurement lies at the heart of sustainable defence. When budget-constrained institutions chase shiny, complex tools, they often inherit systems too intricate to manage. Better is to write tenders that demand security by default: software that enforces patching automatically, hardware that supports encrypted storage, cloud platforms that ship with multi-factor authentication switched on. These requirements cost little at the procurement stage but save fortunes in operational crises. Procurement is not an IT back-office function; it is a governance lever.

Equally essential are drills. Fire drills are mandated in schools and hospitals because they prepare humans to act calmly under stress. Cyber drills deserve equal normalisation. They need not simulate nation-state intrusions; even a rehearsal of what to do if email fails or if records are temporarily inaccessible builds confidence. Drills create muscle memory, reducing panic when the real attack comes. They also reveal bottlenecks—an outdated fax machine that cannot handle patient referrals, or a teacher who alone holds the passwords for grading portals. These human chokepoints matter as much as technical ones.

The civic dimension is unavoidable. A compromised hospital is not just a technical failure but a direct assault on public trust in the state's ability to safeguard life. A breached school is not just an inconvenience but a disruption of the social contract between families and the public institutions that educate their children. This makes cyber resilience in these sectors a democratic concern. It is why boards of governors, health authorities, and local councils must view cyber preparedness not as a "nice-to-have" but as part of their legal and moral duty of care.

There is, however, an uncomfortable tension. Spending scarce funds on cyber resilience means not spending them elsewhere—on extra nurses, more teaching assistants, or repairs to decrepit infrastructure. The question is not whether to spend, but how to prioritise without eroding the mission itself. The most promising approach is to identify high-consequence systems—the electronic health record, the payroll database, the student management portal—and harden them disproportionately. Perfection is impossible; triage is essential.

Citizens, too, have a role. Parents lobbying school boards for cyber drills, patient groups pressing hospitals to demand secure procurement, unions advocating for protected budgets—all create political incentives that shift attention. Attackers exploit inertia; collective voice can counter it. When the public recognises that digital resilience is part of safeguarding children and saving lives, the political calculus shifts.

Yet the unresolved tension lingers. Will these institutions—stretched, underfunded, and focused on their human missions—ever carve out the resources and discipline for sustained resilience? Or will they remain soft targets, shielded only by hope that the next wave of ransomware looks elsewhere? The answer will shape not just the safety of students and patients but the legitimacy of the civic fabric itself.

Insurance and incentives

When the first wave of ransomware attacks swept across Europe in 2017, many victims scrambled to recover not only their data but also their balance sheets. For some, the unexpected lifeline was a cyber insurance policy tucked away in the back pages of their risk portfolio. Claims were processed, ransoms paid, and operations slowly restored. Yet what seemed at the time a relief soon revealed itself as a trap: insurers began to notice that repeated payouts fuelled the very criminal ecosystem they sought to contain. What looked like a shield had, inadvertently, become a subsidy for extortionists.

This paradox lies at the heart of cyber insurance. On one hand, it offers organisations a measure of financial protection against the unpredictable; on the other, it risks creating a moral hazard in which poor practices persist because losses are transferred to an insurer. The central question is whether insurance is merely a safety net, or whether it can become a lever for raising standards across society.

History offers a guide. Fire insurance in the 19th century transformed not only how buildings were rebuilt but how they were constructed in the first place. Insurers demanded fire-resistant materials, reliable hydrants, and inspections. The premiums of those who refused rose sharply, pricing negligence out of the market. Over time, this private mechanism reshaped public safety. A similar opportunity now faces cyber insurers: to condition coverage on hygiene, thereby aligning private incentives with the public good.

Already, we see early experiments. Some policies require multi-factor authentication on all remote access accounts. Others mandate regular patching cycles or tested backups. These are not empty demands; they can be verified through audits and enforced with premium adjustments. By embedding minimum baselines into contracts, insurers create a practical, non-negotiable incentive for organisations that might otherwise relegate cybersecurity to a low priority. The language of exclusions and endorsements becomes, in effect, a new regulatory grammar.

Yet there are limits. Insurance cannot substitute for governance where states have failed to set standards. Nor can it resolve collective problems like systemic vulnerabilities in widely used software, where one flaw ripples across entire economies. A single insurer cannot compel Microsoft or Cisco to re-architect their products. But insurers, through consortia, can lobby for safer defaults, just as they once lobbied for building codes. The boundary between private leverage and public mandate is porous, and fruitful.

The international dimension complicates matters further. Cyber attackers exploit regulatory arbitrage just as financial criminals do. A company in

London may diligently meet its insurer's requirements, but if its supply chain relies on a subcontractor in a jurisdiction with lax standards, the chain remains weak. Here, global insurers possess an unusual form of soft power. By harmonising their clauses across geographies, they can push small suppliers in distant markets to upgrade practices, creating a ripple effect that formal treaties alone have struggled to achieve.

There is also a cultural challenge. Many executives still treat insurance as a simple transfer of risk: a cheque written to absolve them of deeper responsibility. But digital risk does not behave like natural disasters or theft. A hospital that pays out under insurance after a ransomware attack has not only suffered loss—it has been complicit, however reluctantly, in financing the very criminals who may return next year. Leaders must therefore reframe the purpose of cover: not as indemnity against inevitability, but as a contract that disciplines behaviour before crisis strikes.

Critics argue that tying coverage to hygiene will price out those who need protection most: small clinics, local councils, or small businesses. That danger is real. But the alternative—cheap insurance with no strings attached—creates a vicious cycle where the weakest remain perpetually compromised. Here the role of government is crucial: to provide subsidies or shared pools for essential but cash-poor sectors, conditional on adopting best practices. In this way, insurance becomes not a blunt instrument of exclusion, but a guided mechanism for levelling up.

The deeper philosophical insight is that cyber insurance is not really about money at all. It is about accountability. Every clause, every exclusion, every premium adjustment encodes a judgment about which behaviours are acceptable and which are reckless. In aggregate, these judgments shape the behaviour of entire sectors. When written with foresight, policies can elevate the baseline of resilience; when written carelessly, they entrench fragility.

The open question, then, is whether the industry and regulators can rise to the occasion. Will insurers act boldly, as their predecessors did in the age of fire, turning indemnity into reform? Or will they retreat into narrow actuarial logic, paying claims while the systemic risk deepens? For citizens, for boards, and for policymakers, the stakes are clear. Insurance can be a crutch—or it can be a lever. The choice lies in how we design the incentives that will quietly shape the safety of our digital future.

Chapter 11

The New Non-Alignment

At the height of the Cold War, newly independent states sought to chart a course between Washington and Moscow. They called it non-alignment: not neutrality, but agency—an insistence on shaping the world rather than being shaped by it. Today, a similar crossroads appears, not in tanks or treaties, but in cables, chips, and code. In the digital sphere, the duopoly of the United States and China looms large, offering seductive technologies entwined with strategic dependencies. Yet mid-tier nations, small states, and regional blocs are quietly asking whether another path exists: not a seat at one hegemon's table, but a coalition of their own making.

The paradox is stark. Digital interdependence means no country is truly sovereign in the old sense, yet total dependence on a single provider is perilous. An island nation may rely on American cloud services, but its ports on Chinese cranes and its networks on European standards. A West African consortium may deploy shared fibre financed by multiple powers, each with its own agenda. In this patchwork, sovereignty is no longer about drawing a line around one's borders—it is about deciding which dependencies are acceptable, which alliances are sustainable, and which risks are intolerable.

The new non-alignment is not built on slogans or summits; it is built on switches, standards, and shared infrastructure. We see glimpses of it in regional cloud cooperatives, in cross-border internet exchange points, and in joint bids at standards bodies where smaller states, pooling expertise, can outvote larger powers. These are modest steps, but they carry the seeds of a different digital order—one in which states outside the duopoly wield influence not by rejecting interdependence but by shaping its terms.

This chapter explores how such a movement might take shape. It begins with *coalitions of the wired*, where states pool capacity without surrendering control, showing that cooperation need not slide into capture. It turns to *standards diplomacy*, where occupying the dull-seeming chairs of technical committees translates into power more enduring than military hardware. It examines the promise of *neutral clouds and corridors*, where governance and transparency matter as much as fibre and servers. And it addresses *norms and red lines*, where shared prohibitions against targeting hospitals or elections anchor ethics in enforceable commitments.

But ambition is meaningless without accountability. Lofty declarations are plentiful; dashboards that measure downtime avoided or skills gained are rare. In the end, the credibility of a new non-alignment rests not on rhetoric but on results. Can citizens audit the safety of their grids and networks? Can leaders show that cooperation delivers resilience, not dependence under another name?

The stakes extend beyond technology. A world in which only two powers set the rules is a world of diminished choice and fragile sovereignty. A world where mid-tier states act collectively, however imperfectly, is one where leverage can be shared, and risk distributed. The test is whether today's fragmented efforts can be scaled into a coherent movement—whether the quiet work of engineers, diplomats, and regulators can amount to more than a patchwork of half-measures.

What follows is not a utopian manifesto but a map of feasible options, tested by experience and sharpened by constraint. The new non-alignment is not about opting out; it is about building in. The question is not whether the space exists to act outside the duopoly. It does. The question is whether enough states, faced with the pull of giants, will choose to walk that narrower but more sovereign path.

Coalitions of the wired

In 1955, leaders from 29 newly independent states met in Bandung, Indonesia, and declared they would not be dragged into the orbit of either superpower. They had no armies to rival Washington or Moscow, but they discovered leverage in numbers, in shared institutions, and in a refusal to be treated as pawns. Today, a similar impulse emerges in the digital sphere. Countries too small to dominate cloud markets or set global standards are nonetheless asking: what can we achieve if we act together, and what does sovereignty mean if it is practised collectively rather than alone?

The paradox of the digital age is that connectivity is both the source of dependence and the means of liberation. A single small state cannot credibly host a sovereign cloud, finance undersea cables, or influence encryption standards. But five or ten acting together can. Pooling demand creates bargaining power, pooling expertise generates resilience, and pooling infrastructure reduces the asymmetry that locks smaller players into dependency on the duopoly of the United States and China. The task is to find models of cooperation that deliver scale without sliding into capture—coalitions that bind without dominating.

Some examples already exist. The European Union's Gaia-X initiative, though plagued by delays and politics, represents a concerted attempt to design a federated cloud architecture that prevents lock-in. In Africa, the West African Cable System (WACS) and the African Internet Exchange System show how regional investment and shared governance can reduce dependency on external backbones. In Latin America, regional research networks link universities and laboratories across borders, allowing pooled scientific capacity and cheaper bandwidth. None of these projects is perfect, but each proves a basic point: digital sovereignty for smaller players is rarely national; it is almost always regional.

Coalitions also shift the terms of negotiation. A Pacific island nation approaching a hyperscale provider has little leverage when buying server capacity or negotiating data protections. A consortium of ten island states, by contrast, can demand price ceilings, data localisation options, and commitments to renewable energy use. The same principle applies to standards. A single delegate in the International Telecommunication Union may be sidelined; a voting bloc of aligned mid-tier states can secure committee chairs, influence definitions, and insert safeguards into protocols. Here, sovereignty is reframed—not as self-sufficiency, which is impossible in a globally networked world, but as voice and agency within shared arrangements.

Yet coalitions are fragile. They depend on trust among neighbours who often have their own rivalries. They are vulnerable to divide-and-rule tactics from larger powers, who may offer bilateral deals to peel members away. And they struggle with enforcement: what happens when one member accepts subsidised equipment from a major vendor, undercutting the coalition's bargaining stance? The governance structures that sustain cooperation—transparent procurement, shared monitoring, and dispute resolution—become as critical as the technology itself. Without them, coalitions risk dissolving into loose clubs that deliver little.

There is also the tension between inclusivity and efficiency. Larger groupings may be more representative but slower to act; smaller clusters can move faster but risk marginalising outsiders. The digital non-alignment movement will have to balance these pulls. One promising model is modular cooperation: groups of three or four states advancing specific projects—joint data centres, federated identity schemes, shared cybersecurity training—while linking their efforts through interoperable standards. This way, progress does not depend on all members moving at the same pace, but no member is left isolated.

The philosophical shift here is subtle but profound. For centuries, sovereignty has been equated with autonomy: the power to decide alone. In the wired world, autonomy often produces weakness. True sovereignty may now lie in the ability to shape interdependence deliberately, through coalitions that allow small states to punch above their weight. This is not surrender but strategy. It accepts that no nation can master digital infrastructure alone, and turns that fact into leverage rather than liability.

Still, the future of coalitions of the wired remains uncertain. Will they crystallise into lasting institutions, capable of holding their ground against duopolistic pressure? Or will they fragment under the weight of national self-interest, leaving each state to bargain alone? The answer depends less on technology than on political imagination—on whether mid-tier nations can rediscover the Bandung spirit and adapt it to fibre-optic cables and cloud contracts. What is at stake is not just their digital posture, but their role in shaping the rules of a world where sovereignty is increasingly written in code.

Standards diplomacy

A curious truth defines the digital age: the most consequential battles for sovereignty are often fought not on the battlefield or even in boardrooms, but in beige conference centres where engineers debate the syntax of protocols. The design of a header field or the timing of a handshake can determine which vendors dominate, which nations gain visibility into data flows, and which users are left secure or exposed. It is here, in standards bodies, that the rules of the digital world are written—and rewritten.

For decades, many governments treated this domain as technical housekeeping. Participation was delegated to corporate representatives or left to international organisations without close oversight. That neglect carried a cost. When Beijing began systematically sending large delegations to the International Telecommunication Union (ITU) and other forums, many Western states were startled to discover how much influence could be wielded simply by showing up in numbers, chairing working groups, and producing draft proposals. Complaints about "technology sovereignty" rang hollow when those same governments had not invested in the slow, patient work of standards diplomacy.

The lesson is simple yet uncomfortable: standards are politics by other means. They determine whether internet traffic can be inspected in transit, whether encryption defaults are strong or weak, whether a protocol can be deployed cheaply in the developing world or requires expensive licensing. Once set, standards harden into infrastructure; revising them takes decades. Unlike military power, which can be projected quickly, or financial sanctions, which bite immediately, standards confer a subtler form of influence. They accumulate quietly but endure for generations.

Participation, therefore, is strategy. Chairing a standards committee is not glamorous, but it sets agendas and controls drafting language. Sponsoring testbeds—live environments where draft protocols are trialled—provides leverage to define what "works in practice," a crucial filter in standards adoption. Publishing open-source reference code does more than showcase competence: it establishes defaults that others copy, embedding a particular implementation into the DNA of global systems. These tactics, though unassuming, are forms of slow power. They require patience, expertise, and persistence rather than shock and awe.

Consider Wi-Fi. The IEEE 802.11 standards process has been running for decades, with each generation shaping not only consumer connectivity but also industrial automation, military communications, and national security postures. Countries that invested early in influencing spectrum allocation and security protocols found themselves with domestic industries aligned to global adoption. Others, who assumed the market would sort itself out, discovered their firms locked into higher costs or dependent on foreign intellectual property. The same dynamic plays out today in 5G, cloud interoperability, and cryptographic primitives. Complaints about dependency are meaningless unless matched by sustained participation in the slow grind of drafting, testing, and codifying standards.

This is not merely a contest between great powers. Mid-tier nations, too, can play above their weight if they act with intent. Singapore, for instance, has become a respected contributor in cybersecurity standards by leveraging its role as a testbed for pilot projects. Estonia, though small, has built credibility in identity management standards by deploying nationwide digital ID systems that others study and emulate. In both cases, influence stems not from scale but from credibility, consistency, and the ability to contribute working models. For nations that cannot dominate markets, standards diplomacy offers an alternative pathway to relevance.

Yet tension lurks beneath the surface. Standards bodies have long prized openness and technical neutrality. The growing politicisation of their work risks fracturing this culture. Competing blocs have begun to push not only for different technical designs but for different governance philosophies: decentralisation versus centralised control, open-source versus proprietary models, security versus surveillance. Some warn of a "splinternet of standards," where incompatible protocols fragment the global network. Others argue that competition sharpens innovation and allows pluralism rather than monopoly. Navigating these tensions requires not just technical skill but diplomatic subtlety.

Philosophically, standards diplomacy challenges traditional notions of sovereignty. It suggests that autonomy does not flow from rejecting external influence but from embedding one's preferences deep within the connective tissue of global systems. A nation whose engineers shape protocols can exert control far beyond its borders, invisibly yet powerfully. Citizens may never notice the work done in Geneva or Beijing, but their online experiences—their privacy, their costs, their freedoms—are directly affected. Standards, in this sense, are the invisible architecture of liberty or constraint.

The question that remains unresolved is whether states will recognise the value of this slow power in time. Investing in delegations, cultivating technical expertise, and funding open testbeds demands resources and foresight that often sit uneasily with short-term political cycles. But neglect carries its own price: a world where standards are set by others, and sovereignty becomes little more than the right to complain. If coalitions of the wired offer one pathway for smaller nations, standards diplomacy offers another: influence not through dominance, but through persistence. The race is not to the loud, but to the patient. And the world is still deciding which voices will be inscribed into the protocols that shape the century.

Neutral clouds and corridors

In the summer of 2021, internet access in much of West Africa was disrupted by a single severed undersea cable. Banks stalled, hospitals lost records, and ordinary citizens found themselves cut off from services that, in another era, would never have been mediated through a fragile thread of fibre. The incident was not unique. A cable snagged by a ship's anchor in the Red Sea, or a power failure at a European data centre, can ripple outward until millions of people—across borders, across continents—feel the shock. These episodes make visible what is usually invisible: the world's dependence on a handful of digital chokepoints owned, financed, and governed by a small number of states and corporations.

The paradox is stark. Data is borderless, but its conduits are not. The internet's image as a decentralised network obscures the reality that traffic still converges through physical points—cloud data centres, internet exchange points (IXPs), and long-haul corridors of fibre or satellite spectrum. Whoever owns, finances, or governs these points enjoys leverage not unlike that of a canal owner in the age of shipping empires. In the 21st century, sovereignty is exercised not only through territorial borders but through control of clouds and corridors.

This recognition has prompted a search for alternatives. For countries reluctant to depend wholly on either of the great digital blocs—US hyperscale providers or Chinese infrastructure champions—the question is whether genuinely *neutral* digital spaces can be created: shared clouds, jointly governed IXPs, and data corridors with transparent financing and accountability. These are not utopian dreams. They are buildable projects, already emerging in embryonic form from Africa to Europe to South-East Asia.

Shared clouds represent the most ambitious strand. Instead of relying on foreign hyperscalers whose terms of service can change overnight, regional consortia can pool resources to develop sovereign but interoperable cloud platforms. The Gaia-X initiative in Europe is one such attempt, setting out rules for data portability, transparency, and certification rather than simply building a new set of servers. The vision is not a fortress cloud but a federated one—where smaller providers can offer services under common governance frameworks, reducing lock-in and increasing resilience.

Internet exchange points, meanwhile, provide a subtler form of autonomy. IXPs allow local traffic to stay local, rather than bouncing across continents before returning. In Nairobi, Lagos, and Johannesburg, investment in IXPs has reduced latency and costs dramatically, while also diminishing exposure to foreign surveillance. Their neutrality lies not only in their governance but in their technical role: they ensure that citizens of one country do not have to send data through a distant hub just to reach their neighbour. In a crisis, that localisation can prove decisive.

Data corridors, finally, are the arteries of long-haul connectivity. Submarine cables like the Equiano and the PEACE cable, or terrestrial fibre corridors across Eurasia, raise geopolitical questions as acute as those surrounding pipelines of oil and gas. Financing models determine whether they become tools of dependency or instruments of shared prosperity. Transparent governance, with clear rules on access, pricing, and maintenance, can prevent capture by single powers. Just as open shipping lanes underpinned global trade in the 20th century, open data corridors can underpin digital trade in the 21st.

Yet neutrality is easier to declare than to sustain. Shared governance requires trust among states that may disagree on values, politics, or security priorities. Transparent financing demands mechanisms to prevent capture by dominant players who offer attractive but opaque funding. Accountability requires enforcement: audits, service-level guarantees, dispute-resolution processes. Without these, "neutral" projects risk becoming façades for dependency, cloaked in cooperative rhetoric.

The appeal of neutrality, however, is clear. For mid-tier nations—those too small to dominate but too large to accept dependency—the promise of neutral infrastructure is the promise of bargaining power. Instead of aligning wholesale with one bloc, they can diversify risk, participate in governance, and retain leverage. For citizens, neutrality means something more concrete: a greater chance that their hospital data, banking transactions, or communications are not hostage to remote conflicts.

Philosophically, neutral clouds and corridors reframe sovereignty itself. They shift the emphasis from control to cooperation: sovereignty not as isolation, but as the ability to shape shared rules. This is a demanding vision. It requires governments to accept partial interdependence, citizens to trust cross-border governance, and firms to adapt to transparent standards. But the alternative—fragmentation into rival digital empires—may carry higher costs still.

There are precedents. The open skies treaties of civil aviation, the neutral governance of the Suez and Panama canals, even the rules of global postal exchange—all demonstrate that shared infrastructure can be governed in ways that prevent hegemonic capture. None were perfect; all required constant negotiation. Yet they endured because states recognised that absolute control was less valuable than predictable cooperation.

The future of neutral clouds and corridors hinges on whether digital infrastructure can follow a similar path. The technologies exist. The finance can be mobilised. The harder question is political: whether states will cede just enough control to build trust, and whether firms will embrace transparency that may curb short-term profits but secure long-term legitimacy. Neutrality is not the absence of power. It is the art of distributing power in ways that reduce dependency while preserving cooperation.

The story is still being written. Each new cable laid, each exchange point opened, each cloud federation tested carries with it a choice: reinforce the duopoly or widen the field. For nations outside the dominant blocs, the stakes are high. They are not merely consumers of digital infrastructure but potential co-authors of its rules. Whether neutral clouds and corridors remain aspiration or become reality depends on decisions taken now, in boardrooms and ministries, as quietly consequential as any summit or treaty. The open question is whether enough states and firms will choose the harder path of neutrality—messy, negotiated, fragile, but ultimately more resilient—before dependency calcifies into destiny.

Norms and red lines

In May 2017, the WannaCry ransomware tore through networks worldwide, crippling hospitals in Britain's National Health Service. Ambulances were turned away, chemotherapy appointments cancelled, and doctors scribbled notes on paper because computers were locked. The malware's origins lay in a leaked tool from a state intelligence agency, repurposed by criminals and set loose with little regard for consequence. The outrage was palpable: here was digital conflict spilling into operating theatres, where the price was measured not in dollars lost but in lives put at risk.

Episodes like WannaCry sharpen an urgent question: are there lines in cyberspace that must never be crossed? In traditional war, treaties have prohibited chemical weapons, protected Red Cross facilities, and outlawed cluster munitions. Yet in the digital domain—where power grids, elections, and hospitals are all potential targets—the red lines remain blurred. Some states insist that "everything is fair game" in the name of national security. Others argue for restraint but struggle to define what counts as intolerable. Without clarity, cyberspace risks becoming a battlefield where ethics evaporate in the heat of expediency.

Norms in this context are not lofty aspirations but hard, operational rules. To say "no hospital takedowns" is to assert that healthcare infrastructure must be shielded from digital assault in the same way that the Geneva Conventions shield it from bombs. To declare "no election-day outages" is to enshrine the principle that democracy should not be manipulated through the silent lever of digital disruption. These prohibitions are both practical and symbolic: they protect the most vulnerable moments of civic life and mark out the boundaries of acceptable behaviour among nations.

Defining red lines is only the first step. Enforcement is where aspiration meets reality. Unlike traditional arms control, where inspectors can count warheads or measure radiation, verifying cyberattacks requires painstaking digital forensics. Attribution is rarely straightforward. Attackers route traffic through proxies, borrow code fragments from others, and time their operations to sow confusion. This ambiguity benefits the reckless. It is easier to deny than to prove.

Yet forensic science has matured. Investigators can now trace malware families across campaigns, compare linguistic patterns in code comments, and correlate attack timings with political calendars. Attribution reports, once vague, now read like dossiers, weaving technical breadcrumbs with intelligence insights. These investigations supply the evidence that makes naming and shaming credible. Without them, norms collapse into rhetoric. With them, governments, journalists, and courts can hold actors to account.

But naming is not enough. Shaming has bite only when reputational damage translates into material consequence. In the diplomatic theatre, sanctions and indictments are blunt but necessary tools. The United States' indictments of Chinese hackers in 2014, or the coordinated expulsion of Russian diplomats after the 2018 Skripal poisoning and concurrent cyberattacks, signal that bad behaviour carries a price. Critics argue these measures are symbolic, but symbols matter: they establish precedent, deter fence-sitters, and build momentum for broader coalitions of enforcement.

There is also an underappreciated role for positive reinforcement. Norms are not solely prohibitions; they are shared commitments. Just as arms-control treaties were underpinned by verification regimes and mutual monitoring, cyber norms can be bolstered through transparency measures. Joint exercises, incident hotlines, and confidence-building declarations create habits of compliance. Over time, these practices turn red lines from fragile declarations into embedded expectations.

Still, tension persists. What one state deems a justified act of espionage, another may frame as sabotage. Is disabling a propaganda channel an attack on free speech or a countermeasure against disinformation? Is probing an electrical grid a hostile intrusion or a necessary preparation for deterrence? Red lines must be clear enough to constrain, yet flexible enough to adapt.

Their success depends on persuading adversaries that restraint is in their interest—not simply a concession to moralism.

Philosophically, the debate over cyber norms is a debate about the role of ethics in an arena dominated by secrecy and coercion. Can ethics survive in the shadows of zero-day exploits and covert operations? Or do norms inevitably erode under the logic of power politics? The evidence suggests that even in hard security domains, ethics has a role—if only because no state wants to live in a world where everything is permitted. The nuclear age produced not only deterrence but also treaties. The digital age demands its own moral architecture.

The challenge is urgency. Each new cyber crisis forces societies to reconsider what is tolerable. The longer red lines remain undefined, the more space there is for opportunistic actors to normalise behaviour that once seemed shocking. If election-day outages or hospital ransomware are left unchallenged, they risk becoming part of the accepted repertoire of statecraft.

We are at a hinge moment. The technology to attack civilian infrastructure has outpaced the diplomacy to protect it. Forensics has caught up, but enforcement lags. Red lines are being drawn in practice, case by case, rather than agreed in principle. The open question is whether enough political will can be mustered to codify norms before the next crisis erodes them further.

Cyberspace will never be a sanctuary. But it can be governed by rules that preserve a minimum of humanity. The test is whether states, even rivals, can agree on prohibitions that make civilisation recognisable amidst the shadow wars of the digital age. The answer is not yet clear—and until it is, every hospital server, every ballot-counting machine, every emergency call system sits in uneasy suspense, waiting to see whether the world will draw the line.

Measuring success

In the aftermath of a major cyberattack, the first stories that dominate headlines are rarely about what was prevented. Readers see the scale of disruption, the hospitals closed, the airports delayed, the ransoms demanded. What they do not see are the invisible victories: the downtime that never occurred, the attacks quietly blocked, the skills that turned chaos into continuity. Success in cybersecurity, paradoxically, is most often measured in absences—in what did *not* happen. This makes it a difficult subject for politics, where rhetoric and spectacle thrive, and for societies which need reassurance grounded in evidence.

The paradox of prevention has long plagued public safety. No citizen votes in gratitude for the bridge that did not collapse, or the epidemic that never spread. Yet these silent victories shape the true measure of resilience. In the digital realm, this gap is more dangerous still: without credible indicators, leaders are tempted to substitute slogans for substance, and citizens have no way to distinguish competence from complacency. The challenge, then, is to define metrics that reveal real capacity—ones that can be scrutinised, audited, and trusted.

Downtime avoided is one of the clearest such indicators. When Estonia, long a target of Russian cyber pressure, invested in distributed infrastructure and mirrored systems abroad, it ensured that even in the face of attack, government services would remain online. The measure of success was not the absence of probing, which continues daily, but the continuity of services that citizens relied on. This is the language of hours, not headlines: how many minutes a hospital system stayed operational, how quickly a port resumed cargo movements, how long a payment platform remained accessible in the midst of a storm.

Containment of breaches offers another concrete measure. Attacks cannot be wished away, and no system can promise invulnerability. What matters is how far the blast radius extends. In 2021, when a major US pipeline operator was hit by ransomware, containment faltered: disruption rippled from a single corporate system into national fuel distribution, triggering panic buying across states. Contrast that with financial institutions that routinely isolate compromised machines, reroute transactions, and restore integrity within hours—transforming what could be a systemic crisis into a manageable incident. The difference is not luck but design, and measuring containment teaches us which organisations have learnt that lesson.

Skills grown are a subtler but equally vital metric. In cybersecurity, tools age quickly; it is people who sustain resilience. Nations that run regular drills, teach forensic literacy in schools, and embed cybersecurity into vocational training cultivate a workforce able to adapt. Indicators here are not abstract: how many civil servants can perform a tabletop exercise without relying on consultants? How many hospitals rehearse digital downtime as routinely as fire drills? How many small businesses have a recovery plan tested in practice, not just drafted in policy binders? Skills do not announce themselves in press releases, but when a crisis comes, their absence is impossible to hide.

Dashboards that matter combine these elements. They do not tally "attacks detected" in vague millions, a figure inflated by every stray scan on the internet. They report the number of critical services that met uptime targets, the median hours to recover after intrusion, the percentage of institutions that completed mandatory resilience training. Well-designed dashboards are less about showmanship and more about accountability: they give citizens, regulators, and boards a clear view of whether promises translate into protection. They replace fear or complacency with evidence, creating the space for rational debate.

The act of measuring is itself a form of governance. What leaders choose to count signals what they value. When governments obsess over the number of firewalls installed, they reduce cybersecurity to procurement. When they track the resilience of hospitals, schools, and local councils, they elevate protection of the vulnerable to a national priority. Indicators thus shape incentives, steering investment and signalling to adversaries where a nation's core commitments lie.

Yet measurement is fraught with tension. Public dashboards can expose vulnerabilities, giving adversaries a roadmap. Overly optimistic metrics risk breeding false confidence; overly negative ones can paralyse investment. The balance lies in designing indicators that are specific enough to be meaningful yet aggregated enough to avoid tactical exploitation. This is less a technical problem than a political art—deciding how much truth to reveal, to whom, and in what form.

Internationally, measurement also becomes diplomacy. Shared metrics allow allies to benchmark one another, identify laggards, and coordinate assistance. They also allow citizens to hold leaders to account across borders: if one country can demonstrate rapid containment of ransomware in hospitals, others can be pressed to meet that standard. In this way, dashboards become tools of persuasion, soft power expressed through transparency rather than propaganda.

Philosophically, the emphasis on measurement raises a deeper question: can resilience be fully captured in numbers? Trust lost in a breach is not easily reduced to hours of downtime. The confidence of patients, voters, or customers may erode long after systems are technically restored. Metrics illuminate, but they can also obscure—masking the human dimension of security behind the tidy simplicity of percentages. Wise leaders use dashboards as instruments, not substitutes for judgment.

Still, without measurement, there is only rhetoric. And rhetoric, however stirring, cannot patch servers, restore trust, or deter adversaries. Indicators that beat rhetoric do more than provide data: they anchor accountability, sustain investment, and help societies decide what kind of digital future they are willing to defend.

The unresolved challenge is whether societies will insist on such transparency. Will citizens demand dashboards that reveal downtime avoided and skills grown, or will they be satisfied with slogans of "cyber strength"? Will boards press for evidence of containment capacity, or will they wait for the next crisis to learn what was lacking? The answers to these questions will decide whether measurement becomes the backbone of resilience—or another missed opportunity in a field where, too often, failures are visible and successes remain invisible.

Chapter 12

After the Firewall: A Charter for Human Dignity Online

In the early years of the internet, security was imagined as a wall. Firewalls, passwords, and encryption were the bulwarks of an age that saw the digital world as a dangerous expanse from which threats must be kept out. Yet walls, by design, defend infrastructure rather than people. They protect systems, not the dignity of those who live through them. And when systems fail—as they inevitably do—it is the human being who is left exposed: their private messages sold, their labour monitored, their political voice silenced by unseen filters. The firewall was always a tool; what was missing was a charter.

Consider the paradox: our societies enforce strict safety standards for cars, bridges, and medicines, yet online—where the very texture of daily life is mediated—we have tolerated a regime of disclaimers and opaque terms. Children are nudged into addictive loops, patients see intimate records traded as commodities, workers are tracked in ways they cannot contest. These are not the by-products of technical accidents but the consequences of design choices made without human dignity as a constraint. The question, then, is stark: how do we re-centre the human in the digital, not as a customer to be monetised but as a citizen to be respected?

The path forward begins with principles. Dignity, agency, and consent must be treated not as slogans but as constraints—much like gravity or budget. Engineers, policymakers, and corporate boards alike should ask: can this system be built in a way that preserves human agency under pressure? Will the default respect consent when convenience tempts its erosion? This shift in perspective transforms ethics from a public-relations gloss into a design discipline. Principles guide trade-offs when speed, profit, or crisis beckon shortcuts. Without them, systems bend toward exploitation, not empowerment.

Principles, however, mean little without institutions capable of enforcing them. This is where regulatory bodies, ombuds services, and civic technology movements become essential. Just as environmental protection required agencies with teeth, dignity online will need regulators empowered to audit, fine, and even dismantle exploitative practices. Procurement, too, becomes a lever: governments and large buyers can enforce dignity at scale by refusing to purchase tools that fail basic standards of transparency or fairness. Case law, once built, can create precedent and deterrence that outlast electoral cycles. Enforcement, in short, answers the question of *who* ensures dignity—not just *what* dignity requires.

None of this is sustainable without funding and incentives. Ideals without money are lectures; money without ideals is capture. Tax policy, budget allocations, and insurance reforms can embed dignity into the bloodstream of digital economies. An insurer that lowers premiums for firms demonstrating strong privacy-by-design practices creates incentives far more durable than regulatory fines alone. Tax credits for civic technology and digital rights tools could make citizen empowerment scalable. Budgets, more than speeches, reveal priorities. Aligning financial levers with ethical aims is what makes change stick.

Yet the charter is not only for states and corporations. Citizens must move from passive consumers to active participants. This requires acting in unions that negotiate workplace surveillance, councils that oversee local procurement of digital services, and standards groups that decide the protocols of tomorrow. The individual can rarely shift the balance alone; organised citizens can. To build dignity online is to convert knowledge into power, ensuring the governed have a voice in the architectures that shape their lives.

The closing promise of this chapter, and indeed this book, is specificity. Abstract calls for change risk dissipating into the ether. What matters is what households, firms, and councils can do in the next ninety days. A sequenced plan—backups tested, defaults changed, contracts scrutinised—creates early wins that build momentum. Progress accumulates not through grand declarations but through durable habits and enforceable norms.

What follows is not a manifesto to admire but a charter to apply. It demands of its readers not only thought but action: to insist on dignity as a baseline, to engage with the institutions that can enforce it, to shape the incentives that align power with justice. The firewalls of the past defended machines. The charter ahead is about defending people. The question is whether societies, having lived through decades of compromise, are prepared to insist on dignity as the organising principle of the digital age.

First principles

The collapse of the Rana Plaza garment factory in Bangladesh in 2013 was, on the surface, a failure of bricks and mortar. But it was also a failure of principles. Workers had warned of cracks in the walls, yet were ordered inside. Production quotas overrode human dignity. Structural flaws, visible and known, became catastrophic because the system privileged output over safety. That disaster killed more than a thousand people; its lesson reaches far beyond textiles. When humans are treated as variables in someone else's equation—replaceable, secondary, expendable—the system is already broken, regardless of how well it functions technically.

Digital systems today echo the same tension. They run seamlessly, delivering services at scale, but conceal fractures in how they treat human beings. Consent is buried in unread terms, agency is designed away by "dark patterns," dignity is undermined when personal data is harvested without restraint. Like the cracks in Rana Plaza, these flaws are not accidents but design decisions. They remain invisible until the collapse—the breach, the scandal, the disinformation campaign—when the cost becomes undeniable. The challenge, then, is whether societies will wait for such collapses or articulate and enforce first principles before the damage is done.

At the heart of those principles are three anchors: dignity, agency, and consent. Each is deceptively simple, often invoked in political speeches or corporate manifestos. But in practice, they are rarely treated as non-negotiable. To speak of them as *design constraints* means more than affirming them rhetorically; it means recognising them as immovable parameters, akin to laws of physics or the limits of a budget. Just as no architect may build a bridge that defies gravity, no digital architect should build a system that erodes dignity or nullifies consent.

Dignity is the recognition that human beings are ends, not means. In the digital world, this translates into refusing to reduce people to "users" whose worth is measured only in clicks or revenue. A dignified system respects privacy not as a luxury but as a baseline. It avoids designs that degrade attention, manipulate emotion, or render invisible those who do not fit profitable demographics. Consider facial recognition deployed in public housing estates: technically efficient, but stripping residents of dignity by treating them as suspects in their own homes. If dignity had been treated as a constraint, such deployments would have been ruled out from the start, regardless of their market viability.

Agency refers to the capacity to act with understanding and control. In systems design, agency is lost when individuals face choices they cannot meaningfully evaluate, such as labyrinthine privacy settings or opaque recommendation algorithms. A system with agency as a constraint ensures that choices are real, not theatrical. For instance, when Norway fined Grindr for failing to provide meaningful consent options around data-sharing, the case highlighted a deeper truth: options that are hidden, confusing, or tied to punishment are not choices at all. Protecting agency requires designing with clarity and fairness, even when simplicity reduces the volume of exploitable data.

Consent is often invoked but rarely honoured. True consent is voluntary, informed, and revocable. Yet in practice, most consent online is coerced, uninformed, and irrevocable. Treating consent as a constraint means rejecting the familiar "click to accept" model and recognising that consent is not a single act but an ongoing condition. Healthcare provides an analogue: a patient's consent must be informed, and it can be withdrawn. Why should digital consent be weaker than medical consent, when the stakes—identity theft, surveillance, manipulation—are often as intimate? Designing for consent means systems that check back, that allow exit, that treat silence not as assent but as a lack of permission.

What makes these principles vital is not their idealism but their role under pressure. Systems under strain—whether by profit incentives, political urgency, or technical crises—are where values are revealed. A platform facing competition may be tempted to monetise data more aggressively. A government under threat may expand surveillance "temporarily." It is in these moments of pressure that principles must function as guardrails. Trade-offs will be made, but the lines of dignity, agency, and consent should not be crossed. Otherwise, pressure merely accelerates the erosion of human worth.

The philosophical depth here matters because systems talk so often forgets the human. When engineers discuss throughput or uptime, when policymakers debate standards or interoperability, it is easy to frame humans as inputs and outputs. The ethical spine is lost in technical abstraction. By re-centering dignity, agency, and consent, the conversation reclaims what is ultimately at stake: not just efficiency, but the kind of lives that digital infrastructures make possible. Do they allow people to live without humiliation? To act with understanding? To grant and withdraw permission meaningfully? These are not rhetorical luxuries but the measures of legitimacy.

Examples abound of what happens when principles are ignored. Cambridge Analytica exploited consent theatre to manipulate elections. Gig economy platforms have stripped workers of agency by using opaque algorithms to dictate pay and scheduling. Predictive policing tools have undermined dignity by reinforcing racial biases. Each of these cases shows that systems that work technically can still fail ethically. The failures were not inevitable; they were choices. Choices made without principles as constraints.

Yet there are glimpses of what principled design can look like. The General Data Protection Regulation (GDPR), for all its flaws, enshrined meaningful consent and data minimisation as constraints, forcing companies to adapt. The concept of "privacy by design" has nudged firms to consider dignity not as an afterthought but as an engineering requirement. Civic technology projects in places like Barcelona have experimented with giving citizens real agency over how city data is collected and used. These are imperfect steps, but they reveal that systems can be built differently when principles are treated as immovable.

The deeper question is whether societies will demand such constraints consistently. It is tempting, in the face of innovation, to defer ethics until later—to imagine that first principles can be patched in once technologies mature. But by then, power has already been consolidated, habits already shaped, vulnerabilities already entrenched. The longer dignity, agency, and consent are treated as negotiable, the harder they are to recover.

The task ahead is to articulate these principles not as aspirations but as boundaries. To insist that they be coded into procurement contracts, regulatory frameworks, and engineering specifications. To make them visible and enforceable. The reward is a digital world where systems are judged not only by speed and scale but by the respect they show for the people within them.

And yet the unresolved tension lingers: will principles hold when crises demand compromise, when profit promises expansion, when politics demands expedience? Or will they crack, like the walls of Rana Plaza, under the weight of pressures that treat human beings as secondary? The answer depends on whether dignity, agency, and consent remain rhetoric—or whether societies have the resolve to treat them as unbreakable constraints in the systems that increasingly define human life.

Institutions that can enforce

In 2019, the Federal Trade Commission of the United States fined Facebook five billion dollars for violating privacy commitments. It was, at the time, the largest privacy penalty in history—yet the market barely flinched. The company's stock price rose. The fine, though staggering to the public eye, was absorbed as a cost of doing business. The paradox could not be clearer: rules without robust enforcement mechanisms risk becoming theatre. Principles, no matter how eloquently drafted, remain inert unless there are institutions strong enough, independent enough, and well-resourced enough to uphold them.

Enforcement is the bridge between aspiration and reality. Without it, digital ethics dissolve into marketing copy and regulatory frameworks collapse under their own abstraction. But enforcement in the digital sphere is uniquely challenging: technologies move faster than legislation, global platforms straddle multiple jurisdictions, and harms often spread invisibly until it is too late. The critical question is not only *what* standards should govern digital life, but *who* ensures they are followed—and how.

For decades, regulation in the digital domain has been reactive, struggling to keep pace with innovation. National data protection authorities, such as the Information Commissioner's Office in the United Kingdom or Germany's Bundesdatenschutzbeauftragter, offer glimpses of institutional capability. They investigate breaches, issue fines, and sometimes challenge multinational corporations. Yet their budgets pale in comparison to the entities they oversee. A single major platform can spend more on lobbying in a year than a regulator spends on its entire operations. Enforcement, in this landscape, is not merely about legal authority but about resource asymmetry—about whether watchdogs can afford the teeth to bite.

This is where ombuds institutions become vital. Unlike regulators, which set and enforce rules, ombuds offices serve as direct advocates for citizens navigating the system. They provide redress for individuals wronged by opaque algorithms, misleading contracts, or exploitative data practices. The model has roots in Scandinavian administrative law, but its application to digital life is only beginning. An ombuds office dedicated to digital grievances could bridge the gap between abstract regulation and lived experience, translating citizen complaints into systemic reform. Crucially, such institutions must be designed to scale, handling not hundreds but potentially millions of cases—something that demands both procedural innovation and civic technology.

Civic tech itself is increasingly part of enforcement. Platforms that allow citizens to report breaches, audit government surveillance, or track corporate lobbying turn transparency into a form of distributed power. Consider "Have I Been Pwned?," a global database of breached credentials run by a single security researcher. Its popularity demonstrates both the appetite for—and the effectiveness of—public-facing enforcement tools. Imagine this principle scaled: independent dashboards showing compliance with accessibility standards, environmental impact of server farms, or the frequency of takedown requests by governments. Technology, often framed as the problem, can also be the instrument of accountability.

Case law remains another critical lever. Precedent has the capacity to reshape behaviour more rapidly than legislation. The European Court of Justice's "right to be forgotten" ruling forced search engines to implement global systems of removal, a change no parliament had codified in such detail. Similarly, antitrust litigation in the United States redefined corporate mergers for decades. The power of case law lies in its ability to crystallise abstract principles into binding obligations, often with immediate operational effects. Yet case law also relies on courage—judges willing to stretch existing categories, citizens and civil society willing to litigate against deep-pocketed adversaries.

Procurement, though less glamorous, may be the most underappreciated enforcement mechanism. When governments—the world's largest buyers of technology—demand compliance with ethical and security standards as a condition of contracts, vendors adapt. A municipality requiring encryption by default in cloud services can shift markets more effectively than years of public debate. Procurement embeds principles not through coercion but through incentives, turning market competition into a tool for enforcement. This requires competence: procurement officers trained to recognise digital red flags, auditors capable of verifying claims, and political will to privilege long-term resilience over short-term savings.

Of course, enforcement is not without tension. Heavy-handed regulation can stifle innovation; toothless oversight leaves citizens exposed. Institutions face political pressure: regulators attacked as "anti-business," ombuds dismissed as "symbolic," civic tech platforms accused of bias. Enforcement also raises questions of sovereignty: should data breaches by American firms operating in Africa be judged by Washington, Nairobi, or both? Whose norms take precedence when digital services ignore borders? These are not technical debates but geopolitical ones, reminding us that enforcement institutions are also instruments of power.

The deeper philosophical question is whether enforcement is about deterrence or transformation. Should institutions aim merely to punish misconduct, or should they foster a culture of responsibility? A fine may alter behaviour temporarily, but procurement standards, civic audits, and sustained case law create enduring norms. Enforcement, in this sense, is less about policing than about shaping the horizon of possibility: signalling what kinds of systems are acceptable, and which are fundamentally illegitimate.

Yet the challenge persists: institutions that can enforce require not only authority but legitimacy. Citizens must believe that regulators are independent, that ombuds are impartial, that civic tech platforms are transparent. Without trust, enforcement itself becomes another arena of contestation—an instrument of control rather than protection. Can institutions maintain legitimacy when confronting actors wealthier than nations, faster than bureaucracies, and more transnational than treaties?

That tension remains unresolved. The next decade will test whether societies can build institutions agile enough to enforce dignity, agency, and consent in practice. The tools exist—regulators, ombuds, civic platforms, case law, procurement—but their strength depends on whether publics demand their empowerment and leaders grant them the independence to act. The question, lingering and urgent, is whether the guardians of digital life will be capable of defending it—or whether principles will continue to collapse under the weight of institutions too weak to carry them.

Funding and incentives

In the aftermath of the 2008 financial crisis, regulators around the world passed sweeping laws promising that banks would never again gamble recklessly with other people's money. Yet a decade later, it was not legislation alone that had altered the industry's culture, but the incentives buried in capital requirements and insurance premiums. Banks became more cautious not because they suddenly grew more ethical, but because risk became expensive. The lesson is stark and transferable: ideals move when money moves. Lofty charters and ethical pledges matter little if they are not backed by budgets, taxes, and financial levers that make doing the right thing cheaper, safer, and more profitable than doing the wrong.

The paradox of the digital age is that societies loudly debate rights and values while quietly underfunding the institutions meant to uphold them. Data protection authorities often operate on budgets smaller than a mid-sized city council's IT department. Hospitals forced to pay ransoms to recover patient records discover, too late, that insurance markets had little incentive to reward prevention over payouts. Even when standards exist, without financing and enforcement they risk becoming hollow promises. Change sticks not through declarations but through the steady work of aligning incentives so that protecting dignity, agency, and consent is not an act of altruism but of rational self-interest.

Budgets are the starting point. A nation may draft the most ambitious data protection law in history, but if its regulator employs fewer than a hundred staff while supervising firms with millions of customers, enforcement collapses. In cybersecurity, resilience requires long-term investment in infrastructure—segmented networks, secure backups, redundant systems—that rarely yield short-term political credit. Governments that ringfence funding for cyber hygiene, from municipal servers to national grids, demonstrate not merely political will but strategic foresight. A budget is a moral document: it reveals what a society values, not in rhetoric but in arithmetic.

Taxes, meanwhile, can be engineered as steering mechanisms. Consider carbon taxes: they shifted the calculus of entire industries by embedding environmental costs directly into balance sheets. A similar model can be applied to digital risk. Firms that hoard personal data without adequate safeguards could be taxed proportionally to the volume and sensitivity of the data they collect, creating a natural disincentive for excessive surveillance. Conversely, tax credits for firms that adopt certified security standards or implement privacy-enhancing technologies could transform good practice from a competitive disadvantage into a financial advantage. Fiscal policy, in this way, becomes a quiet but powerful tool of digital governance.

Insurance markets represent perhaps the most underutilised lever. Cyber insurance today often functions as a patch: firms pay premiums, insurers pay ransoms, and attackers are quietly emboldened. But insurance could become an engine of prevention. If underwriters demanded evidence of basic controls—multi-factor authentication, incident response plans, employee training—as preconditions for coverage, they could shift industry norms faster than many regulators. Premiums could be calibrated not merely to compensate losses but to reward hygiene, reducing costs for organisations that demonstrably reduce risk. In this way, private incentives align with public safety: fewer breaches, less disruption, more resilience.

Yet incentives cut both ways. Poorly designed schemes can entrench perverse behaviour. A subsidy that rewards hospital cyber upgrades might lead to token compliance if not tied to meaningful audits. An insurance payout for ransomware without strict conditions risks normalising ransom payments as just another operating expense. The architecture of incentives matters: design them well, and they catalyse virtuous cycles; design them poorly, and they amplify the very risks they were meant to suppress.

The interplay of funding and incentives also raises deep philosophical tensions. Should societies make safety a matter of compliance or culture? If firms only secure their networks because it saves them money, have we succeeded in embedding responsibility—or merely in outsourcing ethics to accounting departments? The pragmatist might argue that motives matter less than outcomes: if breaches fall, if citizens are protected, if hospitals remain online, then financial nudges have served their purpose. But the idealist counters that reducing dignity to an actuarial calculation risks hollowing out the very values we seek to defend.

Still, history offers evidence that financial design can do more than enforce compliance; it can reshape norms. When seatbelt laws were paired with insurance discounts, safety became not just a legal requirement but a social expectation. When renewable energy subsidies combined with carbon taxes, clean power moved from fringe idealism to mainstream investment. The same can happen in digital systems. By embedding dignity, agency, and consent into budgets, taxes, and insurance policies, we shift them from slogans to defaults—norms so deeply institutionalised that deviation becomes the exception rather than the rule.

The critical question, then, is not whether ideals can be funded, but how. Who pays for digital safety: the state, the firm, or the individual citizen? Should small businesses shoulder compliance costs that giants can absorb with ease? Do nations risk creating a two-tier internet—one where wealthy states afford robust protections while poorer ones are left vulnerable? Incentives, like code, are never neutral; they embed values, distribute burdens, and shape the future.

We stand at a juncture where money could either entrench surveillance capitalism or enable a more secure, dignified digital sphere. Budgets can starve watchdogs or empower them. Taxes can punish hoarding or reward restraint. Insurance can perpetuate ransom culture or dismantle it through prevention. The architecture of incentives is the architecture of the possible. The challenge is whether societies will design these levers with foresight—or allow them to drift, unexamined, into reinforcing the very harms they claim to oppose. The stakes are not abstract. They are written in the stability of hospitals, the trust of voters, the resilience of grids, and the dignity of citizens navigating a world where money, always, makes ideals move.

From consumer to citizen

When a breach occurs—an identity stolen, a hospital paralysed, an election disfigured—the individuals affected are usually described as *consumers*. They receive apologetic emails, token compensation, perhaps a year of credit monitoring. Their role is passive: to endure, to complain, or at best to switch providers. Yet this framing is itself part of the problem. It locks people into a marketplace logic where harm is treated as a service failure rather than as an assault on dignity and agency. What if, instead, those same individuals acted not as isolated consumers but as citizens—participants in collective structures able to demand, enforce, and shape digital security? The difference is transformative.

The paradox is stark: the digital infrastructures on which society now depends are simultaneously most fragile where collective action is weakest. Workers rely on payroll systems vulnerable to ransomware; parents entrust schools with data that can be sold or leaked; voters expect reliable elections run on networks that can be jammed by outsiders. Alone, none can meaningfully shift the odds. Together—through unions, councils, and standards bodies—they can create accountability that no market or regulator alone can guarantee. Shared security, unlike consumer choice, scales with participation.

History offers lessons. In the nineteenth century, unsafe factories were not reformed by individual buyers choosing less lethal textiles, but by workers organising into unions that fought for safety codes and shorter hours. In the twentieth, environmental protections advanced when citizens forced councils to regulate pollution, not when households merely switched brands of soap. The same logic applies to digital risk today: structural vulnerabilities demand structural remedies, and those remedies require organised citizens, not atomised shoppers.

Consider workplace unions. As offices and factories digitise, payroll systems, shift scheduling platforms, and employee databases become tempting targets. A single ransomware incident can disrupt salaries for thousands, breeding hardship in days. Unions that traditionally fought over wages or pensions now confront a new frontier: demanding cybersecurity audits as part of collective bargaining. In Germany, works councils have begun to exercise co-determination rights over employee data processing, embedding security into labour negotiations. The precedent is profound:

digital resilience treated as a workplace right, negotiated alongside working hours and safety gear.

Local councils represent another locus of power. Municipalities increasingly manage critical services—water, transport, healthcare records—through digital platforms. Individual residents cannot audit these systems, but councils can pool expertise, procure secure solutions at scale, and coordinate regional incident drills. In some Nordic countries, shared municipal data centres have reduced costs while raising security standards, demonstrating that collective ownership and oversight can outperform fragmented procurement. Where councils mobilise, resilience ceases to be the privilege of wealthy cities and becomes a baseline for all.

Standards groups are subtler, yet equally consequential. Much of the internet runs on protocols and specifications decided in committees of engineers and policymakers. These are the places where encryption defaults are set, where interoperability is decided, where privacy protections can be strengthened—or undermined. For decades, participation has skewed towards the well-resourced: large firms, military contractors, and a handful of wealthy states. But when civic organisations, universities, and public-interest technologists engage, the tone and trajectory shift. The adoption of strong encryption in the 1990s was not inevitable; it was secured through activism, code contributions, and principled argument within standards forums. Citizenship here means showing up, voting in committees, writing the reference code that others must adopt.

Tools for organising are not limited to traditional forms. Civic tech platforms now allow distributed communities to pool evidence of breaches, lobby regulators, and benchmark institutional performance. Where once citizens depended on investigative journalists to expose systemic risks, now data collected by affected communities themselves can reveal patterns of neglect or abuse. Platforms tracking outages and mapping cyber incidents, when governed transparently, create collective memory and leverage. They transform isolated harms into systemic pressure.

The transition from consumer to citizen also reframes responsibility. As consumers, people are told to protect themselves with longer passwords and antivirus software. As citizens, they can demand that procurement contracts for hospitals mandate end-to-end encryption, or that insurers only cover firms meeting baseline hygiene. Responsibility expands outward—from the individual keystroke to the collective structures that govern digital life. This is not to absolve personal vigilance but to embed it within a broader ecology of shared security.

Of course, tensions remain. Collective action can be slow, fractured, or co-opted. Unions might prioritise wages over cybersecurity; councils may lack expertise; standards groups can be captured by vested interests. Critics argue that these forums risk paralysis or dilution. Yet the alternative—relying on fragmented individual choice or distant regulators—has already shown its limits. Shared security does not eliminate risk, but it redistributes power: from firms that externalise harm to citizens who insist on accountability.

There is also a philosophical depth to this shift. To be a consumer is to act with the logic of preference: what serves me best, here and now. To be a citizen is to act with the logic of interdependence: what sustains us, over time. Digital systems, by their very architecture, bind people together; one hospital breach can ripple across an entire region. Citizenship recognises this entanglement and insists that dignity and safety are not commodities but common goods. The language changes, and with it the horizon of possibility.

The challenge ahead is whether knowledge can be converted into power. Readers now understand the technical basics of breaches, the incentives that shape firms, the geopolitical struggles over standards. But knowledge, if left at the level of the individual, risks becoming paralysing. Power emerges when that knowledge is pooled, when people act not as isolated endpoints but as organised collectives. From workplace councils to international standards, from local procurement boards to civic tech platforms, the invitation is clear: stop accepting the role of consumer and claim the responsibility of citizen.

The future of digital dignity depends on whether enough people make that shift. Will society continue to treat breaches as customer service failures, to be patched and compensated, or will it demand structural accountability through collective voice? The answer will decide whether shared security remains an aspiration or becomes a lived reality. The transformation begins not in distant capitals but in the decisions of readers to organise—together—where they stand.

The next 90 days

Every great transformation begins not with abstract visions but with the first ninety days. Revolutions in governance, business turnarounds, even personal recoveries are measured not in decades but in what can be achieved in the first three months. The paradox is that while cybersecurity often feels like a problem of daunting scale—global supply chains, geopolitics, artificial intelligence—the most enduring changes come from early, concrete actions. The next ninety days are not about perfection; they are about momentum.

Consider how households across a single town respond after a flood. In the immediate aftermath, no family can rebuild the entire community, but each can clear their own street, check on vulnerable neighbours, and ensure clean water is secured. Within weeks, those modest but coordinated actions compound into something greater than their sum. Cyber resilience follows the same pattern: specific, time-boxed tasks, executed with discipline, create early wins that restore confidence and build the muscle for more ambitious reforms.

The first step is for households to reclaim control of the basics. A family that spends one evening setting up automated backups, updating devices, and enabling multi-factor authentication has already reduced its exposure more than any glossy "security suite" ever could. These are not complex engineering feats; they are habits. Families who choose a long passphrase for their Wi-Fi network, write it down on paper, and lock it in a drawer are not indulging in paranoia. They are acknowledging that their home is also a node in the wider network, and that their diligence protects not only themselves but the community to which they are connected.

For firms, the ninety-day horizon becomes a discipline in prioritisation. Owners and managers cannot address every vulnerability, but they can sequence the most impactful interventions. A small business that ensures payroll and invoicing systems are isolated from general browsing machines, that deploys a hardware security key for email logins, and that rehearses a ransomware response drill within three months will be vastly less attractive to attackers. Insurance providers increasingly recognise these measures; firms that demonstrate them find not only reduced risk but also lower premiums. The ninety-day plan, in other words, is not charity—it is cost-effective governance.

Councils and civic bodies face the steepest challenge, yet also hold the greatest leverage. A council that commits, within ninety days, to auditing its digital suppliers, to convening a regional tabletop exercise, and to publishing a plain-language cyber hygiene checklist for residents creates an anchor of trust. Such actions prove that digital responsibility is not confined to national capitals or to abstract standards bodies. It can be practised at the level where citizens actually experience their lives: schools, clinics, utilities. Councils that act early set a precedent for others, showing that digital resilience is not the privilege of the rich but the obligation of the responsible.

What unites these contexts—household, firm, council—is the philosophy of the early win. By time-boxing tasks to ninety days, the intimidating horizon of "cybersecurity" becomes tangible. Instead of vague commitments to "improve resilience," families can say: *we enabled two-factor authentication this week*. Firms can say: *we isolated payroll from the open internet this month*. Councils can say: *we ran our first incident drill this quarter*. Each milestone is measurable, auditable, and confidence-building.

There is also a deeper cultural shift at stake. Too often, security is discussed as a reactive cost—a line item to satisfy regulators or insurers. The ninety-day plan reframes it as an investment in capacity. Just as a community builds fire brigades not because they expect daily infernos but because readiness is cheaper than rebuilding, so too does a society build cyber capacity not because attacks can be eliminated but because resilience is the foundation of trust. The first ninety days are the training ground where that capacity is forged.

Of course, the danger is that early wins become the ceiling rather than the floor—that households tick a box, firms file a report, councils issue a press release, and then momentum stalls. The art of the ninety-day plan is to design tasks that not only deliver protection but also prepare for the next cycle. A backup drive installed today should prompt a conversation about data retention tomorrow. A ransomware drill should raise questions about supplier dependencies. A council checklist should evolve into procurement standards. Ninety days are not the destination; they are the ignition.

The closing question, then, is whether society can take these first steps not as isolated units but as interlocking pieces of shared security. Will families discuss cyber hygiene at the same table as household budgets? Will firms treat ransomware drills as routine as fire drills? Will councils convene citizens around digital safety as they once did around clean water or public health? The answer will decide whether the next ninety days are a fleeting exercise or the foundation of a durable civic transformation.

The clock, inevitably, is already ticking.

About the Author

Arjun Deshmukh writes where code meets power. Raised among the din of new industries and old institutions, he is preoccupied with a simple question: how do we keep human dignity intact when systems scale faster than laws and habits? His work braids field reporting, historical memory, and systems thinking—moving from the quiet rooms where standards are set to the municipal offices where outages are felt. He has spent years listening to engineers, civil servants, nurses, and small traders describe the same event from different angles, then building frameworks ordinary readers can use. In the tradition of writers who make complex worlds legible without condescension, he argues for security that does not devour liberty, and for sovereignty that does not require empire.

www.ingramcontent.com/pod-product-compliance
Lightning Source LLC
Chambersburg PA
CBHW031325230926
51848CB00001B/91
9789390349678